ZEN SOURCEBOOK

Traditional Documents from
China, Korea, and Japan

ZEN SOURCEBOOK

*Traditional Documents from
China, Korea, and Japan*

Edited by Stephen Addiss
With Stanley Lombardo and Judith Roitman

Introduction by Paula Arai

Hackett Publishing Company, Inc.
Indianapolis/Cambridge

For further information, please address:
  Hackett Publishing Company, Inc.
  P.O. Box 44937
  Indianapolis, IN 46244-0937

  www.hackettpublishing.com

Cover design by Abigail Coyle
Text design by Meera Dash
Composition by Agnew's, Inc.

Library of Congress Cataloging-in-Publication Data
Zen sourcebook : traditional documents from China, Korea, and Japan /
  edited by Stephen Addiss, with Stanley Lombardo and Judith Roitman ;
  introduction by Paula Arai.
        p.   cm.
  Includes bibliographical references.
  ISBN-13: 978-0-87220-909-1 (pbk.)
  ISBN-13: 978-0-87220-910-7 (cloth)
  1. Zen Buddhism—Early works to 1800. 2. Zen literature. I. Addiss,
Stephen, 1935– II. Lombardo, Stanley, 1943– III. Roitman, Judith, 1945–
BQ9258.Z464   2008
294.3'927—dc22   2007038739

CONTENTS

Preface   vii

Introduction   x

Notes on Translation   xxx

Chinese Zen   1

1. The *Heart Sutra* and the *Kanzeon Sutra* (complete)   3
2. Bodhidharma (died c. 532), *The Two Paths* (complete)   9
3. Seng-ts'an (died 606), *Hsin-hsin-ming* (*Trust in Mind,*
    complete)   13
4. Hui-neng (638–713), *Autobiography* (complete), from
    the *Platform Sutra*   19
5. Shih-t'ou (700–790), *Harmony of Difference and Equality*
    (*Sandōkai,* complete)   31
6. Huang-po (died c. 850), *Transmission of Mind* (excerpts)   34
7. Lin-chi (died 866), *Lin-chi Record* (excerpts)   43
8. The P'ang Family: Layman P'ang (740–808), Mrs.
    P'ang (n.d.), and P'ang Ling-chao (d. 808), *Anecdotes
    and Poems* (excerpts)   52
9. Selected Poems by Chinese Nuns   61
10. Chao-chou (778–897), *Recorded Sayings* (excerpts)   72
11. K'uo-an (active c. 1150), *The Ox-Herding Poems*
    (complete)   85
12. Wu-men (1183–1260), compiler, *Wu-men-kuan*
    (*The Gateless Barrier,* complete)   89
13. *The Blue Cliff Record* (excerpts)   112
14. Ta-hui (1089–1163), *Swampland Flowers* (excerpts)   118
15. The Biography of Miao-tsung (1095–1170; complete)   126

Korean and Japanese Zen   133

16. Chinul (1158–1210), *On Cultivating the Mind* (excerpts)   135
17. Dōgen (1200–1253), Selected Writings   140
18. The Awakening of Mugai Nyodai (died 1298) (complete)   173
19. Musō Soseki (1275–1351), Selected Poems   181
20. T'aego (1301–1382), *Collected Sayings* (excerpts)   188

v

21. Ikkyū Sōjun (1394–1481), Selected Poems in Chinese
    and Japanese   197
22. So Sahn (1520–1604), *The Mirror of Zen* (excerpts)   208
23. Bankei Yōtaku (1622–1693), *The Ryūmon-ji Sermons*
    (excerpts)   223
    ○ Illustrated text: Ryōnen Gensō (1646–1711),
    Autobiographical Poems   241
24. Hakuin Ekaku (1684–1768), Autobiographical Writings
    (excerpts) and *Song of Meditation* (complete)   243
25. Daigu Ryōkan (1758–1831), Selected Poems in Chinese
    and Japanese   252
26. Kyong Ho (1849–1912), *The Great Matter of Life and
    Death* (complete)   260

Glossary and Chinese Name Chart   266
Selected Bibliography   271

PREFACE

Zen is believed to have begun when the historical Buddha Shakyamuni, instead of giving a sermon, simply showed a flower to his pupils without a word; one follower understood, smiled, and was enlightened. Later it was said in Zen that when a Master explains too much, his eyebrows fall off. Even more succinctly, Huang-po (see Chapter 6) warned, "Open your mouth—already a mistake." Zen is called a teaching beyond words and writing, and yet there are more books on Zen than any other form of Buddhism. How can this be explained, and why are we publishing still one more Zen volume now?

Although Zen Masters stress that the study of texts is no substitute for actual experience, they have utilized words in their teachings for fifteen hundred years. However, while the most historically significant Zen writings are generally available in English in individual volumes, there is no compendium of fundamental texts by male and female Masters from China, Korea, and Japan. Therefore, in the *Zen Sourcebook,* we offer a collection of sermons, anecdotes, questions, interactions, autobiographical writings, and poems, with the understanding that these words are considered nothing more than guides rather than truths unto themselves. The Zen experience is unique to each individual, and we hope that the works contained here may prove helpful not only to those who wish to understand Zen intellectually but also to those who are engaged in meditation.

Each section is preceded by a brief historical and contextual introduction, but there is no attempt here to provide detailed interpretations of the texts. As the Japanese Zen Master Zenkei Shibayama (1894–1974) wrote in *A Flower Does Not Talk,* "However great the conceptual knowledge and understanding might be, in the face of real experience, concepts are like flakes of snow fallen on a burning fire." We therefore hope that our readers will not only study the texts but also experience them.

After much consideration, we decided not to include writings by modern Zen Masters, despite the many fine books they have published in recent decades. The reasons for this omission are twofold. First, the texts are too new to have become "traditional documents," and second, if we include only one or two of the many outstanding modern teachers, it is impossible not to seem arbitrary. We encourage our readers to seek out these more recent writings on their own, especially since many of them address questions of Zen experience in Western culture.

We should also make clear that this is not a book on the history of Zen. Much of the current scholarship on Zen explores the historicity of early texts, or considers them in terms of what we might call internal Buddhist politics such as disputes between different schools, sub-sects, and traditions. Although these elements are significant in historical research, we feel that they are not as germane to our collection of traditional teachings that have been influential on Zen thought and practice over the centuries. For the same reasons, beyond what is given in the Introduction we have limited our discussions of temple regulations, funeral rites, and other aspects of Zen life that are important in monasteries but not as relevant in the context of this volume.

Our most difficult decisions have come when choosing fundamental texts from the many that we might have included. For example, both Dōgen (Chapter 17) and Hakuin (Chapter 24) wrote extensively, and their traditions have been vital to Japanese Zen; but we could only find room for the texts that seemed to us the most significant for this volume, realizing that others might equally well have been selected.

There are several varieties and levels in Zen writings. Musō Kokushi explained in his *Dream Conversations on Buddhism and Zen* that there is no fixed path for Zen teachers to follow; in spite of the variety of Zen teachings, they all have the same goal, which is to lead people back to the fundamental state. Since Zen teachings vary according to the situation and the listeners, one may question the value of a sourcebook of words from the past. Nevertheless, over the centuries some teachings have been utilized again and again, and their potential is not yet exhausted.

Among the many varieties of Zen texts, the first is a straightforward expounding of teachings in explanatory form. One might characterize these texts as one step removed from pure Zen activity, since they are couched in language that is linear, rational, and therefore inevitably somewhat dualistic. Nevertheless, these teachings have been spoken, written, and published for more than a millennium, so it is clear that they continue to be useful. Second, there are prose texts that move closer to Zen experience in going beyond explanations; these are frequently couched in stories or anecdotes, although they may also be more philosophical in their approach.

A third kind of Zen text consists of autobiographical writings, which can include the record of enlightenment experiences. A fourth category is comprised of anecdotes and kōans. More directly tied to Zen activity, these are often the record of encounters between Masters and pupils; often given as meditation questions, they are frequently paradoxical and go beyond the usual limitations of language. A fifth type is Zen poems; although Masters often counseled against becoming too attached to writing poetry, it was nevertheless a form of Zen activity that could express profound insights.

This sourcebook contains all five kinds of texts (as well as some that combine or defy categories). It also contains something else: examples of the visual expression of Zen Masters in the forms of calligraphy and ink painting. For hundreds of years, leading monks have been asked for examples of their brushwork by students and followers in the East Asian belief that such "ink traces" express the inner character of their maker; these too have become known as expressions of Zen teachings. Especially notable as an artist was Hakuin Ekaku (see Chapter 24), several of whose works grace this volume.

Of necessity, for reasons of space constraints, some of the texts contained in this book are selected from longer originals, but we have tried to include the most significant teachings. Complete translations are cited in the Selected Bibliography, and we hope that readers will be encouraged to delve more deeply into the fascinating historical and contemporary world of Zen.

One of the difficulties posed by compiling this sourcebook was dealing with how the name of the same Zen Master appears in different forms in previous books. For example, Chao-chou, Zhaozhou, Jo Ju, and Jōshū are all the same Chinese Master, first in the traditional Wade-Giles transliteration, second in the Pinyin transliteration that the Chinese government has tried to mandate internationally, third in Korean, and finally in Japanese. For the sake of clarity, we have adopted the Wade-Giles system here, but a list of alternate versions of significant Chinese names is given at the end of this volume in the Glossary and Chinese Name Chart.

In the Notes on Translation, we also invite readers to examine and even participate in the complex and fascinating process of moving from Chinese characters (which are also used in Japanese and Korean writings) to English. No translation can ever encompass every nuance of meaning in the original, but we hope that the translations offered here—many of which were done specifically for this volume—will convey as much as possible of both the meaning and the spirit of the original documents.

We would like to acknowledge those who have contributed so much to making this *Zen Sourcebook* possible. First we must express our great appreciation to Paula Arai for her splendid Introduction, which sets the stage for all the Zen texts that follow. Further, we are grateful to Audrey Yoshiko Seo for her ever-helpful comments, Nelson Foster for his insights into the *Kanzeon Sutra*, Koichi Yanagi for help with the P'ang Ling-chao image, Belinda Sweet for her assistance with Sanskrit, Melissa Foster for technical support at the University of Richmond, and Rick Todhunter, Christina Kowalewski, Abigail Coyle, and Meera Dash from Hackett Publishing. Above all, we thank the many excellent translators who have generously allowed their work to be included in this volume.

Stephen Addiss

INTRODUCTION

The *Zen Sourcebook* is filled with selections from the poetry, letters, stories, sermons, encounters, visual arts, and conversations of great Zen Masters from China, Korea, and Japan. All readers—including undergraduates studying Zen as part of a course in Asian studies, or Zen practitioners seeking to deepen their understanding of this extensive tradition—will find much to consider in the texts collected here. Readers with an academic background in Asian history or religion might hear echoes of an ancient tradition, stretching back to pre-Buddhist India (up to the sixth century B.C.E.), strains of the Taoist and Confucian impulses that gained strength in China's Warring States Period (403–221 B.C.E.), reverberations from the political developments that unified the Silla Dynasty on the Korean peninsula in the seventh century C.E., or the repercussions of the international developments that led to Tokugawa Japan's "Closed Door Policy" of the seventeenth through nineteenth centuries. Readers approaching these texts for the first time, without any previous knowledge of such historical events, will have the valuable opportunity to read this book with the clarity of "Beginner's Mind."

The following overview provides some basic contextualization for the history of, and developments in, the Chinese, Korean, and Japanese Zen traditions; more specific information about each text and its author is provided at the beginning of each chapter. As you read these texts, remember that there is no right or wrong way to read them, only more or less analytic and spiritual ways.

Zen in Its Larger Buddhist Context

The Buddhist path is often referred to as "the Middle Way." It is focused on the practical task of finding balance between the negating behaviors of asceticism and desire. Shakyamuni, a northern Indian prince who lived during the fifth century B.C.E., was the founder of this tradition. He was given the title "Buddha" in recognition of his being an "Enlightened One." His primary teachings are outlined in the "Four Noble Truths."

These truths can be articulated through a medical metaphor. The First Noble Truth—that there is suffering—is the diagnosis. This is an observation, not a condemnation or prediction; people get sick, age, and die. The Second Noble Truth explains the cause of the problem: desire resulting from ignorance of the ultimate nature of reality, which is impermanent and interconnected. In other words, suffering occurs when a person becomes attached to things that cannot create happiness or rejects things out of fear that they will create unhappiness. Decisions and actions made on the basis of the "Three Poisons" of delusion, greed, and aversion will inevitably result in suffering. The prognosis, however, could not be better. There is a cure. According to the Third Noble Truth, it is possible to cease suffering. Delusion, greed, and aversion can be extinguished. The treatment plan, or prescription, lies in the Fourth Noble Truth, which outlines the "Eightfold Path." The eight guidelines are to live in accord with the view, intention, speech, action, livelihood, effort, mindfulness, and concentration that derive from wisdom and compassion.

A major concept in the Buddhist tradition is that there is "no self." This is not a statement that negates existence. It is a shorthand way of saying that there is no independent entity that can ultimately be identified as an individual. The assumption is that everything is interrelated; nothing can exist by itself. Everything is a constant flux in an interdependent web of causation. Considering the idea of the "Two-Reality Theory" can help sort out the important points of the teachings of "no self." The "Two-Reality Theory" suggests thinking of reality in two modes, conventional and ultimate. (It does *not* posit that two such realities actually exist.) Under this theory, conventional reality is perceived through our senses. From the perspective of conventional reality, an individual self exists. But from the perspective of ultimate reality, no distinct self can be discerned in the expansive interdependent flux. Buddhist teachings eventually extended the concept of "no self" to include all sensory phenomena, and they refer to this concept as "emptiness" or "void." It is important not to reify "emptiness"; instead, we should ask, "Empty of what?" The answer is, "Empty of independent existence." For example, this book would not be in your hands were it not for bookstores, publishing companies, and lumberjacks, as well as farmers who grew food to feed the truck drivers who transported the trees and the books—to say nothing of the heat of the sun that provides the conditions for our planet to be hospitable to various plants and animals. In short, everything is connected. Nothing is or acts alone.

According to this tradition, an intellectual understanding of such teachings alone will not alleviate suffering. We must experience the teachings for ourselves. Hence, Shakyamuni Buddha deliberately did not leave his teachings in written form. As the wise and compassionate teacher that he was, he wanted people to test his teachings for themselves and not just follow them blindly. Notwithstanding this pedagogical plan, his disciples gathered and wrote down his teachings to the best of their memories. (Many of these teachings were recounted by his disciple Ananda, which explains why texts designated as *sutras*—or words of the Buddha—contain the phrase, "Thus have I heard." The "I" is Ananda.)

Despite the development of a textual tradition based on the Buddha's teachings, the Buddha's concern that people must experience the teachings for themselves was not lost on his followers. They tested the teachings recorded in the texts. Some then wrote more texts to explain their experiences. Some also wrote commentaries to clarify the meaning of the texts evident to them in their particular sociohistorical context. Hence, no canon of texts has emerged, in the sense of absolutizing the value of certain texts above others. Certain schools or groups prefer certain texts and practices over others, but this preference is within the context that there are countless ways. There is no assumption that "one size fits all." On the contrary, taking seriously the teaching of impermanence has resulted in a plethora of Buddhist texts being developed throughout Buddhist history. Indeed, as Buddhists cultivated different methods and preferences in various regions and time periods, different traditions emerged.

Zen is a lively tradition that started developing in China during the fourth century C.E. It is a school within the Mahayana branch of the vast and diverse Buddhist tradition that was formulated during the fifth century B.C.E. The Mahayana originated in India beginning in the second century B.C.E., and it flourished in East Asia. A fundamental teaching of this tradition is that there are numerous ways to cease suffering and experience the goal of enlightenment, traditionally described with the metaphor "crossing to the other shore." Particular practices or specific articulations of teachings are understood to be tools designed to help one reach "the other shore." They are not absolute truths. We might say that such teachings and practices are vessels to be skillfully navigated in order to cross over the waters of attachment. The vessels are to be left behind upon arrival at "the other shore." This orientation opens up possibilities for crafting historical embellishments and utilizing a range of creative methods, all ideally in the service of helping people cross to a shore where suffering ceases and wisdom and compassion flows.

Bodhidharma (died c. 532?), a South Indian who traveled by sea to China in the fifth century C.E., is generally recognized as the founder of the Zen tradition. The record of his life and teachings is amplified with legendary accounts, which illustrates how people wove elements together with aims that were not always in accord with preserving an accurate historical testimony. Bodhidharma is known to have come to China sometime in the fifth century. As a new development in a tradition that already stretched back nearly a thousand years, the followers of this stream of Buddhism cultivated a view of history that links their approach directly to Shakyamuni Buddha. They "recount" that Shakyamuni transmitted his teachings directly to his disciple Mahakasyapa without using any words. The "mind-to-mind transmission" was accomplished by the Buddha twirling a flower and his disciple understanding what it meant. Zen "history" carefully records each mind that received these teachings. In effect, this record "proves" an unbroken line of transmission. It thereby establishes a lineage of teacher-disciples from Shakyamuni Buddha forward. Through this lineage the expansive family tree of Zen adherents finds nourishment from the root source. This legitimized foundation has proven powerful enough to support an ever-expanding family tree that extends through the centuries to today, with branches reaching across northern and southern China, into the Korean peninsula, onto the Japanese archipelago, and more recently across the North and South American continents, Australia, Africa, and Europe. The Zen stream runs along with other streams of Buddhism, often mixing and crossing paths in an ongoing interaction that fuels the contours of a rich multicultural landscape. As do all traditions over time—especially when moving across cultural, linguistic, historical, and political contexts—Buddhist texts, teachings, assumptions, practices, and questions underwent and continue to undergo a process of transformation in response to the particular concerns of individual people and to specific social structures and aims.

Zen Transformations in China: Ch'an

Zen (Ch'an in Chinese) in China has been deeply influenced by Taoist and Confucian traditions, resulting in a Zen that is both embedded in nature and active in human society. For example, *The Ox-Herding Poems* (Chapter 11) includes a series of ten paintings that depict stages to enlightenment. The eighth *Ox-Herding* painting is of a circle, a vivid illustration of emptiness, the highest Buddhist concept of wisdom. One might interpret this image as an ultimate expression of the Indian Buddhist orientation and view of enlightenment. The Chinese, however, were concerned to bring this concept back into the world. The ninth *Ox-Herding* painting presents a natural scene and may reflect the Taoist influence on Chinese Zen. The tenth painting, of a busy marketplace, might illustrate the Confucian need to participate harmoniously and productively in society. In short, all of these older traditions informed the creation of Zen Buddhism in China, cultivating a Buddhist tradition that relishes embodiment.

Among the many transformations affected by these Chinese traditions was an increased sense that Buddhist practitioners must contribute to society and family. The Zen school also remains notable for its focus on lineage. Establishing a lineage, as noted, legitimizes a school by connecting contemporary Masters, via a genealogical table, to the founder of Buddhism. This lineage links followers in a vast family tree, which reflects the importance of ancestry and familial relationships in Chinese society. Zen teachers have "children" (their students) and "grandchildren" (their students' students). Students have "siblings" (fellow students with the same teacher) and even "cousins" (students of one's teacher's "siblings"). This method of organizing practitioners into lineages also eases tension between traditional Confucian social concerns and the practice of leaving one's family in order to join a monastic community. The literal Chinese translation of "monastic" is "one who leaves home." From a Confucian perspective, leaving home can suggest irresponsible and selfish behavior. Buddhists, on the other hand, interpret leaving home as a demonstration of their concern for family in a broader context. Chinese Zen Buddhists maintain that the merit they accrue helps their ancestors for seven generations past—a benefit they could not reap without the discipline (and departure) required of a monastic.

Monastic discipline in China developed its own distinctive requirements. The book of Buddhist monastic discipline compiled in India, the *Vinaya*, was held in high regard and taken seriously by Chinese Buddhists. Over time an additional set of regulations for monastic life was developed. The distinctive ritual vocabulary and aesthetics of these regulations grew from the basic tenets of Chinese civilization and were embedded with Chinese cultural values and assumptions about human nature. The Confucian work ethic that guided much of Chinese society was at odds with the Indian Buddhist practice of alms-gathering. To followers of Confucian social mores, it appeared that Buddhists were shirking their responsibility to others when they asked for donations. Hence, Buddhist monastic communities began to till fields, or arrange for them to be tended, in order to produce their own food. Not eating after noon—the Indian Buddhist practice—was a strain on those who were engaged in the manual labor of farming fields, fetching water, cutting wood, and cooking. Therefore, a "medicine meal" (often consisting primarily of leftovers) in the evening was added to the schedule. Such innovations gave rise to an additional set of distinctively Chinese regulations for monastics, often attributed to a Zen teacher named Pai-chang (720–814).

In a tremendous display of intellectual energy and cultural confidence, the Chinese, with the assistance of Indian Buddhists who came to China, undertook the project of translating Sanskrit Buddhist texts into Chinese. This project contributed to, and perhaps accelerated, the sinification of Indian Buddhism. The linguistic precision of Sanskrit—perfect for splitting philosophical hairs—did not translate easily into the pictographic script of Chinese with its manifold nuances. This fundamental difference compounded the standard difficulties encountered in any attempt to render one language, and culture, accessible in another.

It should be noted that the translators for this English volume are undertaking a similarly monumental task as part of the American transformation of Zen. The translation process is not simple, and any translator must make numerous judgments and compromises along the way. For example, the cultural conventions of the English language often led translators of Buddhist texts to render words that are gender-neutral (e.g., "person") in the original Chinese as "man"—giving subsequent generations of readers the incorrect impression that women were not included. "Monastic" or "home-leaving one" was rendered as "monk." Nongendered pronouns were translated as "him," "his," or "he." Translators are increasingly aware of this unfortunate gender bias in English and are attempting to produce translations that are in accord with the originals. Some of the English translations in this *Sourcebook* are not by the editors of this volume, however, so you will see examples of the male-gender usage in those texts. Use these as an opportunity to hone scholarly detective skills. Reflect upon how translation can affect interpretation and understanding of a tradition.

Another prominent characteristic of Chinese Buddhism was the relationship between Buddhism and the state. Through stretches of Chinese Buddhist history this relationship was mutually beneficial, with the government offering patronage to Buddhist monasteries and securing their status as non-tax organizations. The state patronage of monasteries may have contributed to the organization of Chinese Buddhism by school rather than sect. (In other words, members of different schools would practice together in the same monastic communities. Sects have distinct administration, teachings, and facilities.) Some state leaders, like Emperor Wu of Liang (464–549), even accepted the Buddhist precepts. At other times, however, the relationship between Buddhism and the state was contentious, even cruel—as it was during the persecutions of Buddhists in 845.

Having noted some of the prominent cultural forces that shaped Buddhism in China, let us now consider some of the major historical forces. Buddhism had entered China in the first century C.E., during the flourishing Han Dynasty (206 B.C.E.–220 C.E.). But it made even deeper inroads into Chinese civilization amid the uncertainty, chaos, and disappointment caused by the civil wars that followed the fall of this powerful dynasty.

By the fifth century C.E., the sinification process was quite advanced, with numerous Buddhist texts translated into Chinese and monastic complexes established on various mountains. The time was ripe for the creation of the "new" school of Buddhism known as Zen. The full picture of Zen's beginnings is complex, and several pieces of the puzzle are buried in history. As mentioned, it is commonly held that Bodhidharma, by providing the crucial link between India and China, is responsible for the founding of Zen.

He is counted as the Twenty-Eighth Buddhist Patriarch in India and recognized as the First Patriarch of Zen in China. He is also said to have been the first to teach that the truth of Zen lies beyond the limits of verbal expression:

> Without relying on words and writings,
> A special transmission outside the scriptures;
> Pointing directly to the human mind,
> See your own nature and become Buddha.
>
> (Chapter 2)

Nonetheless, Zen adherents proved to be prolific and masterful writers. They used words as their tools in dissolving their delusions, aversions, and attachments. As Seng-ts'an (died 606), the Third Patriarch of Zen, advised: "Likes and dislikes / Are the mind's disease" (see Chapter 3). He goes on to explain, "If you choose or reject, / You cannot see things as they are." This early period of Zen produced many of the compelling figures that gave rise to developments in Zen during the T'ang Dynasty (618–907).

Several of the authors included in this volume lived during the T'ang Dynasty. Poetry by the nun Fa-yuan (601–663) offers proof of the participation of women during the early stages of Zen (see Chapter 9). The writings of laypeople from the ninth century indicate that monastics were not the only ones to receive respect from Buddhist adherents. Zen writings regarding the father, mother, and daughter of the P'ang Family are also included here (see Chapter 8).

Hui-neng (638–713) is another figure who animates this period. This illiterate man acquired fame as a result of the controversy surrounding the legitimacy of his position as the Sixth Patriarch of Zen (see Chapter 4). The controversy fueled questions about whether or not there was a proper way to attain enlightenment. Was enlightenment suddenly attained or gradually cultivated? Those siding with the Southern School associated with Hui-neng and led by Shen-hui (670–762) insisted that enlightenment happened "suddenly." Proponents of the Southern School claimed that the Northern School, founded by Shen-hsiu (c. 606–706), erred in teaching a "gradual" approach to enlightenment. Tsung-mi (780–841), a T'ang Dynasty Zen teacher and Hua-yen scholar, described the Northern School's teachings as gradual cultivation followed by a sudden experience. It is important to note, however, that the labels "sudden" and "gradual" were often used for polemical purposes. Therefore, it is best not to make a hard distinction between them; enlightenment in Zen often involves both gradual and sudden experiences.

Three generations after Hui-neng, two Zen Masters forged new trends that came to dominate and define the Zen schools. One Master was Ma-tsu

(709–788), who was remembered for his iconoclastic behavior, especially for shouting at and hitting his students. He was the precursor to Lin-chi (died 866), the founder of Lin-chi or Rinzai Zen (see Chapter 7), whose teacher was Huang-po (died c. 850; see Chapter 6). Another notable Master from this period was Shih-t'ou (700–790; see Chapter 5), who came by his name —literally, "Rock Head"—because he sat on a rock meditating for extensive periods. Shih-t'ou's approach to Zen set the foundation for what would later become the Ts'ao-tung (Japanese: Sōtō) School.

Chao-chou (Japanese: Jōshū, 778–897; see Chapter 10), of the Lin-chi lineage, not only lived long but also survived the persecution of Buddhists under Emperor Wu-tsung (ruled 841–846) in 845. Chao-chou's famous saying—"A monk asked, 'What is Buddha?' The Master said, 'Who are you?'"—is especially poignant when we consider the fear in which monks of his generation were forced to live.

When the persecution ended, Zen divided into what was later to be called the "Five Houses," which developed through multiple lineages of transmission. Of these "Five Houses," the Yün-men, Fa-yen, and Kuei-yang schools did not last long (nor did two earlier schools not included in the "Five Houses," the Ox-Head School and the Hung-chou School). But Lin-chi (Rinzai) and Ts'ao-tung (Sōtō), two of the schools included in the "Five Houses," continue to thrive today.

These schools and figures put down the roots that allowed Zen to blossom during the Sung Dynasty (Northern Sung, 960–1127; Southern Sung, 1127–1279). In addition to the collections of poetry by Sung-era nuns, two of the most heralded Zen texts—*Wu-men-kuan* (*The Gateless Barrier;* see Chapter 12), a collection of kōans (questions and provocations to stimulate enlightenment) compiled by Wu-men (1183–1260), and *The Blue Cliff Record* (see Chapter 13)—were written during this period. Though these texts soon became, and remain, important elements in Zen practice—a point that will be discussed in greater detail shortly—they also generated concern that their rote memorization could prove to be counterproductive, wasting effort that could be directed more directly toward enlightenment.

Zen rose in stature in the eyes of the state during the Sung period. Other Buddhist schools had enjoyed favor with the state prior to the persecution of Buddhists in the ninth century. During the Sung Dynasty, the Lin-chi (Rinzai) School developed a legal system of organization known as "Five Mountains and Ten Temples," which helped establish a high point of Zen Buddhism in its relations to the imperial court. But this close relationship also gave the government a certain measure of control over the school. The Master Ta-hui (1089–1163; see Chapter 14), teacher of the nun Miao-tsung (1095–1170; see Chapter 15), was particularly engaged with the state.

Several poems written by Chinese nuns, each of whom lived during periods of great social and political change, are included in this volume (Chapter 9). The nun Hsing-kang (1597–1654) lived during the Ming Dynasty (1368–1644), a native dynasty that followed the Mongol-ruled Yuan Dynasty (1271–1368). Lay Buddhist activity also flourished in this era. Yun-ch'i Chu-hung (535–1615), who encouraged those studying with him to practice both Zen and Pure Land Buddhism (a school that focuses on Amida Buddha and being reborn in the "Pure Land"), was a leading figure in the Ming Dynasty. Though intellectuals were chiefly preoccupied with Neo-Confucian thought, a revival of interest in Zen took place in the late Ming and early Ch'ing periods.

Five of the nuns whose poetry is collected in this book lived during the Manchu-led Ch'ing Dynasty (1644–1911). Fifteen hundred years after the foundation of Zen in China, Tao-ch'ien, a nineteenth-century nun who died in 1820, wrote of "home" as a place where one can be enlightened. While "home" in this poem could mean one's natural Buddha nature, it may also refer to the domestic sphere over which women presided.

> Eighty years and eight,
> No craving, no attachment.
> Let's go on back home,
> When the water clears, the moon appears.

(Chapter 9)

Meanwhile, Zen had branched out into streams that carried the originally Indian tradition, with a significant Chinese worldview encoded into its practices and articulated in its teachings, into Korea and Japan. This included the stress on lineage and familial genealogy of monastic relationships along with the additional set of monastic regulations and their attending practices. The Koreans and Japanese, however, did not translate the sutras into their native languages as did the Chinese. Nonetheless, both the Korean and Japanese Zen traditions continued to change in the face of their own particular cultural, historical, linguistic, and political dynamics.

Zen Transformations in Korea: Son

Buddhist teachings and practices were carried to Korea along with numerous other influences from Chinese civilization. With Korean state assistance, Buddhism entered Korea in the fourth century C.E. At that time the Korean peninsula consisted of the Three Kingdoms: Koguryo (37 B.C.E.–668 C.E.),

Paekche (18 B.C.E.–660 C.E.), and Silla (57 B.C.E.–668 C.E.). Buddhist influences were carried far into Korea, both during the "Three Kingdoms"
Period and the subsequent Unified Silla Period (668–935 C.E.). Buddhist
law shaped state law, with the result that Buddhists were influential in eco-
nomic and political realms. The king was considered a Buddha himself and
was expected to rule according to Buddhist ethics. Buddhist cosmology began to gain traction. Buddhism flourished as many monastics went to study
in China and even India during the Unified Silla Period. Through all this,
indigenous shamanistic and thaumaturgical (miraculous/magical) practices,
as well as clan-centered customs, began to be woven into Korean Zen.

Koreans added their own flavor to the teachings and practices received from
China. The life of one of the greatest Korean Buddhist scholars, Won Hyo
(617–686), best exemplifies the ways in which this occurred. A brief enumer-
ation of his contributions will help to place the Korean Zen (Son in Korean)
sources included in this *Sourcebook* into a greater historical and cultural context. The civil war that marked Won Hyo's early years may have instilled in
him the sense of urgency and deep concern that resulted in his prodigious
accomplishments. As is often the case with historically important people, a
variety of hagiographical stories surround him. Although the facts of his life
are difficult to establish, we know at least what people *wanted* to think about
his life—as in the story of his visit to a geisha house (where, it is said, he vi-
olated more than one precept). Won Hyo produced some of his finest work
after leaving the formal monastic life. Having never fully identified with the
role of a "house-leaving one," he referred to himself as a "small layman."

As the author of 240 works on Buddhism, including extensive commentaries on numerous sutras, Won Hyo was the first Korean Buddhist to try to
harmonize the vast range of doctrines and teachings that flooded into Korea. It is not hard to imagine why a scholar like Won Hyo would want to
join together such a diverse range of teachings and scriptures, especially after his extensive training in a tradition that developed over centuries, across
a number of regions. The importance placed upon the *Avatamsaka Sutra
(Flower Garland Sutra)* in Korean Buddhism may stem from Won Hyo's
work on this sutra. One of the latest sutras recorded, it offers the organizing
metaphor of the "net of Indra." The metaphor highlights the teaching of "all-
in-one, one-in-all" through its image of a net of jewels reflecting one another.
Of Won Hyo's prodigious writings, twenty works in twenty-five volumes are
extant. He is recognized as the founder of the syncretistic Popsong School—
and, by extension, as having established a paradigm for the development of
a distinctly Korean Buddhism.

Zen initially gained popularity in Korea as Silla Buddhism was on the decline. When it was first imported from China, Zen appealed primarily to the
local Korean gentry. Zen Master Toui (died 825) contributed to the debates

held in this early period over the values of Zen as compared to the established doctrines of the aristocratic state Buddhists. Though Zen gradually began to appeal to the aristocracy, popular religious practices also flourished in the wake of the Silla Dynasty's failure. In 879, the Zen Master Chison founded Huiyang, the first Korean Zen school. Eight other schools, each with its own mountaintop location, were established in the following one hundred years. Together they are known as the Nine Mountain schools. The founders of these schools had all studied with major Zen Masters in China; seven of the founders were first-generation disciples of Ma-tsu, the founder of the Hung-chou School. Of the nine Korean schools, eight drew upon the Chinese Southern School's "sudden enlightenment" teachings and dominated the Korean Zen landscape. Only one school, the Sumi, developed apart from the Sōtō line.

Zen Buddhism made major advances during the Koryo Period (918–1392). The invention of the world's first moveable metal type in 1234 illustrates the sophistication of Korean civilization at this time. The Koryo court also produced two complete woodblock-cut sets of the *Tripitaka Koreana,* the enormous library of traditional Buddhist texts. The first set, completed in 1087, was burned in the Mongol invasion of 1232. The second set, completed in 1251, is currently held in the Haein-sa Temple. Covering both sides of over 80,000 woodblocks, this historic text embodies the state's support of Buddhism. It required no small investment on the part of the government to carry out so massive a project in such expert fashion. Curing the wood tablets so they would not warp, rot, or become infested during the eight hundred years they spent in Korea's humid and fertile climate is a testament to the high quality of the state's work—to say nothing of the skill required to carve millions of intricate Chinese characters, clearly, in wood.

Like Won Hyo, the intellectual giant Chinul (1158–1210; see Chapter 16) was born into a time of civil volatility. Two major currents of thought dominated Korean Buddhism during Chinul's time. Followers of one school treated the study of scriptural teachings as an academic pursuit; adherents of the other school highlighted Bodhidharma's view of Zen as the "special transmission outside the scriptures" (Chapter 2). Just as Won Hyo attempted to combine the different strains of Korean Zen into a unified whole, Chinul wove these two streams together through a practical application of the teachings found in the texts. He drew on a syncretistic variety of Chinese Zen as promulgated by Tsung-mi, teaching above all that gradual cultivation through study of the sutras results in a sudden enlightenment, and that the sutras should be studied both before and after this sudden awakening. Chinul wanted to strike a balance between a practice that strengthens insightful concentration through meditation and the cultivation of wisdom as articulated in the sutras. He was a keen philosopher; his influence on the development of Korean Buddhism has been tremendous, and it continues today. Although Chinul's own lineage is not clear, his insightful writings have been passed down over the centuries, illuminating and inspiring generation after generation.

Most current Korean Zen Buddhists can trace their lineage back to T'aego (1301–1382; see Chapter 20). In keeping with Chinul's work, T'aego taught a combination of sudden enlightenment and gradual cultivation. T'aego also brought Lin-chi (Rinzai) teachings back from China. One of T'aego's most lasting and important achievements was the reunification of all Nine Mountain schools of Zen together into the Chogye order—a sect that currently includes the great majority of Korean Buddhists.

By the time the revolt of 1392 gave rise to the Choson (Yi) Period (1392–1910), Zen Buddhism was no longer held in favor by the state. Where earlier leaders had been pro-Buddhist, the new government favored Confucianism. This change pushed Zen Buddhists to seek refuge in mountain monasteries and limited the involvement of laity in Buddhist institutions. Yet Zen continued to develop despite this change in the political climate.

Already renowned as the greatest Zen Master of the Choson Period, So Sahn (1520–1604; see Chapter 22) became a national hero for his role in resisting the Japanese invasion of 1592, when Shogun Hideyoshi Toyotomi's army burned numerous Buddhist temples, along with the works of art and religious relics they contained. In his Buddhist teachings, So Sahn reinforced Chinul's teachings on the need for gradual cultivation through sutra study, both before and after a sudden enlightenment experience. Eventually, So Sahn's approach to Zen practice stressed the kōan and "capping word" methods of Lin-chi and Ta-hui—methods from which Chinul had been excluded, due to lack of access to the teachings of these Masters—and this emphasis has had a lasting influence on Zen practice in Korea, even today.

Following the invasions of Korea in 1592 and 1598 by Hideyoshi (1536–1598), the country limited its contact with the rest of the world, thereby earning the nickname "Hermit Kingdom." During this phase, Buddhism also declined in Korea despite So Sahn's best efforts. Kyong Ho (1849–1912; see Chapter 26) is best known for reviving Korean Zen from this diminished state. While traveling through a village struck by cholera, Kyong Ho, then a young man, realized the importance of understanding the Dharma: simply studying the teachings of the Buddha would not lead to enlightenment. Following a retreat into a Buddhist temple, he journeyed across Korea teaching at several important monasteries. His teachings revitalized Korean Buddhism. Settling in Haein-sa, Kyong Ho oversaw the printing of the *Tripitaka Koreana* from the woodblock prints carved in the Koryo Dynasty. At the time there were no extant complete copies. Eager to study with this eminent teacher, many students gathered around him. From this influential position, however, Kyong Ho left the public eye and retreated to a remote northern fishing village in his final years. Perhaps it is no surprise that this man, who endured profound suffering and ended up rejuvenating a liberation tradition, would counsel: "Make good medicine from the suffering of sickness."

Zen Transformations in Japan

According to historical chronicles from the period, in 552 the King of Paekche, one of Korea's Three Kingdoms, gave a statue of the Buddha as a gift to the Japanese imperial court under the reign of Emperor Kimmei. The transformation of the Buddhist teachings and practices brought over from Korea—and later directly from China—required conciliation between the indigenous Shinto deities called *kami* and Buddhas. A case was made that Buddhas were more powerful than the local Japanese *kami*. At first this was seen as a threat to the local society, but after some creative political and spiritual adjustments, a long relationship of imperial patronage of Buddhist activities in Japan ensued. Women were central to Shinto rites at the time Buddhism first entered Japan, which may explain why three women were also the first ordained Buddhist monastics in Japan. These women adopted the Buddhist names Zenshin-ni, Zenzō-ni, and Ezen-ni in the 580s. They were the first to study Buddhism abroad, spending the requisite three years of training for full ordination in Paekche and returning to Japan in 590.

By the Heian Period (794–1192), Japanese Buddhists were making regular trips to China for teachings and texts. Unlike Chinese Buddhists, the Japanese were inclined to organize in discrete sects. The major esoteric sects, Tendai and Shingon, established monastic communities on mountains outside the capital. Tendai teachings include various Buddhist sutras and a range of practices. Zen has its beginnings in the Tendai mountain monasteries of the Heian Period. It was not until the Kamakura Period (1185–1333), however, that it took on its distinct form. This was a time of new questions and concerns that gave rise to new responses, of which Zen was one.

In the Kamakura Period—during which Japan was ruled by warriors, not aristocrats—two important Zen sects took hold: Rinzai (Chinese: Lin-chi) and Sōtō (Chinese: Ts'ao-tung). Both sects had their Japanese origins in the Tendai sect. Rinzai is said to have its rather amorphous beginnings in a visit made to Sung China in 1168 by a Tendai monk named Eisai (1141–1215). Upon his return to Japan, Eisai incorporated Chinese Zen teachings and practices into his Tendai setting. Most notably, he placed increased emphasis on seated meditation, or zazen. For this contribution, he is sometimes called the founder of Rinzai Zen in Japan. The efforts of Enni Ben'en (1201–1280) and Shinchi Kakushin (1207–1298)—Tendai disciples of Eisai who brought the *Wu-men-kuan* (see Chapter 12) kōan collection back from China—also contributed to the establishment of Rinzai Zen in Japan. The serious interest in Zen of the Kamakura Shogunal regent, Hōjō Tokiyori (1227–1263), helped solidify Rinzai Zen's place among the samurai and as a distinct sect.

Dōgen (1200–1253; see Chapter 17) is the Master who is considered to be the founder of Japanese Sōtō Zen. Though he had not aimed to found a new sect of Buddhism in Japan, his teachings are nevertheless distinct from others of his time. Dōgen also began as a Tendai monk. According to traditional representation—the details of which have likely been altered to serve the purposes of Zen teachers throughout the ages—Dōgen was compelled to further his training in China. Of the wide range of teachings available under the Tendai umbrella, he felt compelled to find a logical answer to his question: "If we are originally enlightened, why do we have to practice?" He found his answer—"Practice *is* enlightenment"—during his Sōtō Zen training in China. Upon returning to Japan, Dōgen founded a temple just outside the capital in Uji. He later established a monastery, now known by the name Eihei-ji, on the far side of the island, deep in the mountains. Among many students who traveled to this remote location in order to study with him were a number of women who form a continuous link of ordained nuns that continues to the present.

The Muromachi Period (1338–1573) was an especially important era for Rinzai Zen. The new military government, the Ashikaga Shogunate, lavishly supported Rinzai activities. It was in this period that the "Five Mountains," or "Gozan System," was brought from China and employed for organizing a power structure that served both the Rinzai sect and the Ashikaga Shogunate. This system was centered on five main monasteries, the "Five Mountains," under the leadership of which ten lesser temples served. The ten lesser temples were connected to temples in far-reaching areas of the country in an expansive network aimed at protecting the nation and funneling power back to the main temples and the Shogun. Kamakura and Kyoto each had their own "Five Mountains," and nuns had a similar organization called "Niji Gozan." Under the influence of this Gozan culture, the contemplative arts flourished.

Granted the title "National Teacher" ("Kokushi," an indicator of the highest imperial recognition) by Emperor Go-Daigo in 1335, the monk Musō Soseki (1275–1351; see Chapter 19) was a leader in the Gozan community. The translation of his Buddhist name offers insight into his spiritual journey. Upon the death of his Shingon teacher, Soseki undertook a hundred-day prayer, during which he dreamed about T'ang Zen Buddhist monks. This dream apparently reinforced his conviction that Buddhist teachings must be lived, not just learned. He took the names Musō, meaning "dream window," and Soseki, a conflation of the names of the Zen monks who appeared in his dream. In addition to periodically spending time in meditative retreats, Musō became deeply involved in the political affairs embroiling Japan at the time. He also wrote extensively on Zen practice and poetry, designed some of Japan's most heralded gardens, and built and managed temples and monasteries at the pinnacle of beauty and power. Indeed, he lived his life according to his own words: "In the world outside of things there is nothing to get in the way."

Not all Rinzai temples were included in the "Five Mountains" system. The term "Rinka" refers to such non-Gozan Rinzai temples and includes Sōtō temples as well. Though these Rinka temples were not accorded the kind of state-funded support of the "Five Mountains" temples, they made important contributions in their own right. When, toward the end of the Muromachi Period, the fortunes of the Ashikaga waned, so, too, did the Gozan system. The Rinka temples simultaneously rose in power, most notably Myōshin-ji and Daitoku-ji in Kyoto. (Most of the "Five Mountains" monastic compounds, including Tenryū-ji and Tōfuku-ji in Kyoto and Engaku-ji and Kenchō-ji in Kamakura, however, remain important to this day.)

In addition to Sōtō temples, which were located primarily outside the major cities where the major battles for power occurred, first-rate Rinzai Rinka temples also developed in rural areas. Concurrently, Kyoto housed several major Rinzai monasteries. A complicated and controversial Rinzai Zen Master named Ikkyū Sōjun (1394–1481; see Chapter 21) eventually became abbot of Daitoku-ji, an increasingly important Rinka monastery. Ikkyū did not live his life in pursuit of worldly status, so the fact that he reluctantly accepted the position of abbot is an indication of the depth of his compassion, even for those whom he thought were deluded. In his early years, Ikkyū was very serious and disciplined, but in his later years he behaved in ways that seemed calculated to shock. Indeed, a study of his complex life affords the chance to reflect upon the meanings of, and the relationship between, practice and enlightenment.

After a period of warring powers jockeying for control, Japan became unified and stabilized under the feudal rule of the Tokugawa Shogunate (1603–1868). This era is characterized by a carefully controlled response to changes ushered in by international developments. Due to the colonization occurring in other parts of Asia, European interests that included an active Christian missionary effort in Japan were interpreted as a threat to Japanese sovereignty. Japan responded with a "Closed Door Policy" that ended trade and relations with almost all countries and endorsed the persecution of Christianity. The government also implemented an elaborate temple registration system that enabled it to keep relatively tight reins on the populace. Since each family had to register with its neighborhood Buddhist temple, temples flourished during this period. Despite this controlled bureaucratic relationship with the Shogunal government, Buddhism in this era produced a number of important teachers with inspiring, innovative teachings.

The writings of two of the most accessible and cherished of Japanese Zen Masters—Bankei Yōtaku (1622–1693; see Chapter 23), from the Rinzai Myōshin-ji lineage, and Daigu Ryōkan (1758–1831; see Chapter 25), from the Sōtō tradition—offer windows on the concerns and pleasures of the common people of their times. Both of these Masters devoted their teaching efforts to helping everyday people, responding to an important need in this hierarchy-conscious society. They were also both gifted in articulating their teachings in ways that made immediate sense—Bankei with his down-to-earth sermons, and Ryōkan with his unpretentious and reflective poetry.

Though this sourcebook includes only one piece of calligraphy from the third sect of Zen in Japan, any overview of the subject would be incomplete without mentioning the Ōbaku sect. This sect was brought to Japan by the wave of Chinese emigrants arriving in Nagasaki at the end of the Ming Dynasty (1368–1644). The Ōbaku approach to Buddhist practice reflected relatively recent developments in Chinese Buddhism, namely, the intermixing of the Zen and Pure Land traditions. On the surface, these two traditions seem antithetical. Zen is characterized as a method of "Self-Power," because practitioners practice zazen to discipline their body-mind on their own. A practitioner of Pure Land practice must invoke the name of Amida Buddha for aid, and this practice is often referred to as the "Other-Power" method. These distinctions, however, are more rigid in theory than in actual practice. Though the Ōbaku sect never reached the extensive level of the Rinzai and Sōtō sects' widespread temples, it contributed to the development of Zen in Japan. The influx of Chinese Zen monks served to reinvigorate the two older sects and initiated a wave of substantial reforms.

Hakuin Ekaku (1684–1768; see Chapter 24) injected tremendous vitality into Zen. Now recognized as a central figure in modern Zen, Hakuin's contributions to Rinzai transcended the narrow sectarian distinctions of his Myōshin-ji lineage. Hakuin's kōan-centered curriculum still guides Rinzai practice. Deft at finding the right words and images with which to communicate his teachings, Hakuin appealed to people from all levels of the social order. To farmers, he suggested cutting off passions at the roots as if they were weeds. He challenged a sword-wielding samurai named Nobushige: "Here, open the gates of hell." The samurai responded by sheathing his sword and bowing. At this, Hakuin suggested, "Here, open the gates of paradise." His most famous question, however, is the kōan: "What is the sound of one hand [clapping]?"

Zen Practices

Practices that involve specific actions of the body are central to Zen. The assumption is that the mind-body is an organic and dynamic unit. Therefore, entering practice through disciplining the actions of the body is understood to be effective on the mind as well, and every activity in daily life can be an opportunity to practice. No action is too menial for Zen practice, from how to fold a towel to how to wash one's face, from how to sweep the floor to how to place one's slippers. Each act can be done with respect for all involved, whether that be another person, oneself, a utensil, a morsel of food, or even dust. For example, learning the proper form required to wash one's face is in itself treating the water and one's body with the respect accorded a Buddha. Sitting still is simple in form, and it is held as the paradigm for how to learn to act as a Buddha.

A hallmark of Zen-style sitting (zazen) is the focus on body posture, especially a straight spine. Most people try to sit cross-legged in the full-lotus posture, although half-lotus with only one leg up on the opposite thigh is also fine. Followers of the Rinzai communities usually sit with their backs facing the wall, and in the Sōtō communities they sit with their faces toward the wall. Traditionally the length of a session is marked by the length of time it takes to burn a stick of incense, thirty minutes to an hour. Sitting for consecutive sessions is common, and special times (*sesshin*) during the year are devoted to concentrated zazen sessions from early morning to late at night, usually for three to eight consecutive days.

As noted, sociocultural considerations were involved in the development of daily chores as an integral aspect of Zen monastic life. Cooking, cleaning, farming, and other necessary activities, even eating, took on an importance not found in India. Even other East Asian forms of Buddhism did not elevate such activities to the status of "practice" as strongly as did Zen Buddhists. Pai-chang, the Chinese Zen Master known for his book of monastic regulations, is famous for having said, "A day without work—a day without eating." Hence, daily chores are considered a necessary dimension of Zen practice. Often the methods of how to perform each task are prescribed in minute detail, including how to wipe the floor, eat, and wash one's dishes.

In addition to seated meditation and the ritualization of daily activities, numerous ceremonies also punctuate a day in a monastery as well as mark the seasons of the year. The two most common rituals are bowing and chanting the *Heart Sutra* (see Chapter 1). This is also the sutra most commonly chanted by laity as well, whether in their homes or while attending a ritual at a temple. It is also not uncommon for Zen Buddhists, especially in China and Korea, to chant "Homage to Amida Buddha" (Chinese: *namo amito fo;* Korean: *namu amita bul;* Japanese: *namu amida butsu*), a central practice in the Pure Land tradition. Other sutras are also chanted, including the *Kannon Sutra* (a chapter from the *Lotus Sutra*) and, especially in Korea, a small section of the *Avatamsaka Sutra*. The "Four Great Vows" of the Mahayana (Bodhisattva) tradition are also often chanted in the language of a particular community, whether it be Chinese, Korean, Japanese, or English. (The Chinese characters for the "Vows" are given in the Notes on Translation.)

Sutras are usually chanted by the community in the worship hall—or by laity at their home altar—with incense, tea, food, flowers, and light (candles) offered to the Buddha on the altar. Various bells and drums emphasize ritual highlights and transitions, and also help maintain a steady beat for the chant. Such musical instruments are played throughout the day as well, to nonverbally indicate various exacting group activities, including when it is time to wake up, meditate, work, eat, or sleep.

Questions are often a significant aspect of Zen practice, whether written down, shouted out, carefully formulated and articulated, or silently mulled over. Some questions can transport one beyond the limits of dualistic thinking. "Who are you?" has had that effect on some. "Why me?" on the other hand, is the kind of ego-driven question that can cinch the shackles of delusion tighter. Perhaps it is such awareness of the power of asking a well-honed question that led many to seek the kōans of recognized Masters. Written compilations of kōans such as the *Wu-men-kuan* and *The Blue Cliff Record* have helped to form the foundation of kōan practice, an integral aspect of many modes of Zen training.

The use of the kōan is a powerful tool for awakening the Zen adherent to the non-dual nature of ultimate reality, though it is not utilized in all Zen traditions. Kōans are often described as "living words" (as opposed to the "dead words" of doctrine), and they take, therefore, many forms and are employed in a variety of ways. Kōans aim to open one's mind to an expansive perspective of interrelatedness, qualitatively beyond the narrow, self-limiting lenses of delusion, greed, and hatred. The Japanese word *kōan* (*kung-an* in Chinese and *kong-an* in Korean) literally means "public case," and many traditional kōans are brief stories of encounters between early Chinese Zen Masters and their students, such as the eighteenth case of the *Wu-men-kuan:*

> Tung-shan was asked by a monk, "What is Buddha?"
> Tung-shan said, "Three pounds of flax."

> (Chapter 12)

A Master might ask, "What does this mean?" Or, "What is 'three pounds of flax'?" Or, "What is Buddha?" Or, "If you were the monk, what could you say to Tung-shan?" Other kōans are themselves direct questions, such as, "What is the sound of one hand?" as asked by the Japanese monk Hakuin (see Chapter 24 and Figure 20). Hakuin designed his five-tiered kōan curriculum to develop imperturbability in the student, so that he or she would be unshakeable in the midst of daily activity. While most Masters use traditional kōans, new ones also appear; for example, the twentieth-century Master Taizan Maezumi was fond of asking, "How do you do zazen while driving a car?"

In all schools of Zen, kōans are referred to and discussed in public talks and writings by teachers. Students may also be given a kōan in a private interview, especially in the Lin-chi (Rinzai) tradition in which they go alone at regularly scheduled times to receive an appropriate kōan. In such cases, kōans are a focus of meditation; they become mirrors in which the student's mind is revealed. It is not a matter of coming up with the "right answer." One student might imitate a response given by another who successfully moved on to another kōan, but the imitator would not move on. In other words, you cannot cheat. There are no shortcuts. Whether discussed in talks and writings or answered by the student face-to-face with the teacher, kōans point to something more fundamental than the usual categories we draw upon when we speak, and students are expected to reply to kōans in the same way.

One kōan can take a day or a decade to actualize. In manifesting a kōan, words are often secondary, as Wu-men, himself a master of kōans, cautions:

> Words can't explain things,
> Phrases don't connect with spirit;
> Those who cling to words are lost,
> Those attached to phrases are befuddled.
> (Chapter 12)

Regarding kōans, the Korean Master So Sahn wrote, "All of these focused efforts come only from the deepest mind, and are not artificial. It is a kind of intense sincerity. Without such a deeply straightforward striving mind, it is impossible to attain enlightenment" (Chapter 22).

Different concepts of enlightenment are articulated in Zen texts. This is not a problem in the context of the Buddhist tradition, for the aim is practical: the cessation of suffering, which does not require uniform understanding of an absolute truth. Philosophical analysis and stretching the limits of rational thinking can, however, assist in the effort to cease suffering, for they are potent tools for cutting through the delusions that propel one into suffering in the first place. Several Zen Masters throughout history have put their prodigious faculties to use in sorting out whether the nature of enlightenment is such that it occurs suddenly or through gradual cultivation. Their responses indicate that the distinction between these characterizations should not be overstated, for they are more like two ends of a continuum. Dōgen has the shortest answer: "Practice *is* enlightenment." What then is Zen practice?

In sum, Zen practice can include seated meditation (zazen) and kōans. It also often involves sutra study, cleaning, cooking, chanting, making offerings, bowing, working, and eating. Some teachers stress a great deal of lengthy meditation. Others stress actualization in everyday activities like cooking and cleaning. Still others focus on intellectual insight facilitated by study of sutras and commentaries. Many employ kōans. Each school, monastery, temple, teacher, and practitioner strives for a functional balance among these practices, with the aim to act compassionately in the present moment, doing the needful with wisdom.

As you approach the texts in the *Zen Sourcebook,* you are invited to recognize how you are a participant in ongoing interactions and conversations with and about many of the greatest Zen teachers that China, Korea, and Japan have to offer. The multiple points of views, concerns, and aims that each of you as a reader brings to your readings further enhance and develop this body of teachings that were originally intended to goad, inspire, and guide people in pursuit of enlightenment. Even when your aim is purely academic, to engage in reading as a self-conscious reflexive process will refine your critical insights and generate more finely nuanced and sophisticated analyses. For, in reading these texts, several layers of interpretive context come into play—the original historical and cultural contexts of the texts, the social dynamics that have preserved these specific texts enabling us to access them today, the translations into English, and the questions and worldviews of each reader.

Finally, as you read the stories, conversations, encounters, sermons, letters, and poems in this book, you might keep in mind that their original purpose was to express and help guide others to enlightenment. As Hakuin wrote, "All living beings are originally Buddhas . . . look within and find the self-nature beyond the self, / And you will transcend words and explanations."

Paula Arai

NOTES ON TRANSLATION

Most of the texts in this volume, whether they are by Chinese, Korean, or Japanese Masters, were written in Chinese characters. This means that each word has a separate written graph that may equally be a noun, verb, adverb, or adjective; if a noun, it may be singular or plural with no change of form. Unlike Japanese, Chinese verbs and adjectives do not have endings that define their grammatical positions, although a general sentence pattern of subject-verb-object is common, and adjectives usually precede nouns. There is no punctuation, nor are there spaces between phrases, sentences, or paragraphs, and occasionally a two-word compound will mean something different than each word separately. As can be imagined, translation from Chinese into English is difficult, and when dealing with complex Zen texts, the problems only intensify; no translation is, or could ever be, completely definitive.

For example, when Bodhidharma was asked who he was by the Emperor, he answered, 不 (no, not) 識 (know, discriminate). These two words are often translated, "I don't know," but could also mean, "You don't know," "We don't know," or more generally, "Not known," "Not knowing," or "No discrimination."

In order for readers to understand and experience the translation process, the following excerpts are offered with the most common meanings given next to the Chinese characters. Words are read in columns from top to bottom, beginning on the upper right.

Wu-men-kuan Case One (see page 91 for a translation)

還	also, yet, restore	趙	Chao
有	have	州	Chou
佛	Buddha	和	high monk
性	gender, nature, quality	尚	[joins character above]
也	to be, is	因	because, then, therefore
無	*Mu,* no, not, nothing	僧	monk
州	Chou	問	ask
云	say	狗	dog
無	*Mu,* no, not, nothing	子	child, enclitic addition

A second example moves from prose to poetry, in this case a quatrain by Ikkyū in "regulated verse" of seven characters per line (see page 198 for a translation). The poem is entitled "Deluded and Enlightened"; here are the

first two lines, reading downward from the top right, followed by lines three
and four:

不	not	無	*Mu,* no, not, nothing
成	be, become	始	begin
佛	Buddha	無	*Mu,* no, not, nothing
性	gender, nature, quality	終	end, complete
本	original, innate	私	I, me, myself
来	[joins character above]	一	one, single
心	heart, mind	心	heart, mind
衆	humankind	本	original, innate
生	[joins character above]	来	[joins character above]
本	original, innate	成	be, become
来	[joins character above]	佛	Buddha
迷	confusion, delusion	佛	Buddha
道	road, way, path	妄	arbitrary, reckless
心	heart, mind	話	talk

Paula Arai adds that the "Four Great Vows" of the Mahayana (Bodhisattva) tradition are also often chanted in the language of their community, whether it be Chinese, Korean, Japanese, or English. Now reading from
left to right, the "Vows" in Chinese characters and Japanese transliteration
follow:

衆生無辺誓願度	*shu-jō-mu-hen-sei-gan-do*
煩悩無尽誓願断	*bon-nō-mu-jin-sei-gan-dan*
法門無量誓願学	*hō-mon-mu-ryō-sei-gan-gaku*
仏道無上誓願成	*butsu-dō-mu-jō-sei-gan-jō*

Breaking down the vows into discrete words will enable you to
further participate in the translation project underway in the North American transformation of Buddhism and develop your own version of this
vow.

1. 衆生 *shujō*/sentient beings, beings
   無辺 *muhen*/countless, innumerable
   誓願 *seigan*/vow
   度 *do*/cross over [the other shore, a metaphor of
   enlightenment]

2. 煩悩 *bonnō*/defilements, worldly passions
    無尽 *mujin*/inexhaustible, endless
    誓願 *seigan*/vow
    断   *dan*/extinguish, uproot

3. 法   *hō*/dharma, law, truth
    門   *mon*/gate
    無量 *muryō*/immeasurable, nonquantifiable
    誓願 *seigan*/vow
    学   *gaku*/study, master

4. 仏道 *butsudō*/Buddhist Path
    無上 *mujō*/unsurpassable, supreme
    誓願 *seigan*/vow
    成   *jō*/attain, actualize, become

Before you read on, you may enjoy taking the opportunity to render the vows into English yourself.

At this point you can compare your version to one typical translation:

1. However innumerable sentient beings are, I vow to save them.
2. However inexhaustible the defilements are, I vow to extinguish them.
3. However immeasurable the dharmas are, I vow to master them.
4. However incomparable enlightenment is, I vow to attain it.

As you have probably already noticed, the above English translation adds (as is common practice) the subject "I" to suit English grammar conventions, but "I" does not appear in the originals. This insertion of a stress upon the "self" while vowing to realize the wisdom that includes the concept of "no-self" is an unfortunate result of translating across linguistic traditions that developed with different assumptions about reality. The following is an effort to impart a version that carries the resonance of the Chinese characters:

1. Vowing to liberate all beings,
2. Vowing to extinguish inexhaustible defilements,
3. Vowing to master immeasurable dharma gates,
4. Vowing to actualize the supreme way of the Buddhist Path (of wisdom and compassion).

The stress is now on committing to particular activities and results, not on the self.

CHINESE ZEN

1

The *Heart Sutra* and the

Kanzeon Sutra (complete)

*Serving as a prelude to the specifically Zen teachings that follow, two
fundamental Buddhist chants present some of the background that informs
what is called* Ch'an *in China,* Son *in Korea, and* Zen *in Japan.
The* Heart Sutra *is arguably the fundamental text of East Asian
Buddhism. It has been enormously influential, and it is chanted as part of
daily practice in virtually all Zen temples. It was long thought to have been a
section or an abbreviation of the 600-volume Sanskrit* Perfection of Wisdom
Sutra. *A recent study by Jan Nattier suggests that the* Heart Sutra *was actually
composed in China, probably in the seventh century, and later translated into
Sanskrit. Although the center section was indeed taken from the* Perfection of
Wisdom Sutra, *the beginning and end seem to have been originally written
in Chinese, leading to a genuine Sanskrit mantra at the close. This text may
have been originally intended for chanting as a scripture, rather than
composed as a sutra per se, but known as the "*Heart Sutra*" it has become a
major inspiration for many Buddhist sects.*

Since the Heart Sutra *is a text of great power, readers are best served by
experiencing it directly. Therefore we will avoid most of the massive scholarship
and commentary that has arisen around this text over the past fourteen
hundred years and provide only a few brief notes for basic orientation. The
original title is:* Maha prajna paramita hridaya sutra. *Word by word, this
says: "great wisdom perfection heart sutra." Unpacking the syntax, it means:
"the heart of the great perfection of wisdom."*

*One of the significant features that characterizes Mahayana Buddhism is
the idea of Bodhisattvas, enlightened beings who have resolved to stay on earth
until all sentient beings are saved.* Avalokitesvara (Kwan-yin *or* Guanyin *in
Chinese,* Kwan Se Um *in Korean, and* Kannon *or* Kanzeon *in Japanese) is
the Bodhisattva of Compassion. Sariputra, to whom the teaching is directed,
was foremost among the Buddha's disciples in understanding* abhidharma,
the main stream of early Buddhist philosophy.

*Beginning with form and ending with awakening, the long list of
categories that are negated in the* Heart Sutra *largely come from* abhidharma.

*They include the six components of perception (mind is also considered a
sense organ) and an abbreviated list of the twelve links in the chain of
codependence, all of which are contained in the five skandhas, often translated
as elements, aggregates, or constituents of human existence.*

*Although they are philosophically complex, the skandhas can be
approached through experience. Walking through a garden (form), you notice
something red (sensation), see that it's a flower (perception), and reach out to
pluck it or decide to leave it for others to enjoy (volition). Your overall
awareness of yourself in this situation is the fifth skandha (consciousness).
These then are the five elements of existence: form, sensation, perception,
volition, and consciousness.*

*The Heart Sutra also deals with the Four Noble Truths of Buddhism: life
entails suffering, which is caused by our cravings, anger, and ignorance, yet
these can be released, by methods that include meditation. But what then is
the focus of meditation? Early Buddhism emphasized impermanence as the
fundamental nature of all things; in response the Heart Sutra proclaims the
ultimate characteristic to be emptiness (sunyata). This is not nihilism—
emptiness is not nothingness—and Zen Buddhism emphasizes that an
experiential understanding of sunyata can lead to awakening.*

The *Maha Prajna Paramita Hrdaya* Heart Sutra

Avalokitesvara, the Bodhisattva of all-seeing and all-
hearing, practicing deep *prajna paramita*, perceives the
five *skandhas* in their self-nature to be empty.

O Sariputra, form is emptiness, emptiness is form; form
is nothing but emptiness, emptiness is nothing but
form; that which is form is emptiness, and that which is
emptiness is form. The same is true for sensation,
perception, volition, and consciousness.

O Sariputra, all things are by nature empty. They are
not born, they are not extinguished; they are not
tainted, they are not pure; they do not increase, they do
not decrease. Within emptiness there is no form, and
therefore no sensation, perception, volition, or
consciousness; no eye, ear, nose, tongue, body, or mind;
no form, sound, scent, taste, touch, or thought.

It extends from no vision to no discernment, from no ignorance to no end to ignorance, and from no old age and death to no extinction of old age and death. There is no suffering, origination, annihilation, or path; there is no cognition, no attainment, and no realization.

Because there is no attainment in the mind of the Bodhisattva who dwells in *prajna paramita* there are no obstacles and therefore no fear or delusion. Nirvana is attained: all Buddhas of the past, present, and future, through *prajna paramita*, reach the highest all-embracing enlightenment.

Therefore know that *prajna paramita* holds the great Mantra, the Mantra of great clarity, the unequaled Mantra that allays all pain through truth without falsehood. This is the Mantra proclaimed in *prajna paramita*, saying:

> *Gate gate paragate parasamgate*
> *bodhi svaha*
> Gone, gone, gone beyond, gone altogether beyond,
> Awake! All hail!

—Translation by Stephen Addiss
with thanks to Stanley Lombardo

The *Kanzeon Sutra* in Ten Lines

Zen is rooted in Mahayana Buddhism—Hakuin talks of "the Zen meditation of Mahayana Buddhism" in his Song of Meditation *(see Chapter 24)—and these roots are most evident in the texts chanted in most Zen monasteries, Zen temples, and Zen centers around the world. The four great vows of the Mahayana school, homage to the line of ancestors stretching back to the historical Buddha Shakyamuni, and invocations of* Avalokitesvara *(usually under the names of more female forms and often called* Kanzeon) *pervade Zen practice.*

Here we give a brief example of a chant focused on Avalokitesvara, *the* Kanzeon Sutra *in ten lines. Originating in China (no one knows exactly when, but most probably over a thousand years ago), it was championed by Hakuin and is ubiquitous in Japanese Rinzai practice; it also is chanted in some Sōtō sect temples. In its ten lines it conflates* Kanzeon; *homage to* Buddha, Dharma *(doctrine), and* sangha *(congregation); meditation instruction; and difficult philosophical points.*

The compactness of the Chinese text leads inevitably to a wide variation in translations into English, and we provide notes not only to justify this translation but also to signal some of the difficulties inherent in translating Buddhist, and especially Zen, texts.

"At one" is a translation of namu, *which is ordinarily a devotional term.*

The third and fourth lines are about direct and indirect cause (for example, a cigarette butt would be a direct cause of a fire, while the dryness of the vegetation would be an indirect cause), but the word for indirect cause is also associated with notions of affinity and closeness, and that is the approach taken here.

The sixth line is a fairly common Mahayana inversion of terms from early Buddhism (eternal instead of *impermanent, joyous* instead of *suffering, existing* instead of *absence of self, and* pure *instead of* impure). *The third word literally is "self" but in many translations is transformed into "selfless." In effect, this line is another way of contradicting what the* Heart Sutra *also contradicts through its lengthy string of negations.*

In the last two lines, thoughts arise in mind and then turn out to be just this mind. This can be taken both as instructions useful in meditation and as a point about the absolute and the relative, similar to that which is made in the Sandōkai *(see Chapter 5). The word for "mind" here does not distinguish between individual mind and universal mind.*

Since the text is so short, we also include the Sino-Japanese, which is traditionally chanted on one note to the steady beat of a drum (in the shape of a large fish). Nearly every syllable gets its own beat, with the exception of the words underlined, which are two syllables to the beat. The sutra is always repeated without stopping, frequently nine times but often much more.

Kanzeon,
At one with Buddha,
Caused by Buddha,
Close to Buddha
And to Buddha, Dharma, Sangha,
Eternal, joyous, existing, pure.
Morning thoughts are Kanzeon;
Evening thoughts are Kanzeon;
Thoughts, thoughts arise in mind;
All these thoughts are just this mind.

Kanzeon
Namu butsu
Yo butsu u in
Yo butsu u en
Buppo so en
Jo raku ga jo
Cho nen Kanzeon
Bo nen Kanzeon
Nen nen ju shin ki
Nen nen fu ri shin.

—Translation by Stanley Lombardo

Figure 1. Hakuin Ekaku (1684–1768), *Bodhidharma*

Pointing directly to the human mind,
See your own nature and become Buddha.

2

Bodhidharma (died c. 532)

The Two Paths (complete)

The semi-legendary figure Bodhidharma (Japanese: Daruma) is considered both the twenty-eighth generation from the historical Buddha Shakyamuni, and the founder of East Asian Zen. He is therefore the First Zen Patriarch, and later Masters count their generations from him. Because accounts of Bodhidharma's life and teachings were generally written some time after his life, they are historically questionable; a few scholars have even wondered if he existed at all. Nevertheless, Bodhidharma has been of supreme importance in the Zen tradition and is the subject most often depicted in Zen painting, where he represents meditation itself.

According to later accounts, Bodhidharma was the third son of a monarch from South India; he became a Buddhist monk, and traveled to southern China sometime after the year 500 C.E. He was welcomed by the Emperor Wu-ti of the Liang Dynasty, who told him of the many good works he had done, such as building temples. But when the Emperor asked how much merit he had acquired, Bodhidharma said "None."

"What is the first principle of sacred truth?"
"Vast emptiness, nothing sacred."
"Who then is facing me?"
"Don't know."

The Emperor was perplexed, and Bodhidharma departed northward to cross the Yangtze River (supposedly on a reed but more likely on a reed raft), and meditated in front of a wall near the Shao-lin temple for nine years, his famous "wall-gazing" of extraordinary meditation. At this point a Chinese monk named Hui-k'o asked for his guidance, but Bodhidharma was so intent on meditation that he did not notice until the monk cut off one of his arms to show his serious intent. This decisive action is seen as a metaphor for the commitment needed to study Zen. The story of Bodhidharma's subsequent teaching to Hui-k'o became Case Forty-One of the Wu-men-kuan (Japanese:

Mumonkan; *see Chapter 12), a collection of Zen anecdotes and encounters that are given as meditation questions to monks in training.*

Although probably dating to a later century, Bodhidharma's most famous teaching is regarded as the essential statement on Zen, with the understanding that in Chinese and Japanese, the character here translated as "mind" also means "heart" and could be translated either way.

> Without relying on words and writings,
> A special transmission outside the scriptures;
> Pointing directly to the human mind,
> See your own nature and become Buddha.

A story of Bodhidharma's understanding of his four leading followers, although recorded several hundred years later, tells us more about his teaching.

After nine years of teaching, Bodhidharma wished to return to the West [India] and asked his pupils what they had attained from his teaching. Tao-fu said, "In my understanding, the truth neither holds onto words and writings nor is separate from them, yet they can help to realize the Way." The Master replied, "You have attained my skin."

Next the nun Tsung-chih said, "In my understanding, the truth is like a fortunate glimpse of the Eastern Paradise of Akshobya; it can be seen one time and not again." The Master replied, "You have attained my flesh."

Tao-yu then said, "The four elements are originally empty, and the five aspects of personality are nonexistent. In my understanding, there is no teaching to be grasped." The Master replied, "You have attained my bones."

Hui-k'o bowed respectfully and remained silent. The Master said, "You have attained my marrow."

Hui-k'o was then given the transmission as Second Patriarch, and East Asian Zen was firmly established as a continuing tradition.

Several short sermon texts are also attributed to Bodhidharma, one of which teaches two methods of Zen practice.

The Two Paths

Many paths enter the Way, but they do not go beyond two basic kinds. The first is entering through principle, and the second is through practice. To enter through principle means using teachings to awaken the essence and understanding that all beings have the same true nature, which does not shine clearly because it is covered with the dust of delusion. When you abandon the false to cherish the real and meditate in front of a wall, you will discover that there is no separation between self and other; ordinary people and sages are the same. Not bound by words, free from concepts and discriminations, you will be completely in accord with inner truth. This is called entering through principle.

To enter through practice means the four practices that include all others. What are these four? The first is making amends for injustices. The second is accepting worldly conditions. The third is not craving. The fourth is practicing the Dharma.

What is the practice of making amends for injustices? When struggling with difficulties, the person who cultivates the Way should think, "In countless past ages I have deserted the root and followed the branches through a multitude of existences, giving in to feelings of anger and hatred, creating limitless transgressions. Even if I lead a blameless life, the evil deeds of the past have ripened, so any sufferings I feel now are not to be blamed on gods or other humans." You should accept any difficulties that life brings without complaint, for the sutras say, "When you meet with adversity there is no need to be upset, because from a higher viewpoint the basic cause can be understood." If you can keep this attitude in mind, you will be in harmony with truth, and you can make the experience of adversity into practice to enter the Way. This is called making amends for injustice.

What is the practice of accepting worldly conditions? We sentient beings have no true selves but experience happiness and suffering depending upon conditions stemming from cause and effect. If I find fame and fortune, that is the outcome of deeds from the past—but when conditions change, they will disappear, so why be exultant? Gain and loss come from conditions, but Mind neither increases nor decreases. If you are not stirred by the winds of joy or sorrow, you are in silent accord with the Way. This is called accepting worldly conditions.

What is the practice of not craving? People in this world are always seeking one thing or another outside themselves, which is called craving. But those who are wise wake up and maintain the serenity of inner truth while their bodies change with the seasons and laws of causation. All things are empty, so there is nothing to seek and crave. The sutras tell us that seeking leads to suffering, and happiness comes when we cease craving, so we can know that seeking nothing is the Way. This is called not craving.

Finally, what is practicing the Dharma? The Dharma teaches that all natures are inherently pure, and the truth of all manifestations is emptiness. There is no impurity, no attachment, no self, and no other. The sutras say, "In Dharma there are no sentient beings, because it is detached from any impurity of sentient beings; in Dharma there is no self, because it is free from any impurities of selfhood." When the wise understand this truth, they practice the Dharma. Since they have no desire to possess, they practice charity with their bodies, lives, and property without grudging, without partiality, and without attachment to giving. They merely benefit other sentient beings and follow the Way without grasping at forms. As with charity, they also practice the other virtues in order to eliminate delusions, but without being conscious of being virtuous. This is called practicing the Dharma.

—Translation by Stephen Addiss

3

Seng-ts'an (died 606)

Hsin-hsin-ming (Trust in Mind, complete)

Seng-ts'an (Japanese: Sōzan) was the Third Patriarch of Chinese Zen, having received transmission from Bodhidharma's successor, Hui-k'o. Seng-ts'an may have been suffering from leprosy when he met Hui-k'o, and later tradition records their moment of truth, which echoes Hui-k'o's famous encounter with Bodhidharma (see Chapter 12, Wu-men-kuan, Case Forty-One), *along these lines.*

> Seng Ts'an went to Hui-k'o and said, "My body is gripped by a fatal disease. Please, Master, wipe away my sins."
> Hui-k'o said: "Bring your sins out here, and I will wipe them away for you."
> Seng-ts'an sat for a while and then said, "When I look for my sins I cannot find them." Hui-k'o answered, "I have wiped away your sins."

Soon after Seng-ts'an received transmission, Buddhism was persecuted in China and he spent fifteen years wandering and hiding in the mountains. Out of all this hard training comes this poem—the first on record that is attributed to a Zen Master. In the year 582 he met Tao-hsin, who was to become his pupil and thereupon the Fourth Patriarch, and in this way the transmission of Zen continued.

The title Hsin-hsin-ming 信心銘 *has the literal meaning "Trust Mind Inscription." The character for the first* hsin *is composed of two parts* 信, *showing a man on the left standing by his words. The second* hsin *is the character for "heart-mind"* 心, *while* ming *is composed of "metal" and "name"* 銘 *and means "carving" or "inscription." Blending Taoist and Buddhist teachings of oneness, equality, suchness, and interpenetration, the* Hsin-hsin-ming *introduces us to a vast and meticulous world in which time and space no longer have their ordinary meanings and in which*

> Bright and empty,
> mind shines by itself.

The poem consists of 146 lines and differs from standard Chinese verse in that the lines are unrhymed. It also follows an archaic form of poetry with only four characters to each line instead of the usual five or seven, creating a terse, no-nonsense sense of movement.

The Great Way is not difficult:
Just don't pick and choose.
Cut off all likes and dislikes
And it is clear like space.

The slightest distinction
Splits heaven from earth.
To see the truth
Don't be for or against.

Suffering

Likes and dislikes
Are the mind's disease.
If you miss the deep meaning,
It is useless to still your thoughts.

It is clear as vast space,   *mind*
Nothing missing, nothing extra.
If you choose or reject,
You cannot see things as they are.

Outside, don't get tangled in things.
Inside, don't get lost in emptiness.
Be still and become One,
And confusion stops by itself.

Stop moving to become still,
And the stillness will move.
If you hold on to opposites,
You cannot understand One.

If you don't understand One,
This and that cannot function.
Denied, the world goes on.
Pursued, emptiness is lost.

No dualism

The more you think and talk,
The more you lose the Way.
Cut off all thinking
And pass freely anywhere.

Return to the root and understand, *Injustice*
Chase outcomes and lose the source.
One clear moment within
Illumines the emptiness before you.

Huineng

Emptiness changing into things
Is only our deluded view.
Do not seek the truth,
Only let go of your opinions.

dualism

Do not live in the world of opposites.
Be careful! Never go that way.
If you make right and wrong,
Your mind is lost in confusion.

Two comes from One,
But do not cling even to this One.
If one mind does not arise,
The ten thousand things are without fault.

No fault, no ten thousand things,
No arising, no mind.
No world, no one to see it,
No one to see it, no world.

*Life and death,
as they are,
is Nirvana.*

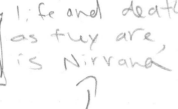

This comes when that goes.
That arises when this sinks.
Understand both
As originally one emptiness.

key

In emptiness the two are the same,
And each holds the ten thousand things.
If you do not see great or small,
How can you prefer one to the other?

key

The Way is calm and wide,
Not easy, not difficult.
But small minds get lost.
Hurrying, they fall behind.

Clinging, they go too far,
Sure to take a wrong turn.
Just let it be! In the end,
Nothing goes, nothing stays.

Follow nature and find the Way,
Free, easy, and undisturbed.
Tied to your thoughts, you lose the truth,
Become heavy, dull, and unwell.

Not well, the mind is troubled,
So why hold or reject anything?
To ride the One Vehicle,
Do not despise the six senses.

Not despising the six senses
Is already enlightenment.
The wise do not act,
Fools bind themselves.

In true Dharma there is no this or that,
So why blindly chase desires?
Using mind to grasp mind
Is the original mistake.

Peaceful and troubled are only ideas.
Enlightenment has no likes or dislikes.
All opposites arise
From faulty views.

Illusions, flowers in the air—
Why try to grasp them?
Win, lose, right, wrong—
Put it all down!

If the eye never sleeps,
Dreams disappear by themselves.

If the mind makes no distinctions,
The ten thousand things are one essence.

See the deep and dark essence
And be free from entanglements.
See the ten thousand things as equal
And return to true nature.

+ the fundamental buddha-Nature

Without any distinctions
There can be no comparisons.
Stop and there is no motion.
Move and there is no stillness.

Without motion or stillness,
How can a single thing exist?
In true nature
There are no goals or plans.

In the mind before thinking
No effort is made.
Doubts and worries disappear
And faith is restored.

Nothing is left behind,
Nothing stays with us.
Bright and empty,
The mind shines by itself.

In the mind without effort
Thinking cannot take root.
In the true Dharma world
There is no self or other.

bc all is one buddha Nature.

To abide in this world
Just say "Not two."
"Not two" includes everything,
Excludes nothing.

monoism

Enlightened beings everywhere
All return to the Source.
Beyond time and space,
One moment is ten thousand years.

Nothing here, nothing there,
But the universe is always before you.
Infinitely small is infinitely large:
No boundaries, no differences.

Infinitely large is infinitely small:
Measurements do not matter here.
What is, is what is not.
What is not, is what is.

Where it is not like this,
Do not bother staying.
One is all,
All is one.

When you see things like this,
You are already complete.
Trust and Mind are not two.
Not-two is Trust in Mind.

The Way is beyond all words:
Not past, not future, not present.

—Translation by Stanley Lombardo

4

Hui-neng (638–713)

Autobiography (complete)

from the *Platform Sutra*

One of the most important Masters in the history of Zen was Hui-neng, an uneducated layman who did not become a monk until many years after he was given transmission to become the Sixth Patriarch. Hui-neng's teachings have been so admired that they have been entitled the Platform Sutra (also known as the Altar Sutra), although strictly speaking a sutra is supposed to represent the words of the historical Buddha Shakyamuni.

The first section of the Platform Sutra consists of the record of a public talk that includes the autobiography of Hui-neng; most of what is known about him comes from this record. As history, it may well have been altered and expanded over the centuries, an occurrence that seems to have happened with several Zen documents; some sections have been used as polemical arguments within Zen traditions, the beginning of longstanding disagreements about the best approaches to Zen practice. As teachings, several sections of this text have become especially celebrated, such as the two poems that were composed in response to a request from the Fifth Patriarch, the significant question that Hui-neng gave to the monk in a mountain pass, and the story of the flag blowing in the wind.

One of the many interesting points in this account is how Hui-neng faced prejudice as a "barbarian" layman from the south. Some interpreters have assumed this to mean that he was an aborigine or otherwise racially different from the northern Chinese, since the text suggests he was visually distinct from other followers of the Fifth Patriarch. The danger posed by prejudice within the large community at the monastery was serious enough to make even the Fifth Patriarch cautious. Yet Hui-neng's background has an important positive meaning as well. If an uneducated layman from a poor family within a subsidiary ethnic group could achieve enlightenment and become the Sixth Patriarch, then seeing one's self-nature is possible for anyone. In this sense Zen is completely democratic.

This narrative emphasizes[sudden enlightenment,]which was to be a feature of "southern school" Zen while the "northern tradition" emphasized gradual attainment, although this distinction is not always clear-cut. In addition, the text stresses the importance of Dharma transmission from one Master to the next, even while making clear that there is nothing to be transmitted beyond symbols such as the robe. One of the effective paradoxes in Zen is that transmission is vital, and yet one must find self-nature, the essence of mind, for oneself.

How much of the text can be certainly ascribed to Hui-neng himself is unsure, but there is so much unique material included that it suggests a certain amount of authenticity. At present, there are two primary versions of this text; the earlier one is shorter and possibly more reliable, but the later version contains several phrases that have become important in Zen teaching, so this is the text given here. As an important source of teachings (Dharma), the Platform Sutra *remains an extremely significant document for early Zen.*

When the Sixth Patriarch arrived at the Pao Lin Monastery, Magistrate Wei of the Shao-chou district, along with local officials, went to the monastery to ask him to deliver public talks on Buddhism in the Ta Fan temple for the benefit of all who would attend. When the Patriarch took his place, the audience included the magistrate, thirty other officials, more than thirty Confucian scholars, and more than a thousand Buddhist monks and nuns, Taoists, and laypeople. They all bowed, wishing to hear the essentials of Buddha-Dharma, so the Patriarch gave this talk.

Good friends, our enlightened self-nature is pure and clean, and it can be used to understand and attain Buddhahood. Let me tell you something about my own life and how I came to understand the Dharma of the Zen school. My father came from Fan-yang, but he was dismissed from his governmental post and banished to become a commoner in Hsin-chou. Unfortunately for me, he died early, so my mother and I lived in poverty and distress. We moved to Nan-hai where I sold firewood to help support us.

One day a customer bought wood from me and requested me to deliver it to his shop. He received the wood and paid me, but as I left the shop I saw a man reciting a Buddhist sutra. When I heard the words, my mind immediately awakened. I asked him what was the name of the sutra, and he said it was the *Diamond Sutra,* so I asked where he came from and why he chanted these words. He replied, "I came from Eastern Meditation Monastery in Huang-mei District of the province of Ch'i, where the Master is the Fifth Patriarch [of Zen]; he has more than a thousand followers. The

Master tells his disciples to read the *Diamond Sutra* in order to reach their own essence of mind and attain Buddhahood."

It must be due to some good cause from one of my former lives that a customer for my firewood gave me ten silver *taels* for the upkeep of my mother and advised me to go seek out the Fifth Patriarch. After I made arrangements for my mother, I left and thirty days later reached Huang-mei, where I paid reverence to the Patriarch. He asked me where I came from and what I wanted, so I replied that I had come as a commoner from afar to pay homage to him, and that I asked for nothing but Buddhahood.

The Patriarch said, "You are a barbarian from the south; how could you expect to become a Buddha?"

I replied, "There are people in the south and people in the north, but their Buddha-nature is the same. As a barbarian I may be different from you physically, but what difference could there be in our Buddha-nature?"

The Patriarch was ready to speak further, but he stopped because of the presence of other people around him and ordered me to join other followers at work. I replied, "May I say that wisdom arises in my mind, and since I do not stray from my essence of mind, I am in a field of blessings; I don't know what work you would have me do."

The Patriarch said, "This barbarian has a sharp mind! Go to the backyard and speak no more," so I went to the back of the monastery and worked, splitting firewood and pounding rice.

More than eight months later, the Patriarch came to see me and said, "I know your understanding is very deep, and I have been considering what to do. I have not spoken to you in case some evil men might do you harm—do you understand?"

"Yes," I replied, "and to avoid having people take notice of me, I haven't come to the main hall."

One day the Patriarch summoned all of his followers and said to them, "The question of birth and death is a most important matter. All day long, you seek out only your own blessings instead of freeing yourself from the sea of death and rebirth. If your self-nature is deluded, blessings will not save you. Go seek for wisdom in your own minds, and then write me a stanza; whoever understands the essence of mind will be given my robe and teachings to become the Sixth Patriarch. Go quickly and don't linger, for thinking and reasoning won't help at all in perceiving your self-nature. The person who can understand will perceive it even if engaged in battle."

After receiving these instructions, the followers withdrew and said to each other, "There's no use in us concentrating our minds to write the verse for his Holiness, since the head monk Shen-hsiu is our instructor and is certain to be the winner. It will only be a waste of effort on our parts to try to write the stanza; let's just follow Shen-hsiu."

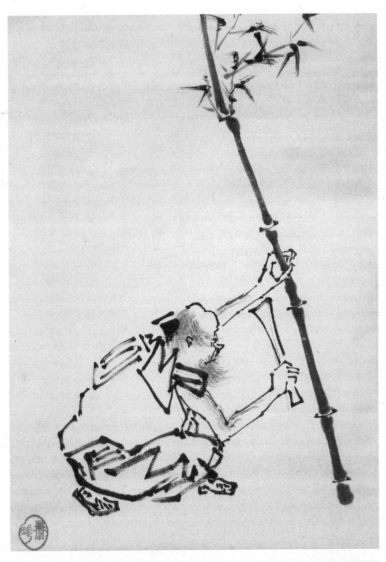

**Figure 2. Stephen Addiss after Liang K'ai, *The Sixth Patriarch
Chopping Bamboo***

Shen-hsiu himself thought, "Since the others would not submit a stanza because I am their instructor, I must certainly compose a verse, for if I don't, how can I know if my understanding is deep or shallow? If my purpose is wisdom, my motive is pure. If I desire to become the next Patriarch, however, my mind is worldly, because I am trying to usurp the rank of a holy person. Yet if I don't submit a stanza, I'll never achieve the Dharma—how difficult, how difficult!"

In front of the Patriarch's hallway there were three corridors that were to be painted by the court artist Lu Chen with images from the *Lankavatara Sutra*. These would depict the transformations of the assembly and the genealogy of patriarchs for veneration by the public.

Shen-hsiu composed a stanza and tried several times to submit it to the Patriarch, but every time he approached the door, his mind became so perturbed that he broke into a sweat. He simply did not have the courage to present it, despite trying thirteen times over the course of four days. Finally he thought to himself, "It would be better to write it on the corridor wall and let the Patriarch see it. If he approves, I will come and bow to him as the writer of the verse, but if he doesn't approve, I will realize that I will have wasted many years here receiving the reverence of others—how could I then practice the Dharma?"

At midnight Shen-hsiu went secretly with his lamp to write his stanza on the south corridor wall, posting the following verse to present his understanding.

> The body is the tree of enlightenment,
> The mind is like a bright mirror's stand;
> Time after time polish it diligently
> So that no dust can collect.

After writing this, Shen-hsiu returned to his room without anyone seeing him. But again he worried, "When the Patriarch sees my verse tomorrow, if he is pleased I will be ready for the Dharma, but if he says it is unfit, it will mean that I must have bad karma from previously lives so I am not qualified—I cannot guess what he will say!" In this manner he could neither sleep nor sit at ease with himself.

The Patriarch already knew that Shen-hsiu had not entered the door to perceiving his own nature. The next morning, he sent for Lu Chen and went with him to the south corridor, where he unexpectedly found the stanza. He said to the artist, "I'm sorry to have caused you this long trip, since there's no need for you to paint the wall now; as the *[Diamond] Sutra* says, 'All forms are transient and unreal.' We will leave this verse here so that people can study and recite it. If they put its teaching into practice, evil realms can be avoided and great merit will be the result." Then he ordered incense to be lit, and for all his followers to pay homage and recite the stanza so that they might come to realize the essence of mind. After they had recited it, they all said, "Excellent!"

At midnight, the Patriarch sent for Shen-hsiu to come to the hall, and asked if he had written the stanza. Shen-hsiu replied, "Yes; I do not dare seek to be Patriarch, but I hope that you will tell me if my verse shows even a grain of wisdom."

The Patriarch said, "Your stanza demonstrates that you have not yet perceived your own nature; you have reached only the doorway and have not yet entered. To seek for complete enlightenment with such a mind cannot succeed, for to achieve supreme enlightenment you must instantly understand your own fundamental nature and essence of mind. This fundamental self-nature has no birth or death, and at every moment you must realize the essence of mind. Once this suchness is known, you will be free from all delusions. Suchness is absolute reality, and when it is perceived, you are in a state of enlightenment. Why don't you go and take a few more days to think it over, and then submit another stanza; if this verse shows that you have entered the gate of enlightenment, I will transmit to you the robe and the Dharma."

Shen-hsiu bowed to the Patriarch and withdrew. For several days he tried his best to write another stanza, but could not because his mind was uneasy and agitated as though in a nightmare; he found no comfort in walking or sitting.

Two days later, a young attendant was passing the room where I was pounding rice, and he chanted the stanza by Shen-hsiu. As soon as I heard it, I knew that the person who had composed it had not perceived his own nature. Even though I had not been taught about it at this time, I already understood the main idea, so I asked the attendant, "Whose verse are you chanting?"

He replied, "You barbarian, don't you know about it? The Patriarch told his disciples that the question of birth and death is a most important matter, and since he was ready to transmit the robe and Dharma to a successor, he ordered his followers to compose a stanza and submit it to him. He said that whoever understood the essence of mind would become the Sixth Patriarch. Our head monk Shen-hsiu wrote this verse on formlessness on the wall of the south corridor and the Patriarch told us to recite it, saying that if we put its teaching into practice, evil realms could be avoided and great merit would be the result."

I told the attendant that I wished also to recite the stanza so that I might gain merit in a future life. I added that I had been pounding rice for eight months but had never been to the main hall, and asked him to show me the stanza so that I might pay homage.

The attendant took me to the corridor, and I asked that the verse be read to me, since I could not read characters. A low-ranking official from Chiang-chou named Chang Jih-yung, who happened to be there, read it aloud to me, and I said, "I have a stanza too. Would you write it down for me?"

The official exclaimed, "You have also composed a verse? How extraordinary!"

I replied, "If you wish to seek out enlightenment, don't despise a beginner, for the lowest rank of person may have wisdom that high-ranking people ignore. If you slight others, you commit a great sin."

The official said, "Dictate to me your stanza, and I will write it down for you. But if you acquire the Dharma, you must liberate me. Please don't forget."

My stanza was this:

> Enlightenment is not a tree,
> The bright mirror has no stand;
> Originally there is not one thing—
> What place could there be for dust?

[Note: In the earliest version of the text, the third line reads "Buddha-nature is always clean and pure," but the third line as given here has become celebrated in Zen.]

When the official wrote this, all the followers who were present were greatly surprised and filled with admiration. They said to each other, "How marvelous! Truly we cannot judge a man by his appearance. How could we have had a Bodhisattva working for us for so long without knowing it?"

Seeing that his followers were amazed, and worrying that jealous people would do me harm, the Patriarch wiped away the stanza with his slipper and expressed the opinion that the author of this verse also had not reached the essence of mind.

The next day the Patriarch came secretly to the room where I pounded rice with a stone tied around my waist [for extra weight on the foot-pedal]. He first asked, "Should not a seeker after the Dharma risk his life this way?" Then he continued, "Is the rice ready?"

"It has been ready for some time," I replied. "It is only waiting to be sieved."

He knocked the foot-pedal three times with his staff and left. I understood the Patriarch's meaning, so that night at the third watch I went to his room. He used his robe as a screen so that no one could see us from outside, and explained the *Diamond Sutra* to me. When he came to the phrase "One should activate one's mind so it has no attachment," I was suddenly and completely enlightened, and understood that all things exist in self-nature. I then exclaimed to the Patriarch, "Who would have thought that self-nature is intrinsically pure? Who would have thought that self-nature is free from birth and death? Who would have thought that self-nature is complete within itself? Who would have thought that self-nature is unchanging? Who would have thought that all things are manifestations of self-nature?"

Characteristics of buddha nature

Knowing that I had realized the essence of mind, the Patriarch said, "For anyone who doesn't know the essence of mind, there is no advantage in studying the Dharma, but anyone who does understand self-nature is a master, a teacher of gods and humans, and a Buddha."

In this way the Dharma was passed to me secretly at midnight, and the Patriarch transmitted to me the doctrine of sudden enlightenment as well as his robe and bowl. He told me, "You are now the Sixth Patriarch. Take care of yourself, save as many sentient beings as you can, and spread the teachings so they will not be lost in the future." He then gave me this stanza:

> Sentient beings sow their seeds
> And cause the earth to bear fruit and return to birth;
> Nonsentient beings have no seeds,
> And their empty self-nature has no rebirth.

The Patriarch also told me, "After the First Patriarch Bodhidharma came to China, people were not sure of the succession, so this robe was transmitted from one Patriarch to the next. As for the Dharma, it is transmitted from mind to mind, to be awakened by self-understanding. From ancient times, Buddhas have taught their followers and Patriarchs transmitted to their successors the realization of self-nature. However, the robe has now become a matter of dispute, and you should not pass it down. If you transmit it, your life will be in great danger. You must leave this monastery quickly before anyone can do you harm."

"Where should I go?"

"You can stop at Huai and then hide yourself at Hui."

Receiving the robe and bowl at midnight, I told the Patriarch that since I came from the south, I did not know the mountain paths, so I could not find my way to the river. He told me that he would accompany me, and took me to the courier's station at Chiu-chiang, where he ordered me into a boat. He then took up the oar and rowed, but I said, "Sir, it is only fitting for me to take the oar."

He replied, "No, it is appropriate for me to row you across."

I said, "While I was deluded, it would have been right for you to row for me, but after my enlightenment I am able to row myself across. I was born on the frontier and do not speak with correct pronunciation, but now that you have transmitted the Dharma to me, my own self-nature can ferry me to the other shore."

The Patriarch replied, "Just so, just so! From this moment, the meditation school will prosper through you. Three years after you leave, I will depart this world, so you should start your journey now and travel as fast as you can to the south. But do not teach the Dharma too soon, or it will be difficult to promote."

After bidding him farewell, I left and traveled to the south on foot; within two months, I reached the Ta-yü Mountains. At this point, I realized that several hundred men were following me with the purpose of robbing me of the robe and bowl of the Patriarch. Among them was a monk whose name was Hui-ming and whose family name was Ch'en. He was a man of fierce temper who had been a military commander, and since he was the most intent on catching up with me, he led the pack. When he was about to overtake me, I put down the robe and bowl on a rock and said, "The robe is nothing but a symbol—what point is there to taking it by force?" Then I hid myself nearby.

When Hui-ming came to the rock, he tried to pick up the robe and bowl, but could not move them. Then he shouted, "Lay brother, lay brother, I have come for the Dharma, not for the robe!"

I came out and sat cross-legged on the rock. Hui-ming bowed and said, "Lay brother, please teach the Dharma to me."

I replied, "Since you have come for the Dharma, first you must empty your mind of feelings so that it does not give rise to a single thought; then I will expound the Dharma." When he had done this for some time, I said, "When you are thinking of neither good nor evil, in that moment, what is your original face?"

Instantly Hui-ming was enlightened. He then asked me, "Beyond the esoteric sayings handed down by the Patriarchs from generation to generation, are there any further teachings?"

I replied, "What you have been taught is not esoteric; if you look inward, that which you call esoteric is inside you."

Hui-ming said, "Although I stayed at Huang-mei, I did not realize my original face. Thanks to your guidance, I now understand, just as someone drinking water knows personally if it is hot or cold. Lay brother, you are now my teacher."

I said, "If this be true, then we are both disciples of the Fifth Patriarch; take good care of yourself." When he asked where he now should go, I told him to travel to Yuan-chou and dwell at Meng-shan.

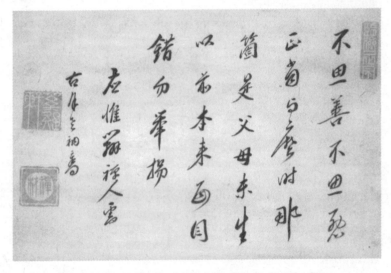

Figure 3. Kogetsu Zenzai (1667–1751), *Original Face*

Not thinking of good or evil,
Just at this moment, who is this?
Before your parents were born,
What was your original face?

After this meeting, I continued to Ts'ao-chi, still pursued by evil men. To avoid trouble, I took refuge in Szu-hui, where I stayed with a group of hunters for a period of fifteen years. I occasionally taught the Dharma to them, in accordance with their capabilities. They often asked me to watch their nets, but when I found a living creature I set it free. At mealtimes, I added vegetables to their pot where they cooked their meat, and when they questioned me, I told them I would only eat the vegetables.

One day I said to myself that it was time to end my seclusion and go preach the Dharma. Accordingly I went to the Fa Hsin temple in Kuang-chou, where the Dharma Master Yin-tsung was lecturing on the *Nirvana Sutra*. One day when the temple pennant was blowing in the wind, two monks were arguing. One claimed that the wind was moving, while the other insisted that it was the pennant that was moving, and they could not come to an agreement. I told them, "It's not the wind moving; it's not the flag moving; it is your minds that are moving."

Everyone was startled by my words, and Yin-tsung asked me to take the seat of honor so he could question me about various difficult points in the sutras. He then said, "Lay brother, you are not an ordinary man. I heard long ago that the person who inherited the robe and Dharma of the Fifth Patriarch would come to the south, and you must be that man."

To this I politely agreed. When he heard this, Yin-tsung bowed to me and asked me to show the robe and bowl to the community of monks. In addition, he asked what instructions the Fifth Patriarch had given me at the time of transmission. I replied that there were no special instructions; apart from looking into one's self-nature, there was no discussion of meditation and deliverance.

Yin-tsung asked, "Why did he not discuss meditation and deliverance?"

I replied, "Because that is a form of dualism, and there is no dualism in Buddha-Dharma."

"What then is the non-dual Buddha-Dharma?"

"The non-dual Dharma is the realization of self-nature. The *Nirvana Sutra*, which you have been teaching, recounts that the Bodhisattva Kao Kuei Te Wang asked the Buddha about those who commit the four major sins or the five perverse sins, or who have no urge for enlightenment—have they lost the roots of their Buddha-nature? The Buddha replied that there are two kinds of roots, permanent and impermanent. Since Buddha-nature is neither permanent nor impermanent, however, the roots can never be eradicated, and this is called non-duality. In addition, the five component parts of one's personality and the eighteen elements of consciousness are separate, but those who are enlightened know that they are not dual in their nature because Buddha-nature is not dual.

Yin-tsung was very pleased with my answers, and putting his palms to-gether in the gesture of respect, he said, "My interpretations of the sutras are as worthless as potsherds, while yours are as valuable as gold." He then shaved my head as initiation into the order of monks and asked to become my pupil. From that time, under the tree of enlightenment, I taught the doc-trines of the Tung-shan School of the Fourth and Fifth Patriarchs.

Since the Dharma was transmitted to me, I have gone through many dif-ficult times, and my life has hung by a thread. Today, the honor of meeting all of you in this assembly—magistrates, officials, monks, nuns, Taoists, and laypeople—is due to our Buddhist merits and the planting of favorable roots in previous incarnations, giving us the opportunity to hear the doctrine of instant enlightenment and the acquisition of wisdom.

This teaching was handed down by former Patriarchs and does not come from my invention. Those who wish to understand the teaching should first purify their own minds, and after listening you should dismiss your doubts so that you will become like Patriarchs of the past.

After listening to this address, the people in the assembly were filled with joy; they bowed to the Patriarch and departed.

—Translation by Stephen Addiss

[Notes: The four major sins are killing, stealing, carnality, and lying; the five perverse sins are patricide, matricide, killing an enlightened being, shedding the blood of a Buddha, and destroying the harmony of the Buddhist assembly.]

5

Shih-t'ou (700–790)

Harmony of Difference and Equality (Sandōkai, complete)

*Shih-t'ou Hsi-chien (Japanese: Sekitō) was born in Guangdong Province in
southern China. When he was twelve years old he became a disciple of the
Sixth Patriarch, Hui-neng. Upon Hui-neng's death two years later, Shih-t'ou
practiced on his own for fifteen years and then studied with Ching-yuan, one
of Hui-neng's main successors. He then established his practice in a hut on a
rocky ledge (hence his name Shih-t'ou, literally "Rock Head") in Hunan
("South of the Lake"). He developed a relationship with his contemporary, the
great Zen Master Ma-tsu (Japanese: Basō), each sending his students to study
with the other. Ma-tsu's center was "West of the River," and it was said of
Zen students of that period that if they did not practice south of the lake and
west of the river, they could never achieve any real attainment.*

Shih-t'ou took the title Sandōkai *(the Japanese form of the word has
became traditional for the Chinese* Ts'an-t'ung-ch'i) *from an earlier Taoist
work. His Chinese text is a poem consisting of forty-four lines, each five
characters long, arranged in twenty-two couplets. The translation here was
produced at the 1997 Sōtō School Liturgy Conference held at Green Gulch
Farm in California. The translation of the title as "The Harmony of
Difference and Equality" is a good index of the main theme of the poem.
The opening lines allude to the doctrinal division between the northern and
southern Zen schools, with their contrasting emphases on sudden and gradual
enlightenment. Their differences are here resolved in the universality of the
Way and Buddha's fundamental teaching. The poem goes on to suggest the
resolution of other dichotomies that arise for the Zen student, and ends with a
memorable exhortation to practice. Dōgen tells us that Shih-t'ou's own solid
and continuous practice of seated meditation gave rise to a vigorous tradition
of Zen. Shih-t'ou's poem was no less influential, since Tung-shan's Five Ranks
(stages of enlightenment) derive from the* Sandōkai, *and the poem became a
fundamental part of the Sōtō School's practice. It is still chanted daily in Sōtō
monasteries throughout the world.*

31

The mind of the great sage of India
is intimately transmitted from west to east.

While human faculties are sharp or dull,
the Way has no northern or southern ancestors.

The spiritual source shines clear in the light;
the branching streams flow on in the dark.

Grasping at things is surely delusion,
according with sameness is still not enlightenment.

All the objects of the senses
transpose and do not transpose.

Transposing, they are linked together;
not transposing, each keeps its place.

Sights vary in quality and form;
sounds differ as pleasing or harsh.

Darkness merges refined and common words;
brightness distinguishes clear and murky phrases.

The four elements return to their natures,
just as a child turns to its mother.

Fire heats, wind moves,
water wets, earth is solid.

Eye and sights, ear and sounds,
nose and smells, tongue and tastes;

Thus for each and every thing,
according to the roots, the leaves spread forth.

From *Branching Streams Flow in the Darkness: Zen Talks on the* Sandokai, by Shun-ryu Suzuki; edited by Mel Weitsman and Michael Wenger (Berkeley: University of California Press, 1999). Reprinted by permission of the publisher.

Trunk and branches share the essence;
revered and common, each has its speech.

In the light there is darkness,
but don't take it as darkness;

In the dark there is light,
but don't see it as light. **NON-duality**

Light and dark oppose one another (key)
like the front and back foot in walking.

proof of non-duality + things flow together

Each of the myriad things has its merit,
expressed according to function and place.

Existing phenomenally like box and cover joining;
according with principle like arrow points meeting.

Hearing the words, understand the meaning;
don't establish standards of your own.

Not understanding the Way before your eyes,
how do you know the path you walk?

Walking forward is not a matter of far or near,
but if you are confused, mountains and rivers block your way.

I respectfully urge you who study the mystery,
don't pass your days and nights in vain.

—Translation by the Sōtō School Liturgy Conference

In useless study
In principle/ useless Intellectualisms w/o practice.

6

Huang-po (died c. 850)

Transmission of Mind (excerpts)

*Huang-po (Japanese: Ōbaku) lived two generations after Hui-neng, during
an era in which a single generational line of Patriarchs no longer sufficed for
the spread of Zen in China. His name as a monk was Hsi-yun, but like
several other early Masters, he is better known for the name of the mountain
where he taught, below Vulture Peak on Mount Huang Po.*

*Born in Fuchou, Huang-po was said to have had a large protruding
forehead that was described as a "great pearl." He entered a monastery in
Fuchou in his youth; he then traveled to practice at Mount T'ien-t'ai, and
also studied with Nan-yang in the capital of Ch'ang-an. One significant
anecdote remains from a visit Huang-po made to the Master Nan-ch'uan;
when asked to recite an "Ode of the Ox-Herd," Huang-po simply replied,
"I am my own teacher right here."*

*We can be grateful to the scholar-official P'ei Hsiu for recording the
teachings of Huang-po, whom he so revered that he had his son become a
novice to study with the Master. In the year 843, when P'ei was governing
Wang-lin Prefecture, he built the Lung Hsing Monastery and invited Huang-po
to come and teach. During this visit P'ei also stayed at the monastery and became Huang-po's pupil; after the Master left, P'ei recorded the teachings he
had heard. Since P'ei was known as a good scholar, and because he gave the
manuscript to two monks who were pupils of Huang-po to check, we can
assume that these writings accurately represent the teachings of the Master.
P'ei then published his manuscript in the year 858, a few years after the death
of Huang-po. The first part of the text consists of short sermons and excerpts
from sermons, while the second section represents further teachings as well as
answers to questions that the Master was asked by his followers; we present
excerpts from both sections.*

*According to P'ei Hsu's preface, Huang-po was in a direct line of spiritual
lineage from Hui-neng and taught the doctrine of "one mind," in which mind
and substance are both void. By describing the mind as "unborn," Huang-po
predates Bankei (see Chapter 23) by nine hundred years, and by stressing that
even the sutras are only temporary remedies, he gives precedence to actual*

experience. *But what is this experience? Huang-po makes clear that it is neither reverential nor intellectual; by his statement that even conceiving of a Buddha makes us obstructed by that Buddha, he urges us to "put mental activity to rest."*

There are many important passages in the following text. For example, as a major Master who transmitted Hui-neng's "sudden enlightenment" tradition for later generations, Huang-po teaches that since "there's never been a single thing," we must enter the Way with "the suddenness of a knife-thrust." Huang-po refers to the historical Buddha as Tathagata ("thus come"), but he considers Buddha-nature as mind (the same character can also mean "heart").

Huang-po's most important pupil was Lin-chi, who tells the story of his interactions with Huang-po in the following section. Since the Lin-chi (Japanese: Rinzai) School survives as one of the most important Zen traditions, we can regard Huang-po as its spiritual ancestor, and, indeed, his powerful and sharply focused teachings are still vital in the transmission of Zen training. In addition, the Chinese monks who emigrated to Japan in the mid-seventeenth century became a sect known in Japan as Ōbaku.

When a sudden flash of thought occurs in your mind and you recognize it for a dream or an illusion, then you can enter into the state reached by the Buddhas of the past—not that the Buddhas of the past really exist, or that the Buddhas of the future have not yet come into existence. Above all, have no longing to become a future Buddha; your sole concern should be, as thought succeeds thought, to avoid clinging to any of them.

If a Buddha arises, do not think of him as "enlightened" or "deluded," "good" or "evil." Hasten to rid yourself of any desire to cling to him. Cut him off in the twinkling of an eye! On no account seek to hold him fast, for a thousand locks could not stay him, nor a hundred thousand feet of rope bind him. This being so, valiantly strive to banish and annihilate him.

I will now make luminously clear how to set about being rid of that Buddha. Consider the sunlight. You may say it is near, yet if you follow it from world to world you will never catch it in your hands. Then you may describe it as far away and, lo, you will see it just before your eyes. Follow it and, behold, it escapes you; run from it and it follows you close. You can neither possess it nor have done with it. From this example you can understand how it is with the true Nature of all things and, henceforth, there will be no need to grieve or to worry about such things.

From *The Zen Teaching of Huang Po*, translated by John Blofeld (New York: Grove Press, 1958). Reprinted by permission of The Estate of John Blofeld and Grove/ Atlantic, Inc.

Thus all the visible universe is the Buddha; so are all sounds; hold fast to one principle and all the others are identical. On seeing one thing, you see all. On perceiving any individual's mind, you are perceiving all Mind. Obtain a glimpse of one way and all ways are embraced in your vision, for there is nowhere at all which is devoid of the Way. When your glance falls upon a grain of dust, what you see is identical with all the vast world-systems with their great rivers and mighty hills. To gaze upon a drop of water is to behold the nature of all the waters of the universe. Moreover, in thus contemplating the totality of phenomena, you are contemplating the totality of Mind. All these phenomena are intrinsically void and yet this Mind with which they are identical is no mere nothingness. By this I mean that it does exist, but in a way too marvelous for us to comprehend. It is an existence which is no existence, a non-existence which is nevertheless existence.

The phenomenal universe and Nirvana, activity and motionless placidity —all are of one substance. By saying that they are all of one substance, we mean that their names and forms, their existence and non-existence, are void. The great world-systems, uncountable as Ganga's sands, are in truth comprised in the one boundless void. Then where can there be Buddhas who deliver or sentient beings to be delivered? When the true nature of all things that "exist" is an identical Thusness, how can such distinctions have any reality? To use the symbol of the closed fist: when it is opened, all beings— both gods and men—will perceive there is not a single thing inside. Therefore is it written, "There's never been a single thing; then where's the defiling dust to cling?" If "there's never been a single thing," past, present and future are meaningless. So those who seek the Way must enter it with the suddenness of a knife-thrust. Full understanding of this must come before they can enter.

Whatever Mind is, so also are phenomena—both are equally real and partake equally of the Dharma-Nature, which hangs in the void. He who receives an intuition of this truth has become a Buddha and attained to the Dharma. No listening, no knowing, no sound, no track, no trace—make yourselves thus and you will be scarcely less than neighbors of Bodhidharma!

Q: What is implied by "seeing into the real Nature"?

A: That Nature and your perception of it are one. You cannot use it to see something over and above itself. That Nature and your hearing of it are one. You cannot use it to hear something over and above itself. If you form a concept of the true nature of anything as being visible or audible, you allow a dharma of distinction to arise.

You people still conceive of Mind as existing or not existing, as pure or defiled, as something to be studied in the way that one studies a piece of categorical knowledge, or as a concept—any of these definitions is sufficient to throw you back into the endless round of birth and death. The man who perceives things always wants to identify them, to get a hold on them. Those who use their minds like eyes in this way are sure to suppose that progress is a matter of stages. If you are that kind of person, you are as far from the truth as earth is far from heaven. Why this talk of "seeing into your own nature"?

If, as thought succeeds thought, you go on seeking for wisdom outside yourselves, then there is a continual process of thoughts arising, dying away and being succeeded by others.

The existence of things as separate entities and not as separate entities are both dualistic concepts. As Bodhidharma said: "There are separate entities and there are not, but at the same time they are neither the one nor the other, for relativity is transient." A man drinking water knows well enough if it is cold or warm. Whether you be walking or sitting, you must restrain all discriminatory thoughts from one moment to the next. If you do not, you will never escape the chain of rebirth.

Only when your minds cease dwelling upon anything whatsoever will you come to an understanding of the true way of Zen. I may express it thus—the way of the Buddhas flourishes in a mind utterly freed from conceptual thought processes, while discrimination between this and that gives birth to a legion of demons!

Q: But how can we prevent ourselves from falling into the error of making distinctions between this and that?

A: By realizing that, although you eat the whole day through, no single grain has passed your lips; and that a day's journey has not taken you a single step forward—also by uniformly abstaining from such notions as "self" and "other." Do not permit the events of your daily lives to bind you, but never withdraw yourselves from them. Only by acting thus can you earn the title of "A Liberated One."

The Master said to me: All the Buddhas and all sentient beings are nothing but the One Mind, beside which nothing exists. This Mind, which is without beginning, is unborn and indestructible. It is not green nor yellow, and has neither form nor appearance. It does not belong to the categories of things which exist or do not exist, nor can it be thought of in terms of new or old. It is neither long nor short, big nor small, for it transcends all limits, measures, names, traces and comparisons. It is that which you see before you—begin to reason about it and you at once fall into error. It is like the boundless void which cannot be fathomed or measured. The One Mind alone is the Buddha, and there is no distinction between the Buddha and sentient things but that sentient beings are attached to forms and so seek externally for Buddhahood. By their very seeking they lose it, for that is using the Buddha to seek for the Buddha and using mind to grasp Mind. Even though they do their utmost for a full aeon, they will not be able to attain to it. They do not know that, if they put a stop to conceptual thought and forget their anxiety, the Buddha will appear before them, for this Mind is the Buddha and the Buddha is all living beings. It is not the less for being manifested in ordinary beings, nor is it greater for being manifested in the Buddhas.

Mind is like the void in which there is no confusion or evil, as when the sun wheels through it shining upon the four corners of the world. For, when the sun rises and illuminates the whole earth, the void gains not in brilliance; and, when the sun sets, the void does not darken. The phenomena of light and dark alternate with each other, but the nature of the void remains unchanged. So it is with the Mind of the Buddha and of sentient beings. If you look upon the Buddha as presenting a pure, bright or Enlightened appearance, or upon sentient beings as presenting a foul, dark or mortal-seeming appearance, these conceptions resulting from attachment to form will keep you from supreme knowledge, even after the passing of as many aeons as there are sands in the Ganges. There is only the One Mind and not a particle of anything else on which to lay hold, for this Mind is the Buddha. If you students of the Way do not awake to this Mind substance, you will overlay Mind with conceptual thought, you will seek the Buddha outside yourselves, and you will remain attached to forms, pious practices and so on, all of which are harmful and not at all the way to supreme knowledge.

This Mind is no mind of conceptual thought and it is completely detached from form. So Buddhas and sentient beings do not differ at all. If you can only rid yourselves of conceptual thought, you will have accomplished everything. But if you students of the Way do not rid yourselves of conceptual thought in a flash, even though you strive for aeon after aeon, you will never accomplish it.

The building up of good and evil both involve attachment to form. . . . Suppose a warrior, forgetting that he was already wearing his pearl on his forehead, were to seek for it elsewhere, he could travel the whole world without finding it. But if someone who knew what was wrong were to point it out to him, the warrior would immediately realize that the pearl had been there all the time. So, if you students of the Way are mistaken about your own real Mind, not recognizing that it is the Buddha, you will consequently look for him elsewhere, indulging in various achievements and practices and expecting to attain realization by such graduated practices. But, even after aeons of diligent searching, you will not be able to attain to the Way.

Our original Buddha-Nature is, in highest truth, devoid of any atom of objectivity. It is void, omnipresent, silent, pure; it is glorious and mysterious peaceful joy—and that is all. Enter deeply into it by awaking to it yourself. That which is before you is it, in all its fullness, utterly complete. There is naught beside. Even if you go through all the stages of a Bodhisattva's progress towards Buddhahood, one by one; when at last, in a single flash, you attain to full realization, you will only be realizing the Buddha-Nature which has been with you all the time; and by all the foregoing stages you will have added to it nothing at all.

This pure Mind, the source of everything, shines forever and on all with the brilliance of its own perfection. But the people of the world do not awake to it, regarding only that which sees, hears, feels and knows as mind. Blinded by their own sight, hearing, feeling and knowing, they do not perceive the spiritual brilliance of the source-substance. If they would only eliminate all conceptual thought in a flash, that source-substance would manifest itself like the sun ascending through the void and illuminating the whole universe without hindrance or bounds. Therefore, if you students of the Way seek to progress through seeing, hearing, feeling and knowing, when you are deprived of your perceptions, your way to Mind will be cut off and you will find nowhere to enter. Only realize that, though real Mind is expressed in these perceptions, it neither forms part of them nor is separate from them. You should not start reasoning from these perceptions, nor allow them to give rise to conceptual thought; yet nor should you seek the One Mind apart from them or abandon them in your pursuit of the Dharma. Do not keep them nor abandon them nor dwell in them nor cleave to them. Above, below and around you, all is spontaneously existing, for there is nowhere which is outside the Buddha-Mind.

Students of the Way should be sure that the four elements composing the body do not constitute the self; that the self is not an entity; and that it can be deduced from this that the body is neither self nor entity. Moreover, the five aggregates composing the mind (in the common sense) do not constitute either a self or an entity; hence, it can be deduced that the (so-called individual) mind is neither self nor entity. The six sense organs (including the brain) which, together with their six types of perception and the six kinds of objects of perception, constitute the sensory world, must be understood in the same way. Those eighteen aspects of sense are separately and together void. There is only Mind-Source, limitless in extent and of absolute purity.

Ordinary people look to their surroundings, while followers of the Way look to Mind, but the true Dharma is to forget them both. The former is easy enough, the latter very difficult. Men are afraid to forget their minds, fearing to fall through the Void with nothing to stay their fall. They do not know that the Void is not really void, but the realm of the real Dharma. This spiritually enlightening nature is without beginning, as ancient as the Void, subject neither to birth nor to destruction, neither existing nor not existing, neither impure nor pure, neither clamorous nor silent, neither old nor young, occupying no space, having neither inside nor outside, size nor form, color nor sound. It cannot be looked for or sought, comprehended by wisdom or knowledge, explained in words, contacted materially or reached by meritorious achievement.

On the first day of the ninth moon, the Master said to me: From the time when the Great Master Bodhidharma arrived in China, he spoke only of the One Mind and transmitted only the one Dharma. He used the Buddha to transmit the Buddha, never speaking of any other Buddha. He used the Dharma to transmit the Dharma, never speaking of any other Dharma. That Dharma was the wordless Dharma, and that Buddha was the intangible Buddha, since they were in fact that Pure Mind which is the source of all things. This is the only truth; all else is false. . . . Nothing is born, nothing is destroyed. Away with your dualism, your likes and dislikes. Every single thing is just the One Mind. When you have perceived this, you will have mounted the Chariot of the Buddhas.

If an ordinary man, when he is about to die, could only see the five elements of consciousness as void; the four physical elements as not constituting an "I"; the real Mind as formless and neither coming nor going; his nature as something neither commencing at his birth nor perishing at his death, but as whole and motionless in its very depths; his Mind and environmental objects as one—if he could really accomplish this, he would receive Enlightenment in a flash. He would no longer be entangled by the Triple World; he would be a World-Transcendor. He would be without even the faintest tendency towards rebirth. If he should behold the glorious sight of all the Buddhas coming to welcome him, surrounded by every kind of gorgeous manifestation, he would feel no desire to approach them. If he should behold all sorts of horrific forms surrounding him, he would experience no terror. He would just be himself, oblivious of conceptual thought and one with the Absolute. He would have attained the state of unconditioned being. This, then, is the fundamental principle.

People are often hindered by environmental phenomena from perceiving Mind, and by individual events from perceiving underlying principles; so they often try to escape from environmental phenomena in order to still their minds, or to obscure events in order to retain their grasp of principles. They do not realize that this is merely to obscure phenomena with Mind, events with principles. Just let your minds become void and environmental phenomena will void themselves; let principles cease to stir and events will cease stirring of themselves. Many people are afraid to empty their minds lest they may plunge into the Void. They do not know that their own Mind *is* the void.

The canonical teachings of the Three Vehicles are just remedies for temporary needs. They were taught to meet such needs and so are of temporary value and differ one from another. If only this could be understood, there would be no more doubts about it. Above all it is essential not to select some particular teaching suited to a certain occasion, and, being impressed by its forming part of the written canon, regard it as an immutable concept. Why so? Because in truth there is no unalterable Dharma which the Tathagata could have preached. People of our sect would never argue that there could be such a thing. We just know how to put all mental activity to rest and thus achieve tranquility. We certainly do not begin by thinking things out and end up in perplexity.

Q: What is the Buddha?

A: Mind is the Buddha, while the cessation of conceptual thought is the Way. Once you stop arousing concepts and thinking in terms of existence and non-existence, long and short, other and self, active and passive, and suchlike, you will find that your Mind is intrinsically the Buddha, that the Buddha is intrinsically Mind, and that Mind resembles a void. Every day, whether walking, standing, sitting or lying down, and in all your speech, remain detached from everything within the sphere of phenomena. Whether you speak or merely blink an eye, let it be done with complete dispassion. This is not something which you can accomplish without effort, but when you reach the point of clinging to nothing whatever, you will be acting as the Buddhas act.

If you would spend all your time—walking, standing, sitting or lying down—learning to halt the concept-forming activities of your own mind, you could be sure of ultimately attaining the goal. Since your strength is insufficient, you might not be able to transcend *samsara* [the cycle of rebirths] by a single leap; but, after five or ten years, you would surely have made a good beginning and be able to make further progress spontaneously.

Anything possessing any signs is illusory. It is by perceiving that all signs are no signs that you perceive the Tathagata. "Buddha" and "sentient beings" are both your own false conceptions. It is because you do not know real Mind that you delude yourselves with such objective concepts. If you will conceive of a Buddha, you will be obstructed by that Buddha! And when you conceive of sentient beings, you will be obstructed by those beings. All such dualistic concepts as "ignorant" and "Enlightened," "pure" and "impure," are obstructions.

Q: If our own Mind is the Buddha, how did Bodhidharma transmit his doctrine when he came from India?

A: When he came from India, he transmitted only Mind-Buddha. He just pointed to the truth that the minds of all of you have from the very first been identical with the Buddha, and in no way separate from each other. That is why we call him our Patriarch. Whoever has an instant understanding of this truth suddenly transcends the whole hierarchy of saints and adepts belonging to any of the Three Vehicles. You have always been one with the Buddha, so do not pretend you can attain to this oneness by various practices.

Discuss it as you may, how can you even hope to approach the truth through words? Nor can it be perceived either subjectively or objectively. So full understanding can come to you only through an inexpressible mystery. The approach to it is called the Gateway of the Stillness Beyond All Activity. If you wish to understand, know that a sudden comprehension comes when the mind has been purged of all the clutter of conceptual and discriminatory thought-activity. Those who seek the truth by means of intellect and learning only get further and further away from it.

Were you now to practice keeping your minds motionless at all times, whether walking, standing, sitting or lying; concentrating entirely upon the goal of no thought-creation, no duality, no reliance on others and no attachments; just allowing all things to take their course the whole day long, as though you were too ill to bother; unknown to the world; innocent of any urge to be known or unknown to others; with your minds like blocks of stone that mend no holes—then all the Dharmas would penetrate your understanding through and through. In a little while you would find yourselves firmly unattached. Thus, for the first time in your lives, you would discover your reactions to phenomena decreasing and, ultimately, you would pass beyond the Triple World; and people would say that a Buddha had appeared in the world. Pure and passionless knowledge implies putting an end to the ceaseless flow of thoughts and images, for in that way you stop creating the karma that leads to rebirth—whether as gods or men or as sufferers in hell.

The Void is fundamentally without spatial dimensions, passions, activities, delusions or right understanding. You must clearly understand that in it there are no things, no men and no Buddhas; for this Void contains not the smallest hairsbreadth of anything that can be viewed spatially; it depends on nothing and is attached to nothing. It is all-pervading, spotless beauty; it is the self-existent and uncreated Absolute. A perception, sudden as blinking, that subject and object are one, will lead to a deeply mysterious wordless understanding; and by this understanding will you awake to the truth of Zen.

—Translation by John Blofeld

7

Lin-chi (died 866)

Lin-chi Record (excerpts)

Lin-chi (Japanese: Rinzai) was one of the most famous Chinese Masters, and his Rinzai tradition of sudden enlightenment is still a major force in East Asian Zen. He was born, probably between 810 and 815, in the western part of Shantung, just south of the Yellow River. It is not known when he became a monk, probably in his teens as was customary at the time. According to his own records, after he had spent some time studying the sutras and monastic regulations, he grew dissatisfied and turned to Zen. Following a period of initial training, he went on pilgrimage to find a Master, settling at Mount Huang Po in Kiangsi. The story that he relates of his enlightenment is a classic, and after this dramatic confrontation Lin-chi became a member of the fourth generation of succession from Hui-neng. He then traveled through China visiting Zen centers before settling in Chen-chou, in northern China, where he lived in a small riverside temple named Lin-chi-yuan, from which his most famous Zen name derives.

Lin-chi's teachings, like the man, are direct, powerful, and straightforward. One of his most celebrated remarks, about killing the Buddha, may seem extremely iconoclastic, but it follows directly upon his teacher Huang-po's comment about not attaching oneself to anything, even the Buddha. Instead, Lin-chi stresses that no extra effort has to be made, for this effort itself can become an attachment. How then should one proceed in one's training, if striving itself may be a mistake? Here is the crux of the matter, and many of Lin-chi's teachings are geared toward helping his followers come to their own understanding that they must let go—even after taking a step forward—and break through their illusions, including those brought on by words. Because of his varied and dynamic teaching methods, Lin-chi has often been portrayed in Zen paintings, sometimes shouting, sometimes holding a stick, and sometimes glowering with a clenched fist.

The following excerpts are taken from talks to his monk followers and from the record of his pilgrimages, collectively known as the Lin-chi Record. In these excerpts, we can see the teacher in several guises, asking questions of his

Figure 4. Hakuin Ekaku (1684–1768), *Portrait of Lin-chi* **(detail)**

followers, prodding them, encouraging them, and challenging them, all in the
effort to support their own quests to find their Buddha-nature.

When first Lin-chi was a monk in Huang-po's assembly, he was simple and direct in his actions. The head monk admired him, saying, "Even though he is still young, he's different from the other monks." He then asked, "How long have you been here?"

Lin-chi answered, "Three years."

"Have you been for an interview yet?"

"No, I've never asked the Master questions—I don't even know what to ask."

"Then why don't you go ask the Reverend Abbot, 'What is the basic meaning of Buddhism?'"

Lin-chi therefore went to ask, but before he had even completed the question, Huang-po hit him. When Lin-chi returned from the interview, the head monk asked, "How did it go?" Lin-chi replied, "Before I had finished my question, the Reverend hit me, but I don't know why."

The head monk said, "Just go and ask him again."

So Lin-chi went back, and once more Huang-po hit him. In total, Lin-chi asked three times, and was hit three times. So he said to the head monk, "At your kind instruction, I have been able to question the Reverend three times, and I have been struck three times. I fear that I am obstructed by my past karma from understanding the Master's profound meaning, so I think I'd better leave this monastery for awhile."

The head monk replied, "If you are going away, be sure to take your leave of the Master." Lin-chi then bowed and withdrew. The head monk went to Huang-po, saying, "The young monk who came to question you is a man of the Dharma, and I hope that when he comes to take his leave, you will find a way to help him. What is planted now can in the future become a great tree that will shade the people of the world in coolness."

When Lin-chi came to say goodbye, Huang-po told him, "You should go nowhere but to Ta-yu's place by the river in Ka-an; he will be sure to explain everything to you."

When Lin-chi arrived there, Ta-yu asked, "Where have you come from?"

Lin-chi replied, "I've just been at Huang-po's monastery."

"What did Huang-po tell you?"

"Three times I asked him about the essence of Buddhism, and three times he hit me—but I don't know if I did anything wrong or not."

Ta-yu said, "Huang-po, like a kindly old grandmother, was wearing himself out on your behalf, and yet you come here to ask if you did something wrong or not?"

Figure 5. Gesshū Sōko (1618–1696)
Nothing Much

"There's nothing much to Huang-po's Buddhism after all."

Hearing these words, Lin-chi attained a great enlightenment and exclaimed, "There's nothing much to Huang-po's Buddhism after all!"

Ta-yu grabbed the young monk and said, "You little bed-wetting devil! You were asking if you had done anything wrong or not, and now you are claiming there's not much to Huang-po's Buddhism—what did you just see? Speak quickly, speak quickly!"

Lin-chi punched Ta-yu three times in the side with his fist, so Ta-yu let go of him and said, "Huang-po is your teacher; this is no business of mine."

Lin-chi then took his leave of Ta-yu and returned to Huang-po, who commented, "This young fellow keeps coming and going, coming and going. When will he ever stop?"

Lin-chi replied, "It's all due to you being a kindly old grandmother." When he had finished his formal greetings, he stood in attendance. Huang-po asked him, "Where have you been?"

"At your Reverend's guidance, I went to see Ta-yu."

"What did he say to you?"

When Lin-chi explained what had happened, Huang-po said, "If I could grab that rascal, I'd give him a beating."

Lin-chi replied, "No need to say what you'd like to do; you can take this right now," and gave Huang-po a good punch.

"You're a madman," exclaimed Huang-po, "returning here to pull the whiskers of the tiger!"

Lin-chi gave a shout.

Huang-po called out, "Attendant, take this madman out of here and into the monks' quarters."

Later Wei-shan told this story to Yang-shan and asked, "Did Lin-chi get his enlightenment from Ta-yu or Huang-po?"

Yang-shan replied, "He not only rode on the head of the tiger, but he also pulled his tail."

•

Lin-chi taught, "Monks, don't be afraid of giving up your bodies and sacrificing your lives for the sake of Buddhism. Twenty years ago when I was at Huang-po's place, I asked him about the essence of Buddhism three times, and three times he was kind enough to hit me with his stick. But it was as though he had touched me lightly with a branch of mugwort. Remembering this, I would like the favor of the stick again—is there anyone who can give me a good smack?"

One of the monks stepped forward and said, "I can do it!"

Lin-chi held out his stick to him, but as the monk was getting ready to grasp it, Lin-chi whacked him.

•

Lin-chi took his place at the high seat of the hall and said, "One person on the top of a solitary peak has no path to come down; another at a busy cross-roads cannot go forward or back. Which one is ahead, and which one lags behind?"

•

Lin-chi ascended the hall and said, "One person is forever traveling but never leaves his home; another has left his house but is not on the way. Which one is worthy to receive the offerings of mortals and gods?"

•

Lin-chi asked his followers, "Do you want to know Buddhas and Patriarchs? They are standing before me listening to this lecture. You don't have confidence in yourselves, so you run around searching. But even if you find something, it will be nothing but words and phrases, not the living spirit of the Patriarchs.

"Followers of the Way, in my understanding we are no different from Shakyamuni. In everything you do each day, is there anything you are missing?

"Followers of the Way, if you want to be the same as Buddha and the Patriarchs, then don't seek outside yourself. The nondiscriminating light of your mind at this instant becomes the essence-body of the Buddha inside you. The nondiscriminating light at this instant becomes the bliss-body of the Buddha inside you. The nondiscriminating light at this instant becomes the corporeal-body of the Buddha inside you. These three bodies are nothing other than you, the person who is listening to me explain the Dharma. But you can only come to this vision when you cease searching for anything outside yourself.

"Followers of the Way, simply follow circumstances and fulfill your karma. When it's time to put on your robe, put it on; when you need to travel, walk onward; when you wish to sit down, just sit; and never have a single thought of entering Buddhahood.

"Followers of the Way, Buddhism requires no special efforts. You have only to lead your everyday life without seeking anything more—piss and shit, get dressed, eat your rice, and lie down when you are tired.

"Fools may laugh at me,
But the wise understand."

•

"In my view, there is no Buddha, no sentient being, no past, and no present. Realization is immediate, needing no time, no practice, no enlightenment, no gain, and no loss. There is no other teaching but this. Were there a special Dharma, I would say it must be a phantom and a dream. This is all that I teach.

"Followers of the Way, the true person knows there is nothing that needs doing, while others lacking inner confidence run around ceaselessly trying to find something; it's like throwing away your own head and then going to look for it."

•

"If you want to live or die, to go or stay as freely as taking off or putting on your clothes, then you should know that each person listening to my talk is without form or characteristics, without root or trunk, and has no dwelling place, yet is as lively as a fish splashing in the water. You are responding to all that happens naturally, yet there is no place where these responses happen. Therefore the more you search, the more this person eludes you, and the more you hunt, the farther away this person will be. This is what I call the mystery."

•

"Whatever comes along, don't let yourself be taken in. If you have a moment of doubt, the demon will enter your mind. Even Bodhisattvas, if they give way to doubt, are assailed by the demon of birth-and-death. Just put a stop to such thoughts, and never seek outside yourself. When something appears before you, shine your inner light upon it; have confidence in what is operating within you—everything else is empty."

•

"Followers of the Way, don't be deluded! Everything in this or any other world is without intrinsic nature, or any nature that manifests itself. They are just empty, as is the word "empty" that describes them. If you regard any name as reality, you are making a big mistake. Even if anything exists, it is in the act of changing.

"A Buddha can enter the world of form without being deceived by form, can enter the world of sound without being deceived by sound, can enter the world of scent without being deceived by scent, can enter the world of taste without being deceived by taste, can enter the world of touch without being deceived by touch, and can enter the world of thought without being deceived by thought. Since these six things—form, sound, scent, taste, touch, and thought—are all empty of fixed characteristics, they cannot imprison the follower of the way, who does not depend on anything.

"Followers of the Way, if you want to understand the Dharma, do not be fooled by others. Whether you turn inward or outward, whatever you encounter, kill it! If you meet a Buddha, kill the Buddha; if you meet a Patriarch, kill the Patriarch; if you meet an enlightened being, kill the enlightened being; if you meet your parents, kill your parents; if you meet your relatives, kill your relatives. Only then will you find emancipation, and by not clinging to anything, you will be free wherever you go.

"Followers of the Way, students come here from every direction, and when guest and host have exchanged greetings, the new student will test out the teacher with a question, throwing out some phrase as if to say, 'Can you explain this?' If you are a teacher and understood that this is just a device, you grab it and throw it into a deep hole. The student then calms down and asks for instruction. The teacher seizes this also and throws it away. The student will now exclaim, 'What surpassing wisdom! What a wonderful teacher!' The teacher responds, 'You can't tell good from bad.'

"Or the teacher may take something and play with it in front of a student. But the student sees through this device and becomes the host, not being fooled by humbug. The teacher then reveals half of himself, and the student gives a great shout. The teacher now enters into the world of verbal differentiations to see if the student gets confused. But the student responds, 'This old baldy can't tell good from bad himself,' whereupon the teacher sighs with admiration, 'Here is a true follower of the way!' "

•

Someone asked, "What was the purpose of Bodhidharma coming from the west?"

Lin-chi replied, "If he had a purpose, he couldn't have saved even himself."

"If there was no purpose, how did the Second Patriarch attain the Dharma?"

"Attaining is not attaining."

"If he did not attain, what do you mean by 'not attaining'?"

Lin-chi answered, "It seems that you can't stop your mind from running around and seeking something. That's why the Patriarch said, 'Such wonderful fellows, using their heads to search for their heads!' Instead of looking outside, you should turn your inner light upon yourself, and you will realize that your body and mind are not different from those of Patriarchs and Buddhas, and there's nothing special that you need to do. This is called attaining the Dharma."

•

"Followers of the Way, don't just accept blindly the things I tell you. Why not? Because they have no proof, they're just pictures drawn in the empty sky.

"My old teacher once said 'open your mouth, already a mistake.' So you'll just have to see for yourselves—that's all there is, or there's no end to talking."

•

One day Governor Wang came to visit Lin-chi, and when they passed the Meditation Hall, the governor asked, "Do the monks at this monastery read the sutras?"

Lin-chi replied, "No, they don't read sutras."

"In that case do they learn meditation?"

"No, they don't learn meditation either."

Governor Wang then asked, "If they don't read sutras or learn meditation, what do they do?"

"They are all in training to become Patriarchs and Buddhas."

The governor said, "Gold dust may be valuable, but in the eye it can cause blindness."

Lin-chi replied, "And to think I used to believe that you were just an ordinary person!"

—Translation by Stephen Addiss

8

The P'ang Family: Layman P'ang (740–808),

Mrs. P'ang (n.d.), and P'ang Ling-chao (d. 808)

Anecdotes and Poems (excerpts)

*One of the main complaints against Buddhism by Confucianists in China
was that it was anti-family. Since monastics left their parents and homes,
they were regarded by some critics as not fulfilling their obligations under
Confucian doctrines. Buddhists replied that the parents were often proud to
have one or more of their children become monastics who could pray for their
families and hold services for them after their deaths. There was also a certain
amount of prestige in having a member of the family in the Buddhist clergy,
at least during times when the religion was being favored by the government.
Nevertheless, the criticism was hard to refute completely.*

*Another concern has been the place of women in Buddhism. Along with
many anecdotes about wise women who frequently got the better of traveling
monks in their interactions, in the stories of the P'ang family there is strong
evidence of Zen going beyond any question of gender. For these reasons, the
story of the P'angs has been very important for Buddhists, especially followers
of Zen, because not only was P'ang a layperson who had become enlightened,
but his wife and daughter were at least his equals, as some of the anecdotes
about them make clear.*

*The son of a minor Confucian official in Hunan, P'ang studied with two
of the great Zen Masters of his time, Shih-t'ou (Japanese: Sekitō; see Chapter
5) and Ma-tsu (Japanese: Basō). In middle age, P'ang gave his house
away and threw his possessions into a river. Thereupon he divided his time,
sometimes settling in one place for a year or two with his wife, son, and
daughter, and sometimes traveling on pilgrimage with his daughter. His Zen
names P'ang Yun ("lofty interior") and Tao-hsuan ("way of mystery") give
some sense of his achievements during his life of poverty and simplicity.*

The text, generally called The Recorded Sayings of Layman P'ang, *is
made up not only of lectures and Dharma discourses, as had been common
with early Zen Masters, but also of Zen encounters and stories from the P'ang*

family's later years, as well as a few poems. The Imperial Prefect Yu Ti (died 818), who had been a vigorous opponent of Buddhism, became an admirer, friend, and pupil of Layman P'ang after a dramatic incident during which the Prefect threatened him with death and P'ang showed no fear. It was Yu Ti who compiled the Recorded Sayings, *probably soon after Layman P'ang's death, adding some brief biographical details. The following anecdotes and poems give an idea of the spontaneous nature of the P'ang family's Zen encounters and show how Zen was a free and active force in the lives of the enlightened.*

Introduction

The layman P'ang Yun of Hsiangchou, whose nickname was Tao-hsuan, was a resident of Heng-yang prefecture in Hengchou. His family had been Confucianists for generations. While yet a youth he became aware of the defiling passions and aspired to seek the absolute truth.

Dialogues with Shih-t'ou

At the beginning of the Chen-yuan era [786–804] of T'ang, the Layman visited Zen Master Shih-t'ou. He asked the Master: "Who is the man who doesn't accompany the ten thousand dharmas?"

Shih-t'ou covered the Layman's mouth with his hand. In a flash he realized!

One day Shih-t'ou said to the Layman: "Since seeing me, what have your daily activities been?"

"When you ask me about my daily activities, I can't open my mouth," the Layman replied. "Just because I know you are thus I now ask you," said Shih-t'ou. Whereupon the Layman offered this verse:

> My daily activities are not unusual,
> I'm just naturally in harmony with them.
> Grasping nothing, discarding nothing,
> In every place there's no hindrance, no conflict.
> Who assigns the ranks of vermilion and purple?—

From *A Man of Zen: The Recorded Sayings of Layman P'ang* by Ruth Fuller Sasaki, Yoshitaka Iriya, and Dana Fraser © 1971. Reprinted by arrangement with Shambhala Publications Inc. Boston, MA. www.shambhala.com.

The hills' and mountains' last speck of dust is extinguished.
[My] supernatural power and marvelous activity—
Drawing water and carrying firewood.

Shih-t'ou gave his assent. Then he asked: "Will you put on black robes or will you continue wearing white?"

"I want to do what I like," replied the Layman. So he did not shave his head or dye his clothing.

Kōan: Facing Downwards

Listen!

The Layman said to Yang-shan: "I have long wanted to meet you, Yang-shan. Now that I have arrived here why are you facing downwards?"

Yang-shan raised up his whisk.

"Exactly!" exclaimed the Layman.

"Is this [whisk] pointing upwards or downwards?" asked Yang-shan.

Striking an open-air post once, the Layman said: "Though there's no one else but us who sees, the post will testify for me."

Yang-shan threw away his whisk, saying: "You may show this wherever you please."

Anecdotes

One day the layman asked Ch'i-feng: "How many *li* is it from here to the top of your peak?"

"Where have you come from?" asked Ch'i-feng.

"It's so dreadfully steep that it can't be asked about," said the Layman.

"How much [steepness] is that?" asked Ch'i-feng.

"One, two, three," said the Layman.

"Four, five, six," said Ch'i-feng.

"Why not say seven?" asked the Layman.

"As soon as I said seven there would be eight," replied Ch'i-feng.

"You can stop there," said the Layman.

"You may go on," said Ch'i-feng.

The Layman shouted and went out.

Then Ch'i-feng shouted.

When the layman was walking with Tan-hsia one day he saw a deep pool of clear water. Pointing to it with his hand, he said: "Being as it is we can't differentiate it."

"Of course we can't," replied Tan-hsia.

The Layman scooped up and threw two handfuls of water on Tan-hsia.

"Don't do that, don't do that!" cried Tan-hsia.

"I have to, I have to!" exclaimed the Layman.

Whereupon Tan-hsia scooped up and threw three handfuls of water on the Layman, saying: "What can you do now?"

"Nothing else," replied the Layman.

"One seldom wins by a fluke," said Tan-hsia.

"Who lost by a fluke?" returned the Layman.

One day Po-ling said to the Layman: " 'Whether you can speak or whether you can't, you cannot escape.' Now tell me, what is it you can't escape?"

The Layman winked.

"Outstanding!" exclaimed Po-ling.

"You mistakenly approve me," said the Layman.

"Who doesn't, who doesn't?" returned Po-ling.

"Take care of yourself," said the Layman and went off.

One day Pen-hsi saw the Layman coming. He gazed at him for quite a while. The Layman then drew a circle with his staff. Pen-hsi came forward and stepped into it. "Thus, or not thus?" asked the Layman. Pen-hsi then drew a circle in front of the Layman. The Layman likewise stepped into it. "Thus, or not thus?" asked Pen-hsi. The Layman threw down his staff and stood still. "You came with a staff, but you go without a staff," remarked Pen-hsi. "Luckily it's made perfect," said the Layman. "Don't trouble to watch it." Pen-hsi clapped his hands, exclaiming: "Wonderful! There's not a thing to be attained!" The Layman picked up his staff and, tapping the ground step by step, went off. "Watch the road, watch the road!" called Pen-hsi.

Pen-hsi asked the Layman: "What was the first word Bodhidharma spoke when he came from the West?" "Who remembers!" said the Layman. "You have a poor memory," said Pen-hsi. "We mustn't speak hit-or-miss about affairs of olden days," said the Layman. "How about affairs right now?" asked Pen-hsi. "There's not a word to say," replied the Layman. "To say that in front of a wise man would be still more brilliant," responded Pen-hsi. "But you have a great eye," disagreed the Layman. "Only when it's thus can one speak without a hint," said Pen-hsi. "Not a single thing can be put into the eye," said the Layman. "The sun is just at the zenith: to raise the eyes is difficult," said Pen-hsi. "The dried skull is bored through," returned the Layman. Snapping his fingers, Pen-hsi said: "Who could discern it!" "What an outstanding fellow you are!" exclaimed the Layman. Pen-hsi returned to his quarters.

The Layman visited Chan Master Ta-mei. Hardly had they met when he said: "I've long wanted to meet you, Ta-mei. I wonder whether the plum is ripe or not."

"Ripe!" exclaimed Ta-mei. "What part do you want to bite?"

"Dried-fruit confection," returned the Layman.

"Then give me back the pits," said Ta-mei, stretching out his hand.

The Layman went off.

As Tse-ch'uan was sitting in his quarters one day, the Layman saw him and said: "You only know how to sit erect in your quarters; you're not aware when a monk comes for an interview."

Tse-ch'uan dropped one leg down.

The Layman went out two or three steps, and then turned back. Tse-ch'uan drew his leg back up.

"You're a man of complete flexibility!" the Layman exclaimed.

"But I'm the host," returned Tse-ch'uan.

Tse-ch'uan called his attendant and had him make tea. The Layman did a dance and went out.

The Layman was once lying on his couch reading a sutra. A monk saw him and said: "Layman! You must maintain dignity when reading a sutra."

The Layman raised up one leg.

The monk had nothing to say.

One day the Layman was in the market place of Hung-thou selling baskets. Seeing a monk begging alms, he took out a cash and said: "Can you tell me how to appreciate alms? If you can, then I'll give you this."

The monk had nothing to say.

"You ask me," said the Layman, "and I'll tell you."

"What is it to appreciate alms?" asked the monk.

"Man seldom hears it," said the Layman. "Do you understand?" he added.

"I don't understand," said the monk.

"Who is the one who doesn't understand?" asked the Layman.

The Layman and His Daughter Ling-chao

The Layman was sitting in his thatched cottage one day. "Difficult, difficult, difficult," he suddenly exclaimed, "[like trying] to scatter ten measures of sesame seed all over a tree!"

"Easy, easy, easy," returned Mrs. P'ang, "just like touching your feet to the ground when you get out of bed."

Figure 6. Anonymous (fifteenth-century Japan), *P'ang Ling-chao*

"Neither difficult nor easy," said Ling-chao. "On the hundred grass-tips, the Patriarchs' meaning."

The Layman was once selling bamboo baskets. Coming down off a bridge he stumbled and fell. When Ling-chao saw this she ran to her father's side and threw herself down.

"What are you doing!" cried the Layman.

"I saw Papa fall to the ground, so I'm helping," replied Ling-chao.

"Luckily no one was looking," remarked the Layman.

Layman P'ang's Death

The Layman was about to die. He spoke to Ling-chao, saying: "See how high the sun is and report to me when it's noon."

Ling-chao quickly reported: "The sun has already reached the zenith, and there's an eclipse." While the Layman went to the door to look out, Ling-chao seated herself in her father's chair and, putting her palms together reverently, passed away.

The Layman smiled and said: "My daughter has anticipated me."

He postponed [his going] for seven days.

The Prefect Yu Ti came to inquire about his illness. The Layman said to him: "I beg you just to regard as empty all that is existent and to beware of taking as real all that is non-existent. Fare you well in the world. All is like shadows and echoes." His words ended. He pillowed his head on Mr. Yii's knee and died.

His final request was that he be cremated and [the ashes] scattered over rivers and lakes. Monks and laity mourned him and said that the Zen adherent Layman P'ang was indeed a Vimalakirti. He left three hundred poems to the world.

Poems by the Layman

People have a one-scroll sutra
Without form and without name.
No man is able to unroll and read it,
And none of us can hear it.
When you are able to unroll and read it,
You enter the principle and accord with the Birthless.
Not to speak of becoming a Bodhisattva,
You don't even need to become Buddha.

White-robed, I don't adhere to appearances;
The true principle arises from Emptiness.

Because my mind's without obstruction
Wisdom goes forth to all directions.
I only consider the lion's roar,
I don't let wild jackals yap!
Bodhi [awakening] is said to be most marvelous,
But I scold it for being a false name.

Without no other, within no self.
Not wielding spear and shield, I accord with Buddha-wisdom.
Well-versed in the Buddha-way, I go the non-Way.
Without abandoning my ordinary man's affairs,
The conditioned and name-and-form all are flowers in the sky.
Nameless and formless; I leave birth-and-death.

Without any cause you lose your mind,
And run out the front gate seeking [it].
Although you try to question old friends,
All's quiet, without any trace [of them].
But returning to the hall, when you carefully consider it,
Transforming sentient beings, [in] accord with tranquility,
You cannot go outside and seek friends;
Of yourself, amidst your family, you enter Nirvana.

The past is already past—
Don't try to regain it.
The present does not stay,
Don't try to touch it from moment to moment.
The future is not come,
Don't think about it beforehand.
With the three times non-existent,
Mind is the same as Buddha-mind.
To silently function relying on Emptiness,
This is profundity of action.
Not the least dharma exists—
Whatsoever comes to eye leave it be.
There are no commandments to be kept,
There is no filth to be cleansed.
With empty mind really penetrated,
The dharmas have no life.
When you can be like this,
You've completed the ultimate attainment.

Not wanting to discard greed and anger,
In vain you trouble to read Buddha's teachings.
You see the prescription, but don't take the medicine—
How then can you do away with your illness!
Grasp emptiness, and emptiness is form;
Grasp form, and form is impermanent.
Emptiness and form are not mine—
Sitting erect, I see my native home.

When the mind's as is,
The spirit of itself is empty.
Without applying medicine,
Ills remove themselves.
With ills removed,
You naturally see the lotus-flower mani-jewel.
Don't trouble over affairs,
Don't bustle around!

—Translation by Ruth Fuller Sasaki,
Yoshitaka Iriya, and Dana Fraser

9

Selected Poems by Chinese Nuns

Although women monastics have been important in Zen history from very early days, there have been few translations of their writings until recent publications, one of which is Daughters of Emptiness *by Beata Grant. She includes poems by forty-eight nuns from the fifth through twentieth centuries, from which a selection is given here.*

The biographies of the nuns often have much in common, although some were taught by female and others by male Masters. Hui-hsu (431–499), from the Chou family, studied with Hsuan-ch'ang and then served as a Buddhist teacher to several members of the royal family. The emperor was so impressed that he built a convent for her; in her later years, she came forth only once, for a religious feast held in her honor, at which she wrote the quatrain given below.

Fa-yuan (601–663) had even stronger imperial connections. She was both the sixth-generation descendant of Emperor Wu Ti of Liang (the same ruler visited by Bodhidharma), and the third daughter of the T'ang Dynasty royal family; she became a noted Buddhist teacher in a convent in the capital city.

There were several outstanding female monastic teachers in the twelfth century. The scholar-husband of Chung-chueh (twelfth century) died while she was still young; she took Buddhist orders rather than marry again, living in the Fayun Convent. Pen-ming (early twelfth century) was a Dharma heir of Yuan-wu (1063–1135), and her verses were published after her death by Master Ts'ao-t'ang (1057–1142) and utilized in sermons by Ta-hui (1089–1163; see Chapter 14). Ta-hui also admired the Buddhist poems of Chen-ju (twelfth century), who left her life at court to become a monastic.

Chih-t'ung (died 1124) had a difficult time becoming a nun, since her scholar-official family at first refused to give her permission, but she eventually took Buddhist orders and lived in a convent in Suchou where she attracted many followers. One of her poems was composed to be inscribed over a monastery bathhouse that she had sponsored.

The nun Miao-tsung (1095–1170) came from a family of scholars and high government officials; she studied Zen with Ta-hui. She was especially noted for her poetry, and her recorded sayings as a Zen Master were also circulated (although they have mostly been lost over time). Her biography appears in this volume as Chapter 15.

"One-eyed" Ching-kang (n.d.) was said to have lost the use of one eye through reading the Diamond Sutra *too assiduously. After giving away all her possessions, she became celebrated for her sermons and discussions on this sutra; although her precise dates are unknown, she lived past the age of seventy.*

Like several of the female monastics here, Hsing-kang (1597–1654) was pressured by her parents to marry, and even lived as a dutiful proto-daughter-in-law after her fiancé died. After both her parents passed away, however, at the age of thirty-four she became a nun and studied with Mi-yun (1566–1642) and his disciple Shih-ch'e (1593–1638). After a decade of meditation, Hsing-kang served as abbess of the Crouching Lion Convent, where she had many followers including seven Dharma heirs.

One of Hsing-kang's students, Yi-k'uei (1625–1679), became a nun after her husband died when she was twenty-three years old. She eventually took her turn as abbess of the Crouching Lion Convent, and her Buddhist prose writings and poems were compiled before her death in 1679.

Born into an elite family, Yin-yueh (seventeenth century) was married at the age of sixteen despite her preference for a life of meditation, but at the age of thirty she studied with, and eventually became a Dharma heir of, Lin-yeh (1595–1652), a follower of Mi-yun. Yin-yueh thereupon lived in a small hermitage and called herself the "Crouching Dragon Abbess."

Ming-hsiu (n.d.) showed her religious spirit by refusing to eat meat as a child and declining to get married so she could care for her parents. After their deaths, she took Buddhist orders, traveling to many of the famous Buddhist sites in China and becoming known for both her teachings and her poetry.

Unlike many of the other nuns included here, Ching-no (late seventeenth century) entered Buddhist orders in her youth and eventually became the senior Dharma heir of the female Master Wei-chi (died 1672). Ching-no had hundreds of followers, and was able to laugh at herself for her love of words after giving up all other attachments.

Chi-fu (late seventeenth century) was a Dharma heir of Ji-ch'u (1605–1672), an heir of Han-yueh (1573–1635). Chi-fu served as abbess of two convents in the Hangchou area, and two collections of her writings were published. Her 1665 poem, "Twelve Hours of the Day" (each hour equals two of ours), gives us an idea of everyday Buddhist life in a convent.

Our final poet, Tao-ch'ien (died 1820), entered a convent at the age of seventeen and, after being tested on the "five obstacles" (that women faced in becoming Buddhas), received Dharma transmission from Pao-lin. Tao-ch'ien later attracted many followers and gained enough support to build a convent where she lived for forty years, combining Zen with Pure Land practices.

Worldly people who do not understand me
Call me by my worldly name of Old Zhou.
You invite me to a seven-day religious feast,
But the feast of meditation knows no end.

Hui-hsu (431–499)

This body without a self
Can be compared to floating duckweed.
This body with its troubles
Is exactly like a leaf in the wind.
This cycle of life and death
Is just like that of night and day.

Fa-yuan (601–663)

Spring morning on the lake: the wind merges with the rain,
Worldly matters are like flowers that fall only to bloom again.
I retire to contemplate behind closed doors, a place of true joy,
While the floating clouds come and go the whole day long.

The hidden birds on the treetops sing without pause,
The sky clears, the rain stops, the window brightens.
From the West came the wondrous meaning without words,
It may be gold dust, but don't let it get in your eyes!

Cheng-chueh (12th century)

Don't you know that afflictions are nothing more than wisdom,
But to cling to your afflictions is nothing more than foolishness?
As they rise and then melt away again, you must remember this:
The sparrow hawk flies through Silla without anyone noticing!

Don't you know that afflictions are nothing more than wisdom
And that the purest of blossoms emerges from the mire?
If someone were to come and ask me what I do:
After eating my gruel and rice, I wash my bowl.
Don't worry about a thing!

Don't worry about a thing!
You may play all day like a silly child in the sand by the sea,
But you must always realize the truth of your original face!
When you suffer the blows delivered by the patriarchs' staff,
If you can't say anything, you will perish by the staff,
If you can say something, you will perish by the staff.
In the end, what will you do
If you are forbidden to travel by night but must arrive by dawn?

                                   Pen-ming (early 12th century)

I suddenly find myself upside-down on level ground;
When I pick myself up, I find there's nothing to say!
If someone should ask me what this is all about,
Smiling, I'd point to the pure breeze and bright moon.

                                   Chen-ju (12th century)

Inscribed over a Monastery Bath-House

Since there is nothing that exists, what are you bathing?
If there is even a speck of dust, from where does it arise?
If you produce a single profound phrase,
Then everyone can come in and bathe.
The most the ancient holy ones can do is scrub your back;
When has a bodhisattva ever illuminated anyone's mind?
If you want to realize the stage beyond impurity,
You should sweat from every last pore of your body.
It is said that water is able to wash away impurities,
But how do you know that the water is also not dirty?
Even if you erase the distinction between water and dirt,
When you come in here, you must still be sure to bathe!

Within the vast expanse of dust essentially a single suchness,
Whether vertical or horizontal, everything bears the seal of
    Vairochana.
Although the entire wave is made of water, the wave is not the
    water;
Although all of the water may turn into waves, the water is still
    itself.

Subject and object from the start are no different,
The myriad things nothing but images in the mirror.
Bright and refulgent, transcending both guest and host,
Complete and realized, all is permeated by the absolute.
A single form encompasses the multitude of dharmas,
All of which are interconnected within the net of Indra.
Layer after layer there is no point at which it all ends,
Whether in motion or still, all is fully interpenetrating.

Chih-t'ung (d. 1124)

Suddenly I have made contact with the tip of the nose,
And my cleverness melts like ice and shatters like tiles.
What need for Bodhidharma to have come from the West?
What a waste for the Second Patriarch to have paid his respects!
To ask any further about what is this and what is that
Would signal defeat by a regiment of straw bandits!

Miao-tsung (1095–1170)

Male or female: why should one need to distinguish false and
   true?
What is the shape in which Kwan-yin would finally take form?
Peeling away the bodhisattva's skin would be of no use whatsoever
Were someone to ask if it were the body of a woman or that of a
   man.

One-Eyed Chin-kang (n.d.)

The First Month of Summer Retreat:
Written in Leisure (Four Verses)

In the gates and halls of the elders, the work of the lineage
   flourishes,
Knowing my own lazy ignorance, I've hidden away in order to be
   still.
Esoteric methods, blows and shouts—I am giving them all a rest,
The myriad dharmas merge in emptiness—stop asking about Zen!

A worn, patched robe hangs lopsided from my shoulders,
When hunger comes, I will eat, when tired, I will sleep.

Sitting still on my cushion, I will completely forget the world
And just let the days and the months drift by my window.

Resting high in the cloudy peaks, a lodging for this illusory body,
White clouds and green bamboo, one leaning against the other.
Before my eyes this magical scene undergoes its transformations,
Fastening shut my brushwood gate, my happiness spills over.

A thatched hut buffeted by high winds—who would dare come
      near?
Blows of wind and shouts of moon keep away the mist and clouds.
Solemnly, I lift up my alms bowl toward the empty heavens;
My unseasoned rice and minced yellow pickle will soon be ready.

The Alms Bowl

How very elegant it is, with not even a single leak or hole!
When thirsty I drink; when hungry I eat, leaving not a crumb.
I understand that once washed, nothing more need be done,
Yet how many lost souls insist on attaching a handle to it!

Understand the ordinary mind, and realize one is naturally
      complete,
Ask urgently who you were before your father and mother were
      born.
When you have seen through the method that underlies them all,
The mountain blossoms and flowing streams will rejoice with you.

Behind Closed Doors

After teaching and preaching, running about for so many years,
Now I've shut my door and retired to the hidden forest spring.
Having kicked open heaven and earth, I can now rest my feet,
Alone I sit before the winter window, the shimmering moon full.

Spending the day in a foolish way: no need for any method,
Here within there is neither existence nor nonexistence.
Straight and tall, I sit, cutting off the path of sage and fool;
Since time immemorial to the present day it has been so.

                                        Hsing-kang (1597–1654)

Summer Retreat

Ninety days of staying put and yet one can find moments of leisure,
Trying to make out a tattered sutra, I read under the light of the
    moon.
Although I have ears, I hear nothing of the dusty affairs of the
    world;
A fragrant breeze slips through the door as I think of the lofty sages.

Ashamed of my meager talents, I flee the world to ancient streams,
Nursing my illness, all day long I keep the double-shuttered gate
    closed.
The vines and creepers grow thick and dense, and no one comes;
Sometimes the forest birds and I discuss methods of self-cultivation.

I watch unmoved as waves recede and Dharma gates fall into
    disrepair,
I draw a circle on the ground within which I will hide myself away.
Suddenly the summer begins to draw to a close, and fall comes
    again;
It is only recently that I have mastered the art of being a complete
    fool.

Zen Meditation

Once the layered gates are shattered, any place is a place of
    tranquility,
Once the mind becomes unattached to things, all things become
    pure.
In moments of leisure, I sit upright in the shade of the pine tree,
Watching as the toad in the moon slowly rises to hover in the east.

When one freely speaks of the Dharma, the heavenly flowers fall,
When one deliberates and debates, one is only confused by things.
With the right opportunity and good fortune nothing is impossible,
Knocking on emptiness, extracting the marrow, becomes a way of
    life.

How wonderfully sublime to discuss mysteries layered like clouds,
It is truly rare to meet someone who can be called a kindred soul.
The red stove blazes forth with an extraordinary determination,
As if it possessed the karmic power to turn the Dharma wheel.

This toiling life disordered and confused by lust, greed, and anger,
But when the mind flower suddenly opens, the world becomes
    spring.
Melting snow to boil water for tea, I while away the entire day,
Feeling inside as vast and expansive as the icy-cold moon above.

A tiny boat in the moonlight stirs up foam-flowers on the water,
Blossoming water lilies send across their fragrances in the dark.
Hearing, seeing, knowledge, and consciousness are all one dharma,
Now this nun can afford to be lazy and let her hair grow long.

Inscribed on a Mirror

We meet and scrutinize each other, I confront my own nature;
If within there is no self, then each and every thing is intimate.
I am fond of this mirror, which like autumn water is completely
    clear,
Always the same, whether reflecting the face of a foreigner or a
    Chinese.

All her life, this "fellow" has been as tough as nails,
Once I dug my heels in, I could not be moved.
At twenty-four, I first found out about this matter
And for ten years struggled to forget outward appearances.
At forty-nine, I cut myself loose from this suffering world
And could see through mundane affairs as if through water.
I'd got to the truth of things and could leave when I wished,
But I stuck to my labors for seven more seasons of spring.
Now in front of your eyes, the iron nails will turn to dust,
And the four great elements will disperse like wind and fire.
When leaves fall, one knows autumn has come,
Now is the time for me to return to the source.
Ha, ha, ha!
Footloose and fancy-free—that's me!

                                        Yi-k'uei (1625–1679)

The World-Honored One Gazes at the Shining Stars

Present, past, heaven and earth—no more rebirth,
So what need for special analysis and explication?

And yet now night after night shining stars appear;
Is it not perhaps a convocation of the compassionate?

Yin-yueh (17th century)

Instructions to the Congregation

Recklessly speaking of wisdom, carelessly talking of religion,
Mistakenly I entice the deaf to learn from my own deafness.
From the beginning form and substance have been complete,
Affairs follow the pattern of the world manifesting in emptiness.

It is because you are attached that opportunities are blocked;
Beings, once free of emotions, can fully penetrate the Way.
Right in the midst of this is where the truth can be realized,
As the sun heads toward the west and the river flows east.

Ming-hsiu (n.d.)

On a Riverbank in Early Summer

A stone pillow and a vine cot: the ten thousand worries forgotten,
Sitting cross-legged, I do not chase after the busyness of the world.
A breeze rises from the rush fan: human emotions grow cold,
The bamboo etched against the gauze window: moon shadows
    grow chill.
No matter where one is, one can mitigate the endlessness of the
    pure night,
In the state of no-mind one can fully enjoy the fragrance of the
    wild lotus.
At my door I greet the running brook, the sounds of the world
    are faraway,
And beyond the railing, the soughing of the pine trees lingers in
    my ears.

Ching-no (late 17th century)

Song of the Twelve Hours of the Day

Middle of the night—the first hour
In my dreams, I go here and there and don't know how to stop
    myself.

Treading into pieces the green of the eastern hills and the western
  peaks,
Then turning over to find one's been nestled in the bedcovers all
  along.

The cock crows—the second hour
All the routines of everyday life, each one naturally in accord.
Over there, by the banks of the river, they scrub their faces until
  they shine,
Over here, rinsing the mouth with tea then swallowing it down.

Dawn breaks—the third hour
I am alone here among ten thousand forms and I can bare my body.
If the Buddha and ancestors came, they'd find it hard to overpower
  me,
Only if a person is herself willing can anyone become intimate
  with her.

The sun rises—the fourth hour
In the coral tree groves, the colors are bright and radiant.
There is no need to look elsewhere for the Buddha, Gautama,
His sixteen-foot-tall golden body is in a single blade of grass.

Mealtime—the fifth hour
In the new pot, fragrant, mouth-watering grains of fresh rice.
When I've finished eating my porridge, I go wash my bowl
Then tell the Dharma master to correct and instruct the others.

Midmorning—the sixth hour
Do not split up the great emptiness into "this" and "that."
Bells and clappers in the wind are very good at preaching,
Explaining everything in detail without using a single word.

The sun shifts south—the seventh hour
Those who are fond of leisure do not pound on Hoshan's drum.
When there's free time, I climb the mountain and stroll about;
And when I'm weary, seat myself on my meditation mat once more.

The sun begins to sink—the eighth hour
From the twelve-sectioned canon we can know how to behave.
With bowed head, I place my trust in the Great One Above
And venture to ask how to apply it to this autumn of 1665.

Late afternoon—the ninth hour
My understanding is still on this side of the river crossing.
I chide myself that my cultivation practice is not stronger.
When all goes well, I am happy; when it doesn't, I get angry!

The sun sets—the tenth hour
A curve of moon hangs over the willow by the window.
I blow on the kindling, and the furnace fills with smoke.
Four or five flecks of dark ash fly up over my head.

Golden dusk—the eleventh hour
Time for the mice to venture out to steal the pale honey.
At the foot of my bed they make a racket late into the night,
Which disturbs this mountain monk so she cannot sleep.

Everyone settled—the twelfth hour
The mustard seed drinks dry the Fragrant-Water Sea.
Beneath my robes, the *mani* jewel suddenly radiates light,
Singing in unison with the lanterns on the outside pillars.

Chi-fu (late 17th century)

Convent Life

You've been earnestly studying the Way year after year
And now no longer cling to either existence or nonexistence.
But having come home, you should not just sit around
But instead go out and till the fields of merit for others.

Eighty years and eight,
No craving, no attachment.
Let's go on back home,
When the water clears, the moon appears.

Tao-ch'ien (d. 1820)

—Translations by Beata Grant

10

Chao-chou (778–897)

Recorded Sayings (excerpts)

*Although the biography of Chao-chou (Japanese: Jōshū) is partly shrouded in
legend, traditional texts indicate that he became a monk on Mount Sung in
his early adolescence and gained his first enlightenment experience at the age
of eighteen. An exemplar of devoted study under a single teacher, he served
under Nan-ch'üan (Japanese: Nansen) for several decades until the Master's
death in 835. After three years of mourning, at the age of sixty, Chao-chou
went on pilgrimage for twenty years, visiting such Masters as Huang-po.
Finally, at the age of eighty, Chao-chou took up residence at a small temple
in northern China and taught there for forty years; his most familiar name
literally means "Province of Chao."*

*Although the persecutions of Buddhism and feudal warfare taking place
around this time limited the number of pupils who were able to study with
him, Chao-chou's teachings reached a wide audience through his recorded
sayings, which include many anecdotes and dialogues that became famous as
kōan texts for meditation. Indeed, the single most famous kōan, which is often
given first in the training of both monks and laypeople, is Chao-chou's famous
Mu (Chinese: Wu, "not have"), his response to the question of whether a dog
has the Buddha-nature (Case One in Wu-men-kuan; see Chapter 12). There
are a total of 525 sayings and poems in the recorded works of Chao-chou, of
which we present a selection here.*

1

The Master asked Nan-ch'üan [Japanese: Nansen], "What is the Way?"
Nan-ch'üan said, "Ordinary mind is the Way."

From *The Recorded Sayings of Zen Master Joshu,* translated by James Green (Boston:
Shambhala Publications, 1998). Reprinted by permission of Rowman & Littlefield.

The Master said, "Then may I direct myself towards it or not?"
Nan-ch'üan said, "To seek [it] is to deviate [from it]."

The Master said, "If I do not seek, how can I know about the Way?"

Nan-ch'üan said, "The Way does not belong to knowing or not knowing. To know is to have a concept; to not know is to be ignorant. If you truly realize the Way of no doubt, it is just like the sky: wide open vast emptiness. How can you say 'yes' or 'no' to it?"

At these words the Master had sudden enlightenment. His mind became like the clear moon.

11

The Master asked Nan-ch'üan, "Mind is not Buddha, Wisdom is not the Way. Then is there any mistake or not?"

Nan-ch'üan said, "Yes, there is."

The Master said, "Please tell me where the mistake is."

Nan-ch'üan said, "Mind is not Buddha, Wisdom is not the Way."

The Master left the room.

12

A monk then asked, "What is the mind that the Patriarch brought from the west?"

The Master said, "Oak tree in the front garden."

The monk said, "Don't instruct by means of objectivity." The Master said, "I don't instruct by means of objectivity."

The monk again asked, "What is the mind that the Patriarch brought from the west?"

The Master said, "Oak tree in the front garden."

17

A monk asked, "The Dharma is not a special Dharma. What is the Dharma?"

The Master said, "Nothing outside; nothing inside. Nothing inside and outside."

25

A monk asked, "What is the one word?"

The Master said, "If you hold on to one word it will make an old man of you."

47

A monk asked, "What is my self?"

The Master said, "Well, do you see the oak tree in the front garden?"

62

Another time the Master said, "I have been here more than thirty years. Not yet has one Zen man ever come here. Even if one did come, after staying a night and grabbing a meal, he would quickly move on, heading for a warm and comfortable place."

A monk asked, "If a Zen man happened to come here, what would you say to him?"

The Master said, "The thousand-pound stone bow is not used to shoot a mouse."

65

A monk asked, "Has someone who cannot be taken in by 'good and bad' liberated himself or not?"

The Master said, "He has not liberated himself."

The monk said, "Why has he not liberated himself?"

The Master said, "Obviously he exists in good and bad."

91

The Master instructed the assembly saying, "I will teach you how to speak. If there is a time when someone questions you, just say, 'I've come from Chao-chou.' If he asks, 'What does Chao-chou say about the Dharma?' just say to him, 'When it's cold, he says it's cold; when it's hot, he says it's hot.' If he further asks, 'I wasn't asking about that kind of thing,' just say to him, 'What kind of thing were you asking about?' If again he says, 'What does Chao-chou say about the Dharma?' just say, 'When I left the Master, he did not give me any message to pass on to you. If you must know about Chao-chou's affairs, go ask him yourself.'"

95

A monk asked, "To a superior man, make one action and he moves on. What about when an inferior man comes?"

The Master said, "Are you superior or inferior?"

The monk said, "Please answer."

The Master said, "In speaking you are not yet the Master."

The monk said, "I've come seven thousand miles, don't play mind games with me."

The Master said, "I have received this question from you, so how can mind games not be played?"

The monk stayed one night and left.

99

A monk asked, "What is Chao-chou?"

The Master said, "East gate, west gate, south gate, north gate."

100

A monk asked, "What is meditation?"

The Master said, "It is not meditation."

The monk said, "Why is it 'not meditation'?"

The Master said, "It's alive, it's alive!"

108

A monk asked, "When great difficulties come upon us, how can they be avoided?"

The Master said, "Well come!"

109

The Master entered the hall and, after sitting quietly for a while, said, "Is everyone here or not?"

Someone said, "Everyone is here."

The Master said, "I'm waiting for one more to come, then I'll speak."

A monk said, "I will tell you that you are waiting for a person who does not come."

The Master said, "It's a person that's really hard to find."

117

A monk asked, "The ten thousand things arise together, then is there any-one who is not deluded [by them]?"

The Master said, "There is."

The monk said, "What is he who is not deluded?"

The Master said, "Do you believe that there is a Buddha-Dharma or not?"

The monk said, "I believe there is a Buddha-Dharma, the ancients have said so. What is he who is not deluded?"

The Master said, "Why don't you ask me?"

The monk said, "I did ask."

The Master said, "Deluded."

132

A monk asked, "Does a dog have a Buddha-nature or not?"

The Master said, "Not [*Mu*]!"

The monk said, "Above to all the Buddhas, below to the crawling bugs, all have Buddha-nature. Why is it that the dog has not?"

The Master said, "Because he has the nature of karmic delusions."

148

A monk asked, "By what means is 'hearing without hearing' accomplished?"

The Master said, "Setting aside not hearing, what do you hear?"

153

A monk asked, "I have just come here and know nothing. What are my du-ties?"

The Master said, "What's your name?"

The monk said, "Hui-han [Japanese: Enan]."

The Master said, "A fine 'knowing nothing' that is."

164

A monk asked, "What about it when 'external form is disregarded'?"

The Master pointed to a water bottle and said, "What's that?"

The monk said, "A water bottle."

The Master said, "A fine 'disregarding external form' that is."

169

A monk asked, "What about it when I'm not wearing a stitch of clothing?"

The Master said, "What are you not wearing?"

The monk said, "I'm not wearing a stitch of clothing."

The Master said, "A fine 'not wearing a stitch of clothing' that is."

175

A monk asked, "What is 'Buddha-mind'?"

The Master said, "You are mind, I am Buddha. Whether to attend upon me or not, you must see for yourself."

The monk said, "You are not lacking it, so shouldn't you be attended upon?"

The Master said, "You teach me."

178

A monk asked, "It is said, 'Do not abandon the root, do not chase after phenomena.' What is the True Way?"

The Master said, "A fine 'monk that has left home' you are."

The monk said, "In the past I never did leave home."

The Master said, "I take shelter in the Buddha, I take shelter in the Dharma."

The monk said, "It's not clear to me; is there a home that can be left or not?"

The Master said, "Just leave home."

The monk asked, "Where does the person who has left home settle down?"

The Master said, "Sitting quietly at home."

183

A monk asked, "What about it when there is a hair's breadth of differentiation?"

The Master said, "Heaven and Earth are far removed from each other."

187

A monk asked, "What is the unmistaken path?"

The Master said, "Awakening to your mind, seeing your nature; these are the unmistaken path."

190

A monk asked, "What about it when I seek to be Buddha?"

The Master said, "What a tremendous waste of energy."

The monk said, "What about it when I'm not wasting any energy?"

The Master said, "In that case, you are Buddha."

214

A monk asked, "What is the practice hall?"

The Master said, "From the practice hall you have come. From the practice hall you will go. Everything [everywhere] is the practice hall. There is no other place."

216

A monk asked, "What is multiplicity?"

The Master said, "One, two, three, four, five."

The monk said, "What is the fact of the state of not relating to multiplicity?"

The Master said, "One, two, three, four, five."

220

A monk asked, "What are the words of the ancients?"

The Master said, "Listen carefully! Listen carefully!"

225

A monk asked, "What sort of person is it that goes beyond Buddha?"

The Master said, "Anyone who is leading an ox and ploughing the fields."

232

A monk asked, "What is Buddha?"
  The Master said, "Aren't you Buddha?"

257

A monk asked, "What is one word?"
  The Master said, "Two words."

270

A monk asked, "What is my teacher?"
  The Master said, "Clouds rising out of the mountains, streams entering the valley without a sound."
  The monk said, "I didn't ask about them."
  The Master said, "Though they are your teacher, you don't recognize them."

291

A monk asked, "What is my self?"
  The Master said, "Have you eaten breakfast or not?"
  The monk said, "I have eaten."
  The Master said, "Then wash out your bowls."

296

A monk asked, "The Second Patriarch cut off his arm, what sort of act is that?"
  The Master said, "He was throwing his whole self into it."
  The monk said, "To whom was the offering made?"
  The Master said, "The offering was made to whoever came."

298

A monk said, "In the day there is sunlight, at night there is firelight. What is 'divine light'?"
  The Master said, "Sunlight, firelight."

299

A monk asked, "What is the perfect question?"
   The Master said, "[That's] wrong!"
   The monk said, "What is 'not asking'?"
   The Master said, "Consider what I just said."

301

A monk asked, "What is non-action?"
   The Master said, "That [asking a question] is action."

315

A monk asked, "I ask you to say something about that which is immediately at hand."
   The Master said, "Pissing is an easy matter, I can do it by myself."

319

A nun asked, "What is the deeply secret mind?"
   The Master squeezed her hand.
   The nun said, "Do you still have that in you?"
   The Master said, "It is you who have it."

331

A monk asked, "For a long time I've heard about the famous stone bridge of Chao-chou, but coming here I saw only a common wooden bridge."
   The Master said, "You saw only the wooden bridge, you have not seen the stone bridge of Chao-chou."
   The monk said, "What is the stone bridge of Chao-chou?"
   The Master said, "Cross over! Cross over!"

343

The King of Chen asked, "You are quite aged, how many teeth do you have left?"
   The Master said, "I have but one tooth."

The King said, "How do you manage to eat?"

The Master said, "Even though there's but one, I chew one bite at a time."

347

A monk asked, "What is the substance of the true person?"

The Master said, "Spring, summer, autumn, winter."

The monk said, "In that case, it is hard for me to understand."

The Master said, "You asked about the substance of the true person, didn't you?"

349

A monk asked, "What is the teacher of the seven Buddhas?"

The Master said, "Sleeping when it's time to sleep, waking when it's time to wake."

355

A monk asked, "What is the fact that goes beyond Buddha?"

The Master clapped his hands and laughed.

358

A monk asked, "What is the state of 'no-thought'?"

The Master said, "Speak quickly, speak quickly!"

The monk asked, "What about it when I don't have anything?"

The Master said, "Throw it away."

389

A monk asked, "What is your 'family custom'?"

The Master said, "Having nothing inside, seeking for nothing outside."

399

A monk asked, "Please point out the state of 'true ease.'"

The Master said, "Pointing it out makes it uneasy."

406

A monk asked, "What is a person who is outside the three worlds?"

The Master said, "But I am inside the three worlds."

426

A monk asked, "I have recently entered the forest and have no understanding. I beg for your teaching."

The Master said, "You have entered the forest. Any more than this is not understanding."

429

A monk asked, "What is Buddha?"

The Master said, "Who are you?"

456

The Master asked a new arrival, "Where have you come from?"

The monk said, "From no direction."

The Master turned his back on the monk.

The monk picked up his bowing cloth and turned around like the Master.

The Master said, "That's a fine 'no direction.'"

459

The Master questioned two new arrivals.

The Master asked the first one, "Have you been here before?'

The monk said, "No, I haven't."

The Master said, "Go have some tea."

The Master then asked the other monk, "Have you been here before?"

The monk said, "Yes, I have."

The Master said, "Go have some tea."

The monk asked, "Setting aside the fact that you told the one who'd never been here before to go have some tea, why did you tell the one who had been here before to go have some tea?"

The Master said, "Head monk!"

The head monk said, "Yes?"

The Master said, "Go have some tea."

Figure 7. Fukushima Keidō (born 1933), *Go Have Some Tea*

480

A monk was on his way to interview the Master, but he saw that the Master was sitting with his robe covering his head, so he went back.

The Master said, "You can't say I didn't answer you."

513

The Master was leaving the main hall when he saw a monk bowing to him.

The Master struck him with his stick.

The monk said, "But bowing is a good thing!"

The Master said, "A good thing is not as good as nothing."

518

There was a monk who asked, "What is nirvana?"

The Master said, "I didn't hear you."

The monk repeated his question.

The Master said, "I'm not deaf."

The Master then recited a verse:

> He who dances and skips on the Great Way,
> Is face to face with the Nirvana Gate.
> Just sitting with a boundless mind,
> Next year spring is still spring.

—Translation by James Green

11

K'uo-an (active c. 1150)

The Ox-Herding Poems (complete)

*The earliest series of ox-herding poems was composed around 1050 by
Ch'ing-chu; they are only partially preserved. Another set composed by
P'u-ming was circulated in Chinese Zen circles, but the series that became
best known in East Asia was written and illustrated by K'uo-an Shih-yuan
in the mid-twelfth century. Woodblock book versions of this series were printed
over the next few hundred years in China and Japan, and it was K'uo-an's
illustrations that became the model for most later painters. As a metaphor for
the path to enlightenment, the ox-herding poems and paintings have often
been utilized by Zen Masters over the centuries; for example, when Zekkai
Chushin was asked in 1395 to explain Zen Buddhism to the Shogun, he used
K'uo-an's book as a point of departure for his explanations.*

*Some sets of ox-herding paintings end with the eighth, the empty circle,
but the final two are also important: after enlightenment, one comes back
to the world—both for one's own continuing practice and to help all others.
The examples here were painted in traditional style by a contemporary
Korean monk.*

1. Searching for the Ox

Searching through tall,
  endless grass,
Rivers, mountain ranges, the
  path trails off.
Weary, exhausted, no place left
  to hunt:
Maples rustle, evening, the
  cicada's song.

2. Finding the Tracks

Along the river, under trees—
    jumbled tracks!
Thick fragrant woods, is this
    the way?
Though the ox wanders far in
    the hills,
His nose touches the sky. He
    cannot hide.

3. Seeing the Ox

Oriole on a branch chirps and
    chirps,
Sun warm, breeze through the
    willows.
There is the ox, cornered,
    alone.
That head, those horns! Who
    could paint them?

4. Catching the Ox

Last desperate effort, got him!
Hard to control, powerful and
    wild,
The ox sprints up a hill and at
    the top
Disappears into the misty
    clouds.

5. Taming the Ox

Don't lose the whip, hold onto
   the rope
Or he'll buck away into the
   dirt.
Herded well, in perfect
   harmony
He'll follow along without any
   constraint.

6. Riding the Ox Home

Riding the ox home, taking it
   easy,
The flute's notes vanish in the
   evening haze.
Tapping time to a folk song,
   happy as can be—
It's all too much for words.

7. Ox Forgotten

Reaching home on the back of
   the ox,
Rest now, the ox forgotten.
Taking a nap under the noon
   sun,
Whip and rope abandoned
   behind the hut.

8. Ox Transcended

Whip, rope, self, ox—no
    traces left.
Thoughts cannot penetrate the
    vast blue sky,
Snowflakes cannot survive a
    red-hot stove.
Arriving here, meet the ancient
    teachers.

9. Returning to the Source

Return to the source, no more
    effort,
Just staying at home, sitting in
    the hut,
Blind and deaf to the world
    outside.
The river runs by itself, flowers
    are red.

10. Entering the Marketplace

Barefoot and shirtless, enter
    the market
Smiling through all the dirt
    and grime.
No immortal powers, no secret
    spells,
Just teach the withered trees to
    bloom.

—Translation by Stanley Lombardo

12

Wu-men (1183–1260), compiler

Wu-men-kuan (*The Gateless Barrier,* complete)

The Wu-men-kuan, *better known in its Japanese pronunciation* Mumonkan, *was compiled in 1228 by the monk Wu-men Hui-k'ai (Japanese: Mumon Ekai). It consists of a series of forty-eight kōans, meditation questions given to Zen students when they have reached a point in their practice where they can quiet and focus their minds. The first kōan given to Zen students has usually been the first case here, Chao-chou's dog and the meaning of* Mu *(Chinese:* Wu, *"not have").*

Kōans are intended to break through conceptual thought, and as such they do not have answers that can be reasoned out but instead act as gateways to reaching enlightenment. Most kōans are Zen encounters between Chinese Masters and their monk pupils, although there are exceptions that refer to Indian Buddhism.

The name Wu-men itself means "no gate," and Wu-men-kuan *means "gateless barrier." In his preface, Wu-men offers a quatrain that has become very well known in the world of Zen:*

> The great way has no gate,
> But there are a thousand paths;
> If you pass through the barrier,
> You can walk alone through the universe.

After each of the forty-eight cases, Wu-men wrote commentaries (which are not given here) and then added four-line verses. His commentaries and poems do not explain the kōans, which would defeat their purpose, but they do add further elements, often paradoxical, to encourage students to go beyond linear thinking.

Since Wu-men's time, a number of Zen Masters have also added their own commentaries to the text, so that a full study of the Wu-men-kuan *would take many volumes. But since its essence consists of the forty-eight kōans, we present them here with Wu-men's verses.*

Figure 8. Nakahara Nantenbō (1839–1925)
Wu-men-kuan (Mumonkan)

Case One

Chao-chou was asked by a monk, "Has a dog the Buddha-nature or not?" Chao-chou said, "*Mu.*"

> *Wu-men's Verse*
> Dog—Buddha-nature—
> Completely manifested, correctly ordered.
> But cross into having and not having,
> You will mourn your body and lose your life.

[Note: Although Buddhists believe that all sentient beings have Buddha-nature, Mu *(Chinese:* Wu*) means "no," "not," "nothing."]*

Case Two

When Pai-chang gave sermons, an old man always followed the monks into the hall and listened; when the monks departed, so did the old man. However, one day he did not leave, so Pai-chang asked, "Who are you, standing before me?" The old man replied, "I am not a human being. In the old days of Kasyapa Buddha, I was the head monk at this mountain temple. One day a monk in training asked, 'Are enlightened people subject to the law of cause and effect or not?' I replied, 'They do not fall into causation.' As a result I have been reborn five hundred times as a fox. I beg you to utter a turning word on my behalf and release me from my life as a fox."

The old man then asked Pai-chang, "Do enlightened people fall into causation?"

The Master said, "They are not in the dark about causation."

At these words, the old man achieved enlightenment. Bowing to the Master he said, "I am released from my fox body, and I shall remain on this mountain. Please have a funeral service for my body as that of a deceased monk."

Pai-chang called his monastery administrator to strike the wooden clapper and inform the monks that after the noon meal there would be a funeral for a dead monk. The monks wondered about this, saying, "Everyone seems in good health, no one is in the Nirvana Hall for the ill, so what could this mean?"

After the meal, Pai-chang led the monks to the foot of a large rock. He poked out the body of a fox with his staff and then performed a cremation ceremony.

That evening Pai-chang ascended to the rostrum and told the whole story to the monks. Huang-po then said, "You have told us that the old man gave

Figure 9. Sozan Genkyō (1779–1868), *Wu-men-kuan Case Two*

> Not caused, not free from causes,
> A pair of dice of the same color.

the wrong answer and had to live as a fox for five hundred generations. But if he had given the correct answer, what would have happened then?"

Pai-chang replied, "Come closer and I'll tell you the answer."

Huang-po went up to the Master and gave him a slap. Pai-chang laughed and clapped his hands, saying, "I thought the Barbarian had a red beard, but right here is a red-bearded Barbarian."

> *Wu-men's Verse*
> Not falling, not in the dark—
> Two faces of the same die.
> Not falling in, not escaping—
> A thousand mistakes, ten thousand errors!

[Note: The "red-bearded Barbarian" is Bodhidharma.]

Case Three

Chü-chih, when asked a question, just raised one finger. Later he had a young follower who, when asked by a visitor what was the primary teaching of his Master, also raised up a finger.

When he heard about this, Chü-chih cut off the boy's finger. The boy ran from the hall screaming in pain, but his Master called to him. When he turned, Chü-chih held up one finger. The boy was instantly enlightened.

When Chü-chih was ready to die, he said to the assembled monks, "I received one-finger Zen from T'ien-lung, and I used it all my life without ever exhausting it." With these words, he passed away.

> *Wu-men's Verse*
> Chü-chih made a fool of old T'ien-lung
> And sliced the boy with his sharp knife,
> Just like the deity Chü-leng raised his hand
> And split the thousand-peak Mount Hua in two.

Case Four

Huo-an asked, "Why has the Western Barbarian no beard?"

> *Wu-men's Verse*
> In front of a fool
> Don't explain your dream;
> The Barbarian with no beard—
> Wisdom accompanying ignorance.

[Note: The Western Barbarian is Bodhidharma.]

Case Five

The monk Hsiang-yen said, "It's as though you are up a tree, hanging onto a branch with your mouth; your hands can't touch a branch and your feet can't reach a bough. Someone under the tree asks you the meaning of Bodhidharma coming from the west. If you don't answer, you fail to help the questioner, and if you do answer, you lose your life. What will you do?"

> *Wu-men's Verse*
> Hsiang-yen is being careless,
> Spreading his poison without end;
> He stops up the mouths of monks
> So their bodies sprout the eyes of devils!

Case Six

Long ago when the Buddha was on Mount Grdhrakuta, he held up a flower before the congregated followers. At this time everyone was silent, but only Mahakasyapa gave a broad smile. The World-Honored One said, "I have the eye of the storehouse of the Dharma, the mysterious mind of nirvana, the true form of no-form, the gate of wondrous process that cannot be set forth by words and writings. This special transmission, beyond all teaching, I now give to Mahakasyapa."

> *Wu-men's Verse*
> He holds up a flower,
> The tail of the snake has already emerged.
> Mahakasyapa smiles—
> Humans and gods, deceived and abandoned.

Case Seven

A monk asked Chao-chou, "I have just entered the monastery; can you give me a teaching?"
    Chao-chou asked, "Have you eaten your breakfast?"
    The monk replied, "I have eaten it."
    Chao-chou said, "Then go and wash your bowl."
    The monk was enlightened.

> *Wu-men's Verse*
> He has made it extremely clear,
> But it takes a long time to get it.
> If you understand that flame is fire,
> Cooking a meal won't take much time.

Case Eight

Master Yüeh-an asked a monk, "Hsi-chung built a cart with one hundred spokes. If you took off both front and rear wheels and the axle, what would you learn?

> *Wu-men's Verse*
> When the wheel goes round and round
> Experts are even more confused;
> Four directions, up, down,
> North, south, east, and west.

Case Nine

A monk asked Ch'ing-jang of Hsing-yang, "The Buddha of Great Penetration and Perfect Wisdom sat for ten kalpas in the Meditation Hall, but the Dharma did not manifest itself and he did not fully attain the Buddha Way—why was this?"

Ch'ing-jang said, "This question is extremely rich in truth."

The monk said, "But why did he not reach the Buddha Way from sitting in the Meditation Hall?"

Ch'ing-jang said, "Because he did not attain Buddhahood."

> *Wu-men's Verse*
> How is calming the body like calming the mind?
> When the mind is peaceful, the body is not distressed.
> When body and mind are both completely serene,
> Why would gods and immortals need to become
> noblemen?

[Note: A kalpa is the time from the beginning of a universe to the beginning of the next universe.]

Case Ten

A monk said to Ts'ao-shan, "I am Ch'ing-shui, alone and poor. I beg the teacher to give me alms."

Ts'ao-shan said, "Master Shui!"

Ch'ing-shui responded, "Yes Sir?"

Ts'ao-shan said, "You have already drunk three cups of the finest wine in China, yet you say you have not moistened your lips!"

> *Wu-men's Verse*
> He is poor like Fan-tan,
> And his spirit is broad like Hsiang-yü;
> Although he has no means of livelihood,
> He quarrels about treasure.

[Note: Fan-tan lived a life of poverty, putting his wife and children in a wheelbarrow and traveling around telling fortunes rather than accepting a high government position; Hsiang-yü was a military hero who sang when facing death.]

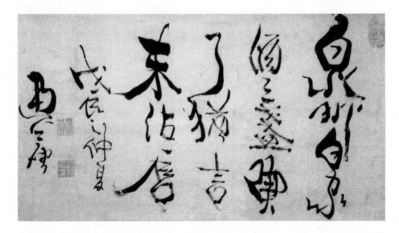

Figure 10. Daien Butsu (died 1825), *Wu-men-kuan Case Ten* **(1808)**

You have already drunk three cups of the finest wine in China,
Yet you say you have not moistened your lips.

Case Eleven

Chao-chou went to the hut of a hermit and asked, "Anyone here, anyone here?" The hermit lifted his fist.

Chao-chou said, "The water is too shallow here to anchor a boat," and went away. He then went to another hermit's hut and said, "Anyone here, anyone here?"

The hermit lifted his fist.

Chao-chou said, "Free to give, free to take away; free to kill, free to bestow life," and made a deep bow.

> *Wu-men's Verse*
> Shooting star eyes,
> Bolt of lightning spirit;
> A killing sword,
> A life-giving sword.

Case Twelve

Every day the monk Jui-yen called to himself "Master," and then responded, "Yes Sir!"

"Wake up, wake up!"

"Yes Sir!"

"From this moment, don't let anyone deceive you!"

"Yes Sir! Yes Sir!"

> *Wu-men's Verse*
> Those searching for the Way do not know truth
> And learn only conscious discriminations.
> These are the origin of endless rounds of birth and
>   death,
> But fools consider them their original self.

Case Thirteen

One day Master Te-shan came down to the dining hall carrying his bowl. Hsüeh-feng asked him, "Old man, where are you taking your bowl? The bell has not yet sounded and the drum has not yet been struck." Te-shan at once returned to his room.

Hsüeh-feng discussed this with Yen-t'ou, who said, "Big or small, Te-shan has not yet penetrated the final word."

Te-shan heard of this, and sent a monk to ask Yen-t'ou to visit him. Te-shan then asked him, "Do you not approve of this old monk?" Yen-t'ou whispered his meaning, and Te-shan silently sent him away.

The next day, Te-shan ascended the rostrum and was not the same. Yen-t'ou, in front of the Monks' Training Hall, clapped his hands and gave a great laugh, saying, "How marvelous. The old man has grasped the final word. After this, no one in the world will be able to match him!"

> *Wu-men's Verse*
> If you understand the first word,
> You understand the last;
> But the last and the first
> Are not a single word.

Case Fourteen

When the monks of the Western and Eastern Halls were quarreling about a cat, Nan-ch'üan held it up and said, "If you are able to speak, I will spare it; if you cannot speak, I will kill it." No one could answer, so Nan-ch'üan proceeded to kill the cat.

That evening Chao-chou returned from afar, and Nan-ch'üan told him what had happened. Chao-chou took off one sandal, put it on his head, and left. Nan-ch'üan said, "If you had been there, you would have saved the cat!"

> *Wu-men's Verse*
> If Chao-chou had been there,
> Everything would have been reversed;
> He would have snatched away the knife,
> And Nan-ch'üan would have begged for his life.

Case Fifteen

When Tung-shan came to study with Yün-men, the Master asked, "Where have you just come from?"

Tung-shan replied, "From Ch'a-tu."

Yün-men asked, "Where were you for the summer sessions?"

Tung-shan answered, "At Pao-tzu in Hunan [South of the Lake]."

"When did you leave there?"

"On August twenty-fifth."

Yün-men said, "I give you sixty blows!"

The next day, Tung-shan came again, knelt down, and said, "Yesterday you gave me sixty blows, but I don't know what I said or did that was wrong."

Yün-men answered, "You dirty rice-bag! Haven't you been meandering west of the river and south of the lake?"

At these words, Tung-shan was enlightened.

> *Wu-men's Verse*
> The lioness has a roundabout way of teaching her cubs—
> She kicks them back so they will come forward;
> He wrongly went to gain equal achievement—
> The first arrow only scratched, but the second went
>   deep.

Case Sixteen

Yün-men said, "The world is vast and broad; at the sound of the bell, why do you put on your seven-piece robe?"

> *Wu-men's Verse*
> If you are enlightened, everything is one;
> If not, ten thousand divisions, a thousand variations.

If you are not enlightened, everything is one;
If you are, ten thousand divisions, a thousand variations.

Case Seventeen

National Teacher Kuo-shih called his attendant three times, and three times the attendant responded. The National Teacher said, "I thought I had failed you, but now I know you have failed me."

> *Wu-men's Verse*
> He has to wear an iron yoke with no hole,
> And his descendants also will have no respite;
> If you want to support the gate and sustain the house,
> You must climb a mountain of swords with bare feet.

Case Eighteen

Tung-shan was asked by a monk, "What is Buddha?"
    Tung-shan said, "Three pounds of flax."

> *Wu-men's Verse*
> Out pour three pounds of flax,
> Intimate words and intimate meaning;
> The person who explains this and that
> Is also a this-and-that person.

Case Nineteen

Chao-chou asked Nan-ch'üan, "What is the Way?"
    Nan-ch'üan answered, "Ordinary mind is the Way."
    Chao-chou asked, "Does it lead in any direction?"
    Nan-ch'üan replied, "To seek it is to lose it."
    Chao-chou asked, "Then how can I know if it is the Way?"
    Nan-ch'üan answered, "The Way does not depend upon knowing, and does not depend upon not knowing. Knowing is illusion; not knowing is blankness. If you can achieve the unquestioned Way, it is like vast emptiness and boundless space, so how can it be this or that?"
    At these words, Chao-chou became enlightened.

Wu-men's Verse
Spring has a hundred flowers, autumn has the moon,
Summer offers a cool breeze, and winter has snow.
When obstructions are not held in the mind,
Then anytime becomes the best season for humanity.

Case Twenty

Master Sung-yüan said, "Why can't a man of great strength lift up his own leg?"

He also said, "When we open our mouths, it is not with our tongues that we speak."

Wu-men's Verse
Lifting a foot, he kicks scented waters from the ocean,
Lowering his head, he looks down at the four heavens.
His body is so big there's no place to put it—
Please add the last line yourself!

Case Twenty-One

A monk asked Yün-men, "What is Buddha?"
Yün-men replied, "A dried shit-stick."

Wu-men's Verse
A flash of lightning,
Sparks of fire from flint—
If your eyes blink,
It's already gone.

[Note: Before the use of toilet paper, a short stick was used in the latrine.]

Case Twenty-Two

Ananda asked Mahakasyapa, "The World-Honored One transmitted to you the golden robe. What else did he transmit?"
Mahakasyapa said, "Ananda!"
"Yes?"
"Take down the flag at the gate!"

Wu-men's Verse
Is the question or answer more intimate?
Many people have knit their brows.
Elder brother asks, younger brother answers, a family
    disgrace,
But this springtime does not belong to yin or yang.

*[Note: Ananda was the Buddha's younger cousin who served as his attendant;
the temple flag was raised when a Master gave a sermon.]*

Case Twenty-Three

The Sixth Patriarch was pursued by Head Monk Hui-ming to Ta-yü Peak.
The Patriarch, seeing Ming coming, laid down his bowl and robe on a rock,
saying, "The robe is nothing but a symbol—what point is there in taking it
by force? I leave them for you to take away."

When Hui-ming came to the rock, he tried to pick up the robe and bowl
but could not move them. Then he shouted, "Lay brother, lay brother, I have
come for the Dharma, not for the robe!"

The Patriarch replied, "Thinking of neither good nor evil, at this instant,
what is the original face of Hui-ming?" At these words Hui-ming had an
awakening, and his entire body dripped with sweat. In tears, he made his
bows and asked, "Beyond these secret words is there anything else even
deeper?"

The Patriarch answered, "What I have said is not a secret; when you realize your true face, anything deeper belongs only to you."

Hui-ming said, "Although I stayed at Huang-mei, I did not realize my
original face. Thanks to your guidance, I now understand, just as someone
drinking water knows personally if it is hot or cold. Lay brother, you are now
my teacher."

I said, "If this be true, then we are both disciples of the Fifth Patriarch,
so maintain with care what you have learned."

Wu-men's Verse
Can't describe it, can't paint it,
Needn't praise or grasp it;
There's no place to hide your original face,
When the world ends, this still remains.

Case Twenty-Four

A monk asked Feng-hsüeh, "Speech and silence are both inward and outward —how can we go beyond dualism?"

Feng-hsüeh said,

> "I often think of Chiang-nan in March;
> Partridges chirp among the fragrant blossoms."

> *Wu-men's Verse*
> You don't need fine phrases;
> Before you speak, the answer is there.
> If you just chatter on and on,
> Knowing will become deceiving.

Case Twenty-Five

Yang-shan had a dream that he went to the realm of the future Buddha and was given the third seat. A senior monk pounded the gavel and announced, "Today the sermon will be given by the monk in the third seat."

Yang-shan stood up and pounded the gavel, saying, "Mahayana teachings go beyond the Four Propositions and transcend the Hundred Negations. Listen carefully! Listen carefully!"

> *Wu-men's Verse*
> Bright sun, blue sky,
> A dream explained within a dream—
> Falsehood and fabrication!
> He deceived the entire congregation.

[Note: Mahayana is the "greater vehicle" of Buddhism.]

Case Twenty-Six

Fa-yen of Ch'ing-liang went to the Monks' Hall to speak before the noon meal. He pointed to the bamboo blinds, and immediately two monks went to roll them up. Fa-yen said, "One wins, one loses."

> *Wu-men's Verse*
> When they are rolled up, bright, bright, the great sky;
> But the great sky does not match our teachings.

Why not cast away everything including the sky?
Then even the wind can never pass through.

Case Twenty-Seven

A monk asked Nan-ch'üan, "Is there a teaching that has never been taught?"
Nan-ch'üan replied, "There is."
The monk asked, "What is the teaching that has never been taught?"
Nan-ch'üan said, "Not mind, not Buddha, not things."

> *Wu-men's Verse*
> Too much kindness loses its virtue;
> Not speaking is more truly useful.
> The blue ocean may be transformed,
> But in the end, it cannot be explained.

Case Twenty-Eight

One night Te-shan visited Lung-t'an and asked for his teaching. Lung-t'an said, "It has grown late, so you had better retire."

Te-shan made his bows, lifted the curtain, and went out. Seeing that it was dark outside, he came back in and said, "It's very dark out there."

Lung-t'an lit a candle and handed it to him. Just when Te-shan was about to take it, Lung-t'an blew the candle out. Te-shan was immediately enlightened, and made a deep bow.

Lung-t'an asked, "What have you understood?"

Te-shan replied, "From this moment, I will never again doubt what the sages of old have taught."

The next day Lung-t'an went up to the rostrum and said, "There is one among you with fangs like a tree of swords and a mouth like a bowl of blood. Hit him with a stick, and he won't even turn his head to look at you. One day he will climb to the highest peak and establish the Way."

Te-shan then made a bonfire of his commentaries on the *Diamond Sutra* in front of the Monks' Hall and said, "Even the most profound doctrines are like a single hair in vast emptiness; the greatest wisdom is just a drop of water thrown into a deep ravine." When he had burned his commentaries, he took his leave.

> *Wu-men's Verse*
> Hearing the name is not as good as seeing the face;
> Seeing the face is not as good as hearing the name.

Even though he was able to save his nose,
He has lost his eyes!

Case Twenty-Nine

In front of the Sixth Patriarch, a temple pennant was blowing in the wind, and two monks were arguing. One claimed that the wind was moving, while the other insisted that it was the pennant that was moving, and they could not come to an agreement.

The Sixth Patriarch said, "It's not the wind moving; it's not the flag moving; it is your minds that are moving." The two monks were amazed.

Wu-men's Verse
The wind, the flag, the mind moves—
A single appearance, and understanding passes by.
We only know to open our mouths
But don't realize how we indulge in talk.

Case Thirty

Ta-mei asked Ma-tsu, "What is Buddha?"
Ma-tsu answered, "Mind is Buddha."

Wu-men's Verse
Blue sky, bright sun,
How foolish to search to and fro;
And asking about Buddha—
Holding the loot, you still declare your innocence.

Case Thirty-One

A monk training under Chao-chou asked an old woman the way to Mount T'ai.

The old woman said, "Go straight ahead." After the monk had taken three or five steps, she added, "He looks like a real monk, but he goes just like that!"

Later another monk told Chao-chou about it, and he replied, "Wait, and I'll go check on her."

The next day he went, asked the same question, and got the same reply.

On his return, Chao-chou told the monks, "I have now completely investigated the old woman of Mount T'ai for you."

> *Wu-men's Verse*
> The question is the same;
> The answer is also the same:
> There's sand in the rice
> And thorns in the clay.

Case Thirty-Two

A non-Buddhist asked the World-Honored One, "I don't ask for words; I don't ask for non-words." The Buddha just remained seated.

The non-Buddhist said admiringly, "The World-Honored One, with great pity and compassion, had parted the clouds of my illusions and allowed me to enter the Way." Making his bows, he departed.

Ananda then asked the Buddha, "What did this outsider realize that he can praise you in this manner?"

The World-Honored One replied, "A first-class horse moves at even the shadow of the whip."

> *Wu-men's Verse*
> Moving over a sword-edge,
> Walking on ridges of ice;
> Without steps or ladders,
> Climbing the peaks with open hands.

Case Thirty-Three

A monk asked Ma-tsu, "What is Buddha?"

Ma-tsu replied, "Without mind, without Buddha."

> *Wu-men's Verse*
> To a swordsman, give a sword,
> But don't give poems to non-poets.
> To those you meet, explain just three-quarters;
> It's no good to give people the final part.

Case Thirty-Four

Nan-ch'üan said, "Mind is not Buddha; wisdom is not the Way."

> *Wu-men's Verse*
> The heavens are clear and the sun appears;
> Rain falls and the earth gets wet.
> With exhaustive kindness he explains everything,
> But through fear, people do not trust him.

Case Thirty-Five

Wu-tsu asked a monk, "Ch'ien and her soul were separated—which is the real Ch'ien?"

> *Wu-men's Verse*
> Moon and clouds, always the same;
> Valleys and mountains, always different;
> Ten thousand blessings, ten thousand blessings,
> This one and this two.

[Note: In a famous ghost story, Ch'ien's body stayed with her family while her soul was with her lover.]

Case Thirty-Six

Wu-tsu said, "When you meet true followers of the Way, do not greet them with words, do not greet them with silence. How will you greet them?"

> *Wu-men's Verse*
> Meeting attained persons on the road,
> Not using words or silence,
> Smash them with your fist—
> Those who can understand will understand!

Case Thirty-Seven

A monk asked Chao-chou, "What is the meaning of the Patriarch coming from the west?"
    Chao-chou answered, "Oak tree in the front garden."

Wu-men's Verse
Words can't explain things,
Phrases don't connect with spirit;
Those who cling to words are lost,
Those attached to phrases are befuddled.

Case Thirty-Eight

Wu-tsu said, "Suppose a water buffalo passes by a window. The head, horns, and four legs go past—why can't the tail pass by?"

Wu-men's Verse
If it passes by, it falls in a ditch;
If it goes back, it is destroyed;
But this little tail,
How wondrous it is!

Case Thirty-Nine

A monk said to Yün-men, "The radiance shines over the entire universe . . ." but before he could finish the first poetic line, Yün-men asked, "Aren't those the words of Chang-cho?"

The monk replied, "Yes," so Yün-men said, "You have made a slip of the tongue."

Later, Master Ssu-hsin took this matter up and asked, "Tell me, in what way did the monk make a slip of the tongue?"

Wu-men's Verse
Fishing in a swiftly flowing stream,
The greedy will be captured;
Just open your mouth,
And your life is already lost.

Case Forty

When Kuei-shan was studying with Pai-chang, he was the monastery's head cook. Pai-chang wanted to choose an abbot to found a temple on Mount Ta-kuei, so he invited the head monk and his other disciples to make presentations. Then he took a water-bottle and placed it on the floor, saying, "Don't call this a bottle, so what is it?"

The head monk said, "It can't be called a tree-stump."

Pai-chang then asked Kuei-shan, who walked up and kicked the bottle over.

Laughing, Pai-chang said, "The head monk has been defeated by Kuei-shan," and therefore ordered Kuei-shan to found the temple.

> *Wu-men's Verse*
> Throwing baskets and ladles aside,
> With one blow he cuts off all obstructions;
> Pai-chang's barrier did not stop him,
> From his toes come innumerable Buddhas.

Case Forty-One

Bodhidharma sat facing the wall. The Second Patriarch, standing in snow, cut off his arm and said, "Your disciple's mind is not at rest. I beg you, teacher, give it peace."

Bodhidharma replied, "Bring me your mind and I will give it peace."

The Second Patriarch said, "I have searched for my mind, but I cannot find it."

Bodhidharma answered, "Then I have given peace to your mind."

> *Wu-men's Verse*
> Coming from the west and pointing directly—
> That's what caused all the trouble!
> All the fuss and bother at temples
> Is just because of you.

Case Forty-Two

Long ago, Manjusri came to a place where Buddhas assembled with the World-Honored One, but they had departed. Only a young woman remained, seated in deep meditation, near the seat of Buddha. Manjusri asked the Buddha, "Why is this woman so close to your seat when I cannot be?"

Buddha told Manjusri, "Try to awaken this woman from her meditation and ask her yourself."

Manjusri walked around her three times, snapped his fingers once, then took her up to the Brahman Heaven and practiced supernatural powers, but he could not awaken her. The World-Honored One said, "Even a hundred

thousand Manjusris could not bring her out of meditation, but down below, past twelve hundred million lands as numerous as sands on the Ganges,
there is the Bodhisattva Mōmyō who will be able to bring this woman out
of her profound contemplation."

Instantly the Bodhisattva Mōmyō emerged from the earth and bowed to
the World-Honored One, who gave him an order. Mōmyō went to the
woman, snapped his fingers once, and she came out of her deep meditation.

> *Wu-men's Verse*
> One could bring her out and one could not,
> Yet both are completely free.
> The god face opposes the devil face;
> The failure is quite marvelous.

*[Note: Manjusri is the evolved Bodhisattva of Wisdom, while Mōmyō is a be-
ginning Bodhisattva.]*

Case Forty-Three

Shou-shan held up his bamboo staff and said, "Monks, if you call this a staff,
you offend; if you don't call it a staff, you bear its burden. Tell me, everyone,
what will you call it?"

> *Wu-men's Verse*
> Lifting up the bamboo staff—
> The law of killing and giving life;
> Where offending and bearing the burden interfuse,
> Buddhas and Patriarchs beg for their lives!

Case Forty-Four

Pa-chiao said to the assembled monks, "If you have a staff, I will give you a
staff; if you don't have a staff, I will take it away from you."

> *Wu-men's Verse*
> In every direction deep and shallow,
> Everything in his hand;
> Holding up heaven and earth,
> Everywhere spreading the truth.

Case Forty-Five

The Patriarch Wu-tsu said, "Shakyamuni and Maitreya are servants of another. Tell me, who is this other?"

> *Wu-men's Verse*
> Don't draw another's bow,
> Don't ride another's horse,
> Don't discuss another's faults,
> Don't stick your nose into another's business.

[Note: Shakyamuni is the historical Buddha; Maitreya is the Buddha of the future.]

Case Forty-Six

Shih-shuang said, "How do you step forward from the top of a hundred-foot pole?"

Another sage of old said:

> "The person sitting on a hundred-foot pole
> Has entered the Way but not fully penetrated truth;
> This person must step forward from the hundred-foot pole
> And reveal the complete self in every direction."

> *Wu-men's Verse*
> The eye in the forehead is darkened,
> The pointer on the scale misleads us;
> Throwing away body and spirit,
> The blind are leading the blind.

Case Forty-Seven

Tou-shan created three barriers to test his followers.

"Penetrating your way through the underbrush is accomplished by seeing our own nature. Monks, at this moment where is your self-nature?

"When you see your own nature, you are free from life and death. When the final light dims in your eyes, how can you be released from birth and death?

"When you are free from birth and death, you know where you have been. When the four great elements of life have separated, where will you go?"

Wu-men's Verse
One instant of full attention fills immensity,
Endless time exists right now;
If you focus on this moment of attention,
You can see the person who is seeing.

Case Forty-Eight

A monk asked Kan-feng, "The Buddhas of the ten directions have a single road to nirvana. I wonder, where does this road begin?"

Kan-feng drew a line in the air with his stick and said, "Right here."

Later, the monk asked Yün-men for help on this question.

Yün-men held up his fan and said, "This fan jumps up to the thirty-third heaven and hits the nose of the god residing there. The carp of the eastern sea leaps up, and rain falls in buckets."

Wu-men's Verse
Before you lift your foot, you have already arrived:
The tongue has not yet moved, but the teaching is
    complete;
Although each step comes before the next,
Know that you must still face the great void.

—Translation by Stephen Addiss

13

The Blue Cliff Record (excerpts)

Best known by its Japanese name, Hekiganroku, The Blue Cliff Record *(Chinese:* Pi-yen-lu*) is one of the two most famous collections of kōans, the other being the* Wu-men-kuan *(Japanese:* Mumonkan; *see Chapter 12), which is often studied first by Zen monks but was actually compiled a century later.*

The Blue Cliff Record *was originally organized by Hsüeh-tou (Japanese: Setchō, 980–1052), who selected and added verses to one hundred kōans. A half century later, Yuan-wu (Japanese: Engo, 1063–1135) gave a series of talks on the kōans, which were then organized and added as introductions, notes, and commentaries. Yuan-wu's monastery was on Mount Chia in Hunan; in his room there hung a two-character calligraphy reading "Blue Cliff," which gave a name to the text as now completed. However, so many monks began studying this compendium that a successor to Yuan-wu named Ta-hui (Japanese: Daie, 1089–1163; see Chapter 14) decided that Zen students were memorizing the introductions, kōans, poems, and commentaries instead of working primarily on their own practice, so he had the printing blocks destroyed.*

Ta-hui was celebrated for his strictness and for rejecting all "answers" to kōans, but his stringent school of Zen lasted only a few generations. Other Masters believed that a kōan collection could be useful for their disciples, and around the year 1300, The Blue Cliff Record *was reassembled from secondary manuscripts; it is believed that although some of the original commentaries might now be incomplete, the kōans themselves have been retained from the original.*

The Blue Cliff Record *was first brought to Japan and taught by Dōgen (1200–1253) of the Sōtō (Chinese: Ts'ao-tung) sect (see Chapter 17), demonstrating that this sect did not reject kōan study as is sometimes claimed. The compendium had even more impact on the Rinzai (Chinese: Lin-chi) tradition in Japan, particularly since this sect descended from Yuan-wu, who was sometimes considered "the second coming of Lin-chi." Hsüeh-tou himself, however, was a follower of an important Master named Yün-men (Japanese: Ummon, 864–949), so a number of kōans relating to this teacher can be found in* The Blue Cliff Record. *These include his famous phrase usually* rendered *"Every day is good day,"* here translated as *"Day after day, this is a good day."* The actual five Chinese characters are 日 日 是 好 日, which literally mean *"day day this good day."*

Due to the length of the complete text, for this volume we have chosen a group of seventeen kōans, which are presented without introductions, notes, poems, or commentaries until the final two selections, which are presented as the text became known with its additions. For further study, readers are encouraged to read one of the full-length translations now available of the entire work.

Case One

Emperor Wu of Liang asked the great teacher Bodhidharma, "What is the first principle of sacred truth?"

Bodhidharma said, "Vast emptiness, nothing sacred."

The Emperor asked, "Who then is facing me?"

Bodhidharma replied, "Don't know."

The Emperor failed to understand, and Bodhidharma crossed the river to the land of Wei. Later the Emperor inquired of Master Chih about this, and Chih asked him, "Do you know who this person is?"

The Emperor said, "Don't know."

Master Chih explained, "He is the Bodhisattva Kwan-yin, transmitting Buddha-mind."

The Emperor was regretful and wanted to send someone after Bodhidharma, but Master Chih said, "There's no use in Your Majesty dispatching someone to bring him back. Even if everyone in the country went, he would not return."

Case Three

The great teacher Ma-tsu had not been well. The chief monk came to pay his respects and asked, "How is your health these days?"

The Master replied, "Sun-faced Buddha, Moon-faced Buddha."

Case Five

Hsüeh-feng, addressing the assembly, said, "The entire world, held in the fingers, becomes the size of a grain of rice. Thrown before your face, it's as dark as a lacquer tub, so beat the drum and call everyone to search for it."

Case Six

Yün-men addressed the assembly, "I don't ask you about the first half of the month, but say even one word about the second half." He then answered himself, "Day after day, this is a good day."

Case Seven

A monk questioned the Master Fa-yen, saying, "My name is Hui-ch'ao—what is Buddha?"

The Master replied, "You are Hui-ch'ao."

Case Eleven

Huang-po, instructing the assembly, said, "You all stuff yourselves with the dregs of food and drink, but as you keep going like this, where are you right now? Don't you know that in all of China there are no Zen teachers?"

One monk came forward and asked, "What about all those who instruct followers and lead assemblies?"

Huang-po replied, "I'm not saying there is no Zen, but only that there are no Zen teachers."

Case Seventeen

A monk asked Hsiang-lin, "What is the meaning of the First Patriarch coming from the west?

Hsiang-lin said, "Sitting long, getting tired."

Case Twenty

Lung-ya asked Ts'ui-wei, "What is the meaning of the First Patriarch coming from the west?

Ts'ui-wei said, "Pass me the chin rest."

Lung-ya gave him the chin rest, and Ts'ui-wei hit him with it.

Lung-ya said, "If you want to hit me, go right ahead, but ultimately there's no meaning in the First Patriarch coming from the west."

Lung-ya also asked Lin-chi, "What is the meaning of the First Patriarch coming from the west?"

Lin-chi said, "Pass me the cushion."

Lung-ya gave him the cushion, and Lin-chi hit him with it.

Lung-ya said, "If you want to hit me, go right ahead, but ultimately there's no meaning in the First Patriarch coming from the west."

Case Forty-One

Chao-chou asked T'ou-tzu, "What if someone who has experienced the great death should come back to life?"

T'ou-tzu said, "Not allowed to go at night, submitting to brightness."

Case Forty-Three

A monk asked Tung-shan, "When we are beset with cold or heat, how can we avoid them?"

Tung-shan replied, "Why not go where there is no cold or heat?"

The monk asked, "But where is there no cold or heat?"

Tung-shan said, "When cold, let the cold kill you; when hot, let the heat kill you."

Case Fifty-Three

When the Master Ma-tsu and Pai-chang were out walking, they saw some wild ducks fly past. The Master said, "What was that?"

Pai-chang replied, "Wild ducks."

The Master asked, "Where have they gone?"

Pai-chang answered, "They've flown away."

The Master then grabbed and twisted Pai-chang's nose, and Pai-chang cried out in pain.

The Master then asked, "How could they ever fly away?"

Case Sixty

Yün-men held up his staff before the assembly and said, "This staff has become a dragon and swallowed the universe. Mountains, rivers, the great earth—where can clouds arrive?"

Case Seventy-Seven

A monk asked Yün-men, "What is the teaching that goes beyond Buddhas and Patriarchs?"

Yün-men said, "A sesame bun."

Case Eighty-Six

Yün-men addressed the assembly, "Every one of you has bright light, but when you look, you see nothing but darkness. What is this bright light?"

He answered himself, "The kitchen hall and the main gate." He also said, "A good thing cannot match nothing."

Our final selections here are presented with the introductions by Yuan-wu and the poems by Hsüeh-tou, the form in which The Blue Cliff Record *has become known to later generations of Zen students. Further commentaries were often added by other Zen Masters, sometimes case-by-case and sometimes line-by-line.*

Case Forty-Six

Introduction

Completing a single stroke goes beyond ordinary and sacred; a few words smash bindings and unravel attachments. Beyond walking on ice and treading the edge of a sword, sitting amid sound and form and traveling over sound and form, following the wondrous in every direction, what about knowing what's appropriate in every instant? Try this and see:

Case

Ching-ch'ing asked a monk, "What is this voice outside the gate?"

The monk replied, "The voice of the raindrops."

Ching-ch'ing said, "Humans are topsy-turvy; deluding themselves, they chase after things."

The monk asked, "What about you?"

Ching-ch'ing replied, "I have reached not deluding myself."

The monk asked, "What does that mean, 'I have reached not deluding myself'?"

Ching-ch'ing said, "Going out from the body is easy, but explaining how to escape the body must be difficult."

Poem

An empty hall with the voice of raindrops—
Even a master finds it hard to answer.
If you say you understand entering the stream,
You still don't understand.
Understanding, not understanding—

Southern mountains, northern mountains more and more suffused with rain.

[Note: In a commentary to this kōan, Hakuin Ekaku wrote, "Drip, drip, this is exactly the present moment—in the empty hall, the voice of the raindrops has never stopped even for a second—but who is it that hears the sound of the rain?"]

Case Eighty-Seven

Introduction

The clear-eyed man has no nest, sometimes appearing on a solitary peak amid boundless grasses, sometimes in the noisy marketplace naked and free. Suddenly, he screams in rage with three heads and six arms; suddenly, sun-faced and moon-faced, he sends forth a benevolent radiance to everyone. Within a single particle he manifests all embodiments, and for different kinds of people he harmonizes with mud and unites with water. If he suddenly stirred up transcendental openings, even the eyes of a Buddha could not see them; if one thousand sages came forth, they would have to fall back three thousand miles. Will there come again someone with the same abilities and the same attainment? Try this and see:

Case

Yün-men addressed the assembly, "Medicine and sickness cure each other, and the entire earth is medicine. What is the self?"

Poem

    The entire earth is medicine—
    From old times to new, what great mistakes!
    With the gate shut, there's no need to build a cart,
    The road to travel is naturally empty and wide.
    Mistakes, mistakes!
    Stick up your nose to heaven, you're still bound to earth.

[Note: Hakuin commented, "There's no kōan more lofty than this one, but how many people past and present have misunderstood it! Medicine is the entire earth: is it the self, or what is it?"]

—Translations by Stephen Addiss

14

Ta-hui (1089–1163)

Swampland Flowers (excerpts)

One of the leading Zen Masters of the Sung Dynasty, Ta-hui Tsung-kao was born in Anhui and left home at the age of seventeen, receiving ordination a year later. Studying under several teachers, including Yuan-wu, he made such progress that by the time he was thirty-seven he received a ceremonial purple robe and an honorific title from the prime minister. Social and political unrest made him relocate his training center several times, and during one such period he compiled a six-volume collection of the records of earlier teachers along with their kōans, The Treasury of the True Dharma Eye.*

Ta-hui is remembered today as a major teacher of the Lin-chi (Japanese: Rinzai) Zen school and a fervent proponent of kōan training. The fact that his writings come primarily from letters and sermons to laypeople shows his determination to make Zen training possible for everyone who wished to practice. He believed strongly that each teaching must fit the person, time, and place, and as noted earlier he even stopped the printing of his teacher Yuan-wu's compilation of kōans, The Blue Cliff Record *(Chapter 13), because he felt that monks were memorizing it rather than finding their own enlightenment experiences.*

On the eighth day of the ninth month of 1163, Ta-hui told his disciples that tomorrow he was going on a journey, and the next day he wrote out his final poem and died peacefully. His final verse is:

> Birth is just like this
> Death is just like this—
> Composing a verse?
> What purpose could it have?

All you disciples of Buddha, real mind is not fixed, and real wisdom is not bounded. Even if I let these two lips go on talking from now till the end of

From *Swampland Flowers*, by J. C. Cleary © 2006. Reprinted by arrangement with Shambhala Publications Inc. Boston, MA. www.shambhala.com.

time without a break, you still can't depend on another person's power: this is a matter in which each and every person is fully sufficient in his own right. It can neither be augmented nor diminished the least little bit. Here at my place there's no doctrine to be given to people: I just wrap up the case on the basis of the facts. It's just as if you bring a crystal pitcher which you cherish like anything, and as soon as I see it, I smash it for you. And if you bring a wish-fulfilling gem, I'll take it away from you. The Dharma cannot be seen, heard, perceived, or known. If you employ seeing, hearing, perception, or knowing, then this is seeing, hearing, perception, or knowing—it's not seeking the Dharma. Since it's outside of seeing, hearing, perception, and knowing, what then will you call "the Dharma"? When you get here, it's like a man drinking water—he knows for himself whether it is cold or warm. Only if you personally witness it and awaken to it can you see the Dharma: for a person who has really witnessed and awakened, when a single hair is picked up, he at once can understand the whole great earth.

Existence cannot be grasped; nonexistence cannot he grasped either. Winter's cold and summer's heat cannot be grasped; inside, outside, and in between cannot be grasped. The one who speaks like this cannot be grasped; the one who hears such talk cannot be grasped either. Not even a fine hair can be grasped. Neither you nor I can be grasped. Ungraspability itself also cannot be grasped. The void is not subject to being obstructed by things, nor does it hinder the coming and going of all things within it. The subtle wisdom of true emptiness is also thus: birth and death, ordinary and holy, stains and defilements, cannot touch it at all. Although they can't touch it, the subtle wisdom does not hinder birth and death, ordinary and holy, from coming and going in its midst. Basically things have no inherent nature: those who lose themselves pursue them on their own. Originally objects are undifferentiated: those who lose themselves do their own differentiating.

Studying Ch'an requires a straightforward mind and straightforward conduct, direct words and direct speech. Since mind and words are straightforward and direct, from beginning to end, through all the stages, there will never be all the petty detailed aspects within them. The Ancestral Teacher came from the West, directly pointing to the human mind, (letting people) see their inherent nature and achieve buddhahood.

So right now you want such realization. It's not hard, either: simply be equanimous in your mind, without any defiling attachments. What are defiling attachments? Thoughts of sentient beings and buddhas, thoughts of the world and leaving the world, thoughts of seeking detachment and enlightened knowledge—all these are called defiling attachments. Just boldly apply your spiritual energy before desire arises, and leap out with a single bound—This Mind will be shining bright, alone and liberated. The instant you awaken to this, turn above it: then naturally it will be clear everywhere and revealed in everything. And when you get to such a stage, you must not watch over it. If you watch over it, then there's something you consider important; as soon as there's something considered important, this mind leaks—then it's called the leaking mind, not the equanimous mind of even sameness. "Even sameness" means good and evil are equal, turning away and turning towards are equal, inner truth and outer events are equal, ordinary and sage are equal, finite and infinite are equal, essence and function are equal. This truth can only be known by those who experience it. All of you people who haven't yet experienced it simply must do so. Only when you've experienced it completely can you be called a true leaver of home. Those whose minds don't experience this, and who seek the experience outside of mind, are called home-leaving outsiders: they're not fit to plant weeds.

This Mind is broad and vast, without divisions, without sides or surface: all the buddhas, numerous as the sands, attaining true awakening, the mountains, rivers, and the great earth, the profuse array of myriad images—all are within This Mind. This Mind can put names on everything, but nothing can put a name on it. Therefore all the buddhas and ancestral teachers could not but go along with your mistake and attach names to it, calling it True Suchness, Buddha-nature, Enlightenment and Nirvana, imposing all kinds of different appellations. Because in the world of you sentient beings, views are biased and insensitive, with all sorts of differentiation, they set up these different names to enable you, amidst differentiation, to recognize This Mind that has no difference—it's not that This Mind has differences.

Buddha said, "One may wish to reveal it with comparisons, but in the end there is no comparison that can explain this." Saying it's broad and vast has already limited it, to say nothing of wanting to enter this broad and vast realm with the limited mind. Even if you managed thereby to enter, it would be like taking a ladle in order to ladle out the ocean: though the ladle is filled, how much could it hold? Nevertheless, the water in the ladle, before it went in there, was identical to the limitless water (of the ocean). Likewise, because your world is just this big, and you feel satisfied with it, this limitless world adapts to your capacity and fills it up. It's not that the water of the great ocean is only this much. Therefore Buddha said, "It's like the great ocean, not deferring whether mosquitos or titans drink its water—all get their fill." Mosquitos and titans symbolize the difference between great and small: basically, in essence, This Mind doesn't have so many differences. Just don't create so many views, and recognize This Mind: then you'll be able to know all kinds of differences too.

The former sages didn't even hold to This Mind as real: outside of mind, what else is there real that can obstruct you? Today I have dragged through the mud and water—again, it's for lack of alternative. It's from old ladylike kindness, admonishing a beloved child, soothing a favorite son, that I've drawn out so many ramifications. Don't remember what I've said, and consider it right. Today I speak this way, but then tomorrow I'll speak otherwise. As soon as you're thus, I am not thus; when you're not thus, then I am thus. Where will you search out my abiding place? Since I myself don't even know, how can anyone else find where I stay?

This is the living gate: you can enter only when you've put to death your fabricated "reality." The obstruction of the Path by the mind and its conceptual discrimination is worse than poisonous snakes or fierce tigers. Why? Because poisonous snakes and fierce tigers can still be avoided, whereas intelligent people make the mind's conceptual discrimination their home, so that there's never a single instant, whether they're walking, standing, sitting, or lying down, that they're not having dealings with it. As time goes on, unknowing and unawares they become one piece with it—and not because they want to, either, but because since beginningless time they have followed this one little road until it's become set and familiar. Though they may see through it for a moment and wish to detach from it, they still can't. Thus it is said that poisonous snakes and fierce tigers can still be avoided, but the mind's conceptual discrimination truly has no place for you to escape.

Good and evil all arise from one's own mind. But tell me, besides your activities, thoughts, and discrimination, what do you call your own mind? Where does your mind come from? If you can discern where your own mind comes from, then boundless karmic obstruction will be cleared away instantly, and all sorts of marvels will come of themselves without being sought.

Where do we come from at birth? Where do we go at death? If you know where we come from and where we go, then you can be called a student of Buddha. Who is it who knows of birth and death? And who is it who experiences birth and death? Again: who is it who doesn't know where we come from and where we go? Who is it who suddenly realizes where he comes from and where he goes to? And who is it who, contemplating these words, blinks his eyes unable to understand, his belly churning up and down, as if a mass of fire were placed in his heart? If you want to know, just apprehend him at the point where he can't understand. If you can recognize him then, you'll know that birth and death surely have nothing to do with him.

Whenever you're reading the scriptures or the stories of the ancient worthies entering the Path, when your mind doesn't understand clearly and it seems bewildering and stifling and flavorless, as if you're gnawing on an iron spike, this is just the time to apply effort: above all you must not give up. This is the place where conceptual knowledge doesn't operate, where thought doesn't reach, where discrimination is cut off and the path of reason is annihilated. Where you can always explain reasons and apply discrimination, this all pertains to emotional consciousness. Time and again people take this thief as their son. Don't be unaware of this!

That which flows out from one's own breast, as he calls it, is one's own beginningless present awareness, fundamentally complete of itself. As soon as you arouse a second thought, you fall into comparative awareness. Comparative awareness is something gained from external refinements; present awareness is something from before your parents were born, something from the other side of the Primordial Buddha. Power gained within present awareness is strong; power gained from comparative awareness is weak.

In the conduct of your daily activities, just always let go and make yourself vast and expansive. Constantly calculating and making plans, flowing along with birth and death, becoming afraid and agitated—all these are sentiments of discriminating consciousness. Yet people studying the Path these days do not recognize this disease, and just appear and disappear in its midst. In the Teachings it's called acting according to discriminating consciousness, not according to wisdom. Thereby they obscure the scenery of the fundamental ground, their original face.

Gentlemen of affairs who study the Path often understand rationally without getting to the reality. Without discussion and thought they are at a loss, with no place to put their hands and feet—they won't believe that where there is no place to put one's hands and feet is really a good situation. They just want to get there in their minds by thinking and in their mouths to understand by talking—they scarcely realize they've already gone wrong.

Gentlemen of affairs make their living within the confines of thought and judgment their whole lives: as soon as they hear a man of knowledge speak of the Dharma in which there is nothing to attain, in their hearts there is doubt and confusion, and they fear falling into emptiness. Whenever I see someone talking like this, I immediately ask him, is this one who fears falling into emptiness himself empty or not? Ten out of ten cannot explain. Since you have always taken thought and judgment as your nesting place, as soon as you hear it said that you shouldn't think, immediately you are at a loss and can't find your grip. You're far from realizing that this very lack of anywhere to get a grip is the time for you to let go of your body and your life.

Gentlemen of affairs often get a glimpse of the unexpected, but lose it when things are as intended. I must let you know: when things are going according to your ideas you must always be mindful of the times when they don't follow your intentions—don't forget even for a moment! Your whole life you've made up so many little word games, when the last day of your life arrives, which phrase are you going to use to oppose birth and death? To succeed you must know clearly where we come from at birth and where we go at death.

If views of delusion and enlightenment perish and interpretations of turning towards and turning away are cut off, then this mind is lucid and clear as the bright sun and this nature is vast and open as empty space; right where the person stands, he emits light and moves the earth, shining through the ten directions. Those who see this light all realize acceptance of things as unborn. When you arrive at such a time, naturally you are in tacit accord with this mind and this nature. Only then do you know that in the past there was basically no delusion and now there is basically no enlightenment, that enlightenment is delusion and delusion is enlightenment, that turning towards and turning away are identical, that inherent nature is identical to mind and mind is identical to inherent nature, that buddhas are delusive demons and delusive demons are buddhas, that the One Path is pure and even, that there is no equal or not equal—all this will be the constant lot of one's own mind, not dependent on the skills of another.

I ask you to abandon at once all the joy you've ever felt in reading the words of the scriptures yourself or when being aroused and instructed by others. Be totally without knowledge and understanding, as before, like a three-year-old child—though the innate consciousness is there, it doesn't operate. Then contemplate what's there before the thought of seeking the direct essentials arises: observe and observe. As you feel you're losing your grip more and more and your heart is more and more uneasy, don't give up and slack off: this is the place to cut off the heads of the thousand sages. Students of the Path often retreat at this point. If your faith is thorough-going, just keep contemplating what's before the thought of seeking instruction in the direct essentials arises. Suddenly you will awaken from your dream, and there won't be any mistake about it.

You shouldn't think about past events, whether good or bad; if you think about them, that obstructs the Path. You shouldn't consider future events; to consider them is crazy confusion. Present events are right in front of you: whether they're pleasant or unpleasant, don't fix your mind on them. If you do fix your mind on them, it will disturb your heart. Just take everything in its time, responding according to circumstances, and you will naturally accord with this principle.

Unpleasant situations are easy to handle; pleasant situations are hard to handle. For that which goes against one's will, it boils down to one word: patience. Settle down and reflect a moment and in a little while it's gone. It's pleasant situations that truly give you no way to escape: like pairing magnet and iron, unconsciously this and that come together in one place.

In the conduct of their daily activities sentient beings have no illumination. If you go along with their ignorance, they're happy; if you oppose their ignorance, they become vexed. Buddhas and bodhisattvas are not this way: they make use of ignorance, considering this the business of buddhas. Since sentient beings make ignorance their home, to go against it amounts to breaking up their home; going with it is adapting to where they're at to influence and guide them.

When you bring up a saying, don't use so many maneuvers at all, just don't let there be any interruption whether you're walking, standing, sitting, or lying down. Don't discriminate joy and anger, sorrow and bliss. Just keep on bringing up the saying, raising it and raising it, looking and looking. When you feel there's no road for reason and no flavor, and in your mind you're oppressed and troubled, this is the place for each person to abandon his body and his life. Remember, don't shrink back in your mind when you see a realm like this—such a realm is precisely the scene for becoming a buddha and being an ancestral teacher.

"The Ancestral Teacher's coming from the West only means that winter is cold and summer is hot, night is dark and day is light." It's just that you vainly set up meaning where there is no meaning, create concern where there is no concern, impose "inside" and "outside" where there is no inside or outside, and talk endlessly of this and that where nothing exists.

A monk asked Chao-chou, "Does a dog have Buddha nature or not?" Chao-chou said, "No." As you contemplate this, don't try to figure it out, don't try to explain it, don't demand clear understanding, don't take it verbally, don't construe the raising of it as the principle, don't fall into empty quiescence, don't consciously anticipate enlightenment, don't take your understanding from the explanations of the teachers of our school, don't drop it into the bag of unconcern. Whether walking, standing, sitting, or lying down, just constantly call the story to mind: "Does a dog have Buddha-nature or not? No." When you can keep your attention on it fully, when verbal discussion and intellectual consideration cannot reach it and your heart is agitated, when it's like gnawing on an iron spike, without any flavor, then you must not falter in your intent—when you get like this, after all it's good news.

Both torpor and excitation were condemned by the former sages. When you're sitting quietly, as soon as you feel the presence of either of these two diseases, just bring up the saying, "A dog has no Buddha-nature." Don't exert effort to push away these two kinds of disease, just be peaceful and still right there. Over a long time, as you become aware of saving power, this is the place where you gain power. Nor do you have to engage in quiet meditation—this itself is meditation.

Just take the mind, so long-lasting, and bring it together with the saying "A dog has no Buddha-nature." Keep them together till the mind has no place to go—suddenly, it's like awakening from a dream, like a lotus flower opening, like parting the clouds and seeing the moon. When you reach such a moment, naturally you attain unity. Through the upsets and errors of your daily activities, just contemplate the word "No." Don't be concerned with awakening or not awakening, getting through or not getting through.

Once awareness is correct, then in your daily activities twenty-four hours a day, when seeing form, hearing sound, smelling scent, tasting flavor, feeling touch, or knowing phenomena, whether walking, standing, sitting, or lying down, whether speaking or silent, active or still, there's nothing that's not profound clarity. And since you don't engage in wrong thinking, all is pure whether there is thinking or not. Once you've attained purity, when active you reveal the function of profound clarity, and when inactive you return to the essence of profound clarity. Though essence and function are distinguished, the profound clarity is one: like when you cut up sandalwood, each and every piece is sandalwood.

> Two exist because of one
> Don't even keep the one!
> When the one man isn't born
> The myriad phenomena are without fault.

—Translation by J. C. Cleary

15

The Biography of

Miao-tsung (1095–1170; complete)

Miao-tsung is a woman Zen Master who has only recently received scholarly attention, although she is mentioned in several early Zen records. From an illustrious family, she turned to Zen (Chinese: Ch'an) in her mid-teens, studying with Ta-hui (see Chapter 14). Celebrated in her own day for her command of Buddhist, Taoist, and Confucian literature, Miao-tsung also wrote notable poetry (another translation of one of her poems is included in Chapter 9), as well as poetic commentaries to The Blue Cliff Record. *Nevertheless, her life and work has been little known in the West until the different sources about her life and Zen understanding were gathered and translated by Miriam Levering.*

(Note: The Taoist story mentioned below is about Chuang-tzu, who dreamed he was a butterfly. Upon awakening, he couldn't be sure if he was a person who had dreamed he was a butterfly, or a butterfly now dreaming that he was a person.)

Tse-shou Miao-tsung Ch'an Master, lay surnamed Su, was the grand-daughter of a Grand Councilor named Su Sung (1020–1101). When she was 15 years old she was ignorant of Ch'an. She only wondered about how human beings are born into the world—we are born and we do not know where we come from, we die and do not know where we go. From collecting her thoughts and focusing on this, she had an insight. But she did not think this was different from that of others. She thought that humans, as the most numinous of sentient beings, must all be like this. And so she never mentioned it to others.

Later she was forced to obey her father's and mother's order, and married Hsu Shou-yuan of Hsi-hsu. But before long she began to dislike deeply the forms of this world, and performed abstinences and purified her mind as be-

From *Women Saints in World Religions,* edited by Arvind Sharma (Albany: State University of New York Press, 2000). Reprinted by permission of the publisher.

fore. She wanted to transcend the mundane world and leave it behind, to discipline her will and emulate the ancients. So she went to visit the Ch'an Master Chien-yen Yuan.

Master Yuan said: "A well-brought-up lady from a wealthy family [protected from any knowledge of the world], how can you be prepared for the business of a great (male) hero?"

Miao-tsung replied: "Does the Buddha Dharma distinguish between male and female forms?"

Master Yuan questioned her further. He said: "What is the Buddha? This mind is the Buddha. What about you?"

Miao-tsung replied: "I've heard of you for a long time, but you still say that kind of thing."

Master Yuan said: "When someone came in the door, Te-shan immediately hit him."

Miao-tsung replied: "If you would carry out that mandate, you would not receive the offerings of humans and gods in vain."

Master Yuan said: "You are not there yet."

Miao-tsung hit the incense stand with her hand.

Yuan said: "There is an incense stand for you to hit. What if there were no incense stand?"

Miao-tsung immediately left.

Yuan called after her: "What truth have you seen that has made you like this?"

Miao-tsung turned her head around and said: "Everywhere there is not a single thing."

Yuan said: "That is what Yung-chia said."

Miao-tsung said: "Why shouldn't I take it out on him?"

Yuan said: "A real lion cub!"

At the time Ch'an Master Chen-hsieh was living in a small cloister at I-hsing. Miao-tsung went directly to see him there. Chen-hsieh was sitting upright on a rope mat. The instant that Miao-tsung was inside the door, Chen-hsieh said: "Are you ordinary or a sage?"

Miao-tsung said: "Where is the third eye?"

Chen-hsieh said: "The real thing appears right in front of your face— what is that like?"

Miao-tsung held up her kneeling and bowing cloth.

Chen-hsieh said: "I did not ask about that."

Miao-tsung said: "Too late—it's gone!"

Chen-hsieh shouted: "Ho!"

Miao-tsung also shouted: "Ho!"

Miao-tsung had visited various famous masters in Kiangsi and Chekiang when she went with her husband to Chia-ho where he was to take up an official post. Her only remaining thought was that she had not yet met Ta-hui. Just then it happened that Ta-hui and Feng Chi-ch'uan arrived by boat at the city wall. Miao-tsung heard about it and went there, but she only bowed silently in respect.

Ta-hui said to Feng, "That woman who just came, she has seen something. But she has not yet encountered the hammer and tongs, forge and bellows. She is just like a ten thousand ton ship in a closed-off harbor—she still cannot move." Feng said: "How can you say that so easily?" Ta-hui said: "If she turns her head back this way, I will have to make a finer discrimination."

The next day Miao-tsung's husband Hsu Shou-yuan commanded Ta-hui to preach the Dharma. Ta-hui looked at the assembly and said:

"Today among you there is a person here who has seen something. I inspect people like a customs officer—as soon as they arrive, I know whether or not they have dutiable goods." When he stepped down from the seat, Miao-tsung asked him for a name in the Way. He gave her the name "No Attachments [Wu-cho]." The following year she heard that the Dharma-seat at Ching-shan [where Ta-hui was then teaching] was flourishing, and went there to spend the summer retreat. In a formal instruction to the whole assembly by Ta-hui she heard raised the kōan of when Yao-shan Wei-yen [774–827] first went to study with Shih-t'ou Hsi-chien [700–790], and then later saw Ma-tsu Tao-i. It included the line:

> Shih-t'ou said: "This way won't do; not this way won't do. This way and not this way both won't do."

As Miao-tsung listened she suddenly awakened. But after the sermon was over she did not immediately go to Ta-hui's chamber to describe her awakening. At the time during the sermon the Vice Director Feng Chi, who was below the seat on which Ta-hui was preaching, suddenly had an insight. He hastened to the abbot's quarters to report to Ta-hui, saying: "A moment ago you brought up Shih-t'ou's saying. I understand it."

Ta-hui said: "How do you understand it?"

Feng Chi said: "This way won't do, *shabaho*. Not this way won't do, *hsi-li shabaho*. Both this way and not this way won't do, *soro hsi-li shabaho*."

At this moment Miao-tsung arrived. Without telling him whether it was good or bad, Ta-hui brought up the Vice Director's answer to Miao-tsung. She laughed and said: "Kuo-hsiang commented on Chuang-tzu. Those who know say that Chuang-tzu commented on Kuo-hsiang. "

Ta-hui saw that her words were different. So he raised another kōan for her, asking her about the story of Yen-t'ou and the woman. The story goes as follows: "Yen-t'ou became a ferryman by the shores of Lake Ou-chu in Hupei. On each side of the lake hung a board; when someone wanted to cross he or she would knock on the board. Yen-t'ou would call out, 'Which side are you crossing to?' Then he would wave his oar, come out from the reeds and go to meet the traveler. One day a woman carrying a child in her arms appeared. Eventually he asked her, 'Where did the child you are holding in your arms come from?' She said, 'I have given birth to seven children; six of them didn't meet anyone who understood them. If this remaining one does not prove to be of any use, I will throw it in the river right away.' "

Miao-tsung replied with a four-line *gatha:*

> One tiny boat drifts across a vast stretch of water;
> He makes his oars dance, chanting his tunes wonderfully;
> The clouds, mountains, sea, and moon are all thrown in;
> Alone I doze off into Chuang-tzu's butterfly dream.

Ta-hui remained silent and departed.

The next day Ta-hui hung up the sign for individual interviews, so she entered his chamber. Ta-hui asked: "Since the ancient virtuous ones did not go out of their gates, how were they able to eat oil-fried rice cakes in the village?

Miao-tsung said: "Only if you promise to let me off easily will I say."

Ta-hui said: "I will let you off easily, try giving your reply."

Miao-tsung said: "I will also let you off easily."

Ta-hui said: "But what about the oil-fried rice cakes?"

Miao-tsung then shouted "Ho," and went out.

Miao-tsung composed a verse on the occasion of her awakening.

> Suddenly I came across my nose.
> My cleverness was like ice melting and tiles crumbling.
> Why did Bodhidharma need to come from India?
> The second patriarch did not need to give three bows.
> If you still want to ask "what's it like?"
> The whole troupe of bandits is defeated utterly.

Ta-hui repeated the verse, saying:

> You have awakened to the living intention of the patriarchs,
> Cutting all in two with one stroke, directly finishing the job.
> As you meet karmic occasions one by one, trust to
>   naturalness;

Whether in this world or outside of it there is no excess or lack.

"I compose this *gatha* as testimony to your enlightenment. The four ranks of sages and six types of ordinary beings are in shock. Stop being in shock; even the blue-eyed barbarian still does not know."

Once when Miao-tsung entered Ta-hui's chamber for personal instruction, he asked her: "The monk who was just here answered you—tell me, why didn't I agree with him?"

She replied: "How can you suspect me?"

Ta-hui raised his bamboo stick and said: "What do you call this?"

She said: "Blue sky, blue sky!"

Ta-hui then hit her.

She said: "Someday you will hit someone mistakenly."

Ta-hui said: "When the blow lands, I'll stop. Why worry about whether it is a mistake or not?"

Miao-tsung said: "Only for the sake of circulation."

According to one account, when Miao-tsung, who was not yet a nun, studied with Ta-hui at Ching-shan, Ta-hui lodged her in his abbot's quarters. The Head Monk Wan-an always made disapproving noises. Ta-hui said to him, "Even though she is a woman, she has strengths." Wan-an still did not approve. Ta-hui then insisted that he should interview her. Wan-an reluctantly sent a message that he would go.

When Wan-an came, Miao-tsung said: "Will you make it a Dharma interview or a worldly interview?"

The Head Monk replied: "A Dharma interview."

Miao-tsung said: "Then let your attendants depart." She went in first, then called to him, "Please come in."

When he came past the curtain he saw Miao-tsung lying face upwards on the bed naked. He pointed at her [womb] and said: "What kind of place is this?"

Miao-tsung replied: "All the Buddhas of the three worlds and the six patriarchs and all the great monks everywhere—they all come out from within this."

Wan-an said: "And would you let me enter, or not?"

Miao-tsung replied: "It allows horses to cross; it does not allow asses to cross."

Wan-an said nothing, and Miao-tsung declared: "The interview with the Senior Monk is ended." She then turned over and faced the inside. Wan-an became embarrassed and left.

Ta-hui said: "It is certainly not the case that the old beast does not have any insight." Wan-an was ashamed.

One day Miao-tsung bowed and took her leave to return to her home. Ta-hui asked: "When you leave this mountain, if someone asks about the teaching here, how will you answer?"

She said: "Before I arrived at Ching-shan, I could not help doubting."

Ta-hui said: "And after you arrived?"

Miao-tsung said: "As of old, the early spring is still cold."

Ta-hui said: "Does not such an answer make me out to be a fool?"

Miao-tsung covered her ears and left.

The Layman Feng [Chi] doubted that her awakening had any real roots. Later he specially invited Miao-tsung to come from P'ing-chiang-fu to meet him. When he went to her boat, he asked her the following:

" 'A woman gave birth to seven sons. . . . Six had never found anyone who really understood them. If this last one is also not any use, I will immediately abandon him in the water.' My teacher [Ta-hui] says that you have understood this. What is it that you understand?"

Miao-tsung said: "What you have testified to is the truth."

Feng was greatly startled.

Thereafter she was greatly admired by the monastic assembly and became famous throughout the world. After a long time in concealment, she put on the robe. Even though she was advanced in years, she kept the precepts with great strictness, and polished herself with austerity and frugality, having models from older generations. Because of her fame in the Buddhist Way, the governor of P'ing-chiang-fu [Kiangsu province] Chang An-kuo ordered her to come out from her reclusive life and become the abbess and Ch'an teacher of Tse-shou Nunnery. Before long she asked leave to retire, and returned to her old home.

—Translation by Miriam Levering

KOREAN AND
JAPANESE ZEN

16

Chinul (1158–1210)

On Cultivating the Mind (excerpts)

Chinul, one of the most important figures in Korean Buddhism, worked both to reform the Buddhist monastic order by recentering it in Zen meditation practice, and to give Zen meditation itself a philosophical and doctrinal basis derived from the sutras.

Chinul was sickly as a child, and his father vowed that if his son's health improved he would have him ordained as a monk. The boy accordingly entered a Zen monastery when he was seven and was ordained at the age of fifteen. He does not seem to have had a permanent teacher or ever to have received transmission in a lineage, displaying rather a penchant for self-reliance and seclusion and developing his practice using the sutras and the works of Chinese Zen Masters as guidelines. It was when he was reading a passage from the Platform Sutra *on the freedom and self-reliance of true nature that he had his first enlightenment experience. Later, while searching the* Hua-yen Sutra *for a passage confirming the approach of Zen, he had a profound awakening when he read: "As one particle of dust contains thousands of sutras, so the wisdom of all Buddhas is complete in the bodies of ordinary people who do not realize it." Much of Chinul's later writing aims at reconciling Hua-yen philosophy with Zen practice.*

In 1188, Chinul assembled a group of fellow meditators called the Concentration and Wisdom Community. Ten years later the community had attracted such a large following that Chinul had to relocate it. The site he chose, on Songgwang Mountain, developed into one of the most important monasteries in Korea. There Chinul introduced a method of Zen meditation, derived from the Chinese Zen Master Ta-hui (1089–1163; see Chapter 14), known as hwa-du *(Chinese:* hua-t'ou*) practice. Hwa-du means "word-head" and signifies the meditation technique of silently observing a brief phrase that sums up the essential point of a* kōan. *Due largely to the influence of Chinul,* hwa-du *practice became the standard form of Zen meditation in Korea.*

On Cultivating the Mind, *written in 1205 and excerpted here, presents Chinul's urgent recommendation to practice meditation in the context of sudden awakening and gradual cultivation, together with his belief in the inherent possession of the luminous mind by all human beings.*

Revealing Truth through Suffering

The three worlds are burning with suffering like a house on fire. How long can we endure this? The best way to escape the wheel of suffering is to seek Buddhahood, but before you seek Buddhahood you should know that Buddha is nothing but your own mind. Do not look for your mind far away: it is within this body of yours.

The physical body does not truly exist; it is subject to birth and death. But true mind is like empty space, infinite and indestructible. Therefore, it is said:

> The hundred bones will crumble
> And return to fire and wind.
> But one thing is eternally clear,
> Embracing heaven and earth.

Confused Practice Cannot Help

It is sad that people have been confused for so long. They do not understand that their own minds are Buddha and that their own natures are Dharma. They look for Dharma by searching out sages far away. They look for Buddha but do not observe their own minds.

If they aspire to Buddhahood while clinging to their opinion that Buddha is outside the mind and that Dharma is outside their own nature, then even if they burn their limbs and break their bones for a million kalpas to show their sincerity, even if they sit constantly and never lie down to sleep, write out sutras in their own blood, eat only one meal a day, and practice every austerity—it would be like trying to cook rice by boiling sand, and in the end they will only wear themselves out.

The Same Enlightenment for Sages and Ordinary Beings

If you see the nature of your mind, gates to the Dharma as countless as grains of sand in the Ganges will open, and limitless subtle meanings will make themselves known. The World-Honored One saw this and said, "Sentient beings everywhere are all endowed with the wisdom and virtue of a Tathagata." And also, "The various illusory forms that sentient beings take all come from the Tathagata's perfect enlightenment." And so it is clear that Buddhahood cannot be attained apart from the mind. All the Buddhas of the past were simply ordinary people who understood their minds. Likewise, all the masters of the present have simply cultivated their own minds. And all future practitioners will have to depend upon cultivation of mind. So if you wish to follow the Way, do not seek for it outside yourself.

> The nature of mind is without blemish.
> It is originally whole and complete.
> If you leave behind delusory karma
> You will be Buddha just as you are.

The One Thing Is within Us But We Do Not See It

Student: If Buddha-nature is present now within the body, it is not separate from ordinary people. Then why can't I see it? Would you please explain this more?

Chinul: It is present within your body; you just don't see it. Who is it exactly who feels hungry and thirsty during the day, feels hot and cold, angry and happy? The body is a temporary compound of four elements: earth, water, fire, and wind. Matter itself is lifeless and insentient, so how can it see, hear, feel, and be conscious? But seeing, hearing, feeling, and being conscious are exactly your Buddha-nature. This is why Lin-chi said:

> This corpse's four elements
> Cannot speak or hear Dharma.
> Empty space
> Cannot speak or hear Dharma.
> Only the formless thing before your eyes,
> Clear and bright of itself,
> Can speak and hear Dharma.

This thing without any form is the Dharma-seal of all Buddhas. It is your original mind.

Sudden Enlightenment and Gradual Cultivation

Student: If enlightenment is by its very nature sudden, why is gradual cultivation necessary? And if cultivation is necessarily gradual, how can we talk about sudden enlightenment? Would you please clear up our doubts about sudden enlightenment and gradual cultivation?

Chinul: First, then, sudden enlightenment. If you are an ordinary person, you mistakenly believe that your real body is the four elements and that your deluded thoughts are your mind. You do not understand that your self-nature is the Dharma-body, and that your own luminous mind is the Buddha. As you wander around looking for the Buddha outside your mind, a wise mentor might point out to you the entry point. If in one moment of thought you then turn the light around and see your original nature, you will realize that it is free from all delusion and is fundamentally complete. You will see that you are not a bit different from all the Buddhas. This is why enlightenment is called sudden.

Now, gradual cultivation. Even after you have realized that your original nature is no different from that of the Buddhas, you still have to deal with the energy of your beginningless habits, which cannot be eliminated all of a sudden. So you must continue to practice after enlightenment until gradually your efforts reach completion and you conceive a spiritual embryo. Then, after a long time, you may become a sage.

It is just like when a newborn baby arrives, perfectly endowed with all its faculties but still weak. It will take many months and years before it is a mature adult.

Looking for Techniques for Awakening Is Wrong

Student: What technique can we use to reflect inward and awaken to our self-nature in one moment of thought?

Chinul: Self-nature is just your own mind. Why do you need some technique? If you look for a technique to see your mind, you are like someone who because he cannot see his own eyes thinks that he doesn't have any eyes and so looks for another way to see. But he does have eyes, and how could he see except with his own eyes? If he realizes that he never lost his eyes, that is the same as seeing his eyes. Then there is no notion that he cannot see, or of finding some other way to see.

It's the same with spiritual awareness. It's just your own mind. How else could you understand?

> If you look for your mind,
> You cannot find it.
> See that it cannot be found,
> And you will see self-nature.

Direct Apprehension of the Luminous Mind

Student: A person of superior faculties will get this right away. But those of us who are just average will still have some doubts. Could you describe some methods for those who are confused about how to get enlightenment?

Chinul: The Way has nothing to do with knowing or not knowing. Just get rid of the mind that clings to delusion and wants enlightenment. Listen to this:

> Each and every existent
> Is like a dream, like a phantom.
> Deluded thoughts are originally calm;
> The sensory world is originally empty.

Where everything is empty, luminous awareness is not obscured, and this empty, calm, luminous mind is your original face. It is also the Dharma-seal transmitted in direct succession by all the Buddhas, Patriarchs, and enlightened beings of the past, present, and future. If you awaken to this mind, there are no steps in between, no stairs to climb. You go directly to the stage of Buddha, and with each step you transcend the three worlds. You will return home, all doubts resolved. Filled with both compassion and wisdom, you will become the teacher of Heaven and Earth. It will be as if gods and humans offered you thousands of gold coins every day, with the promise of more. You will indeed have finished the great work of life and death.

—Translation by Stanley Lombardo

17

Dōgen (1200–1253)

Selected Writings

Dōgen, one of the two most significant Japanese Zen Masters along with Hakuin, is considered the founder of the Sōtō sect in Japan. His writings are very extensive, culminating in the long and complex text Shōbōgenzō (Treasury of the Dharma Eye).

Born to a noble family in Kyoto, Dōgen became aware of the transience of life early when he was orphaned at the age of seven. He began studying the esoteric Buddhism of the Tendai sect at the age of thirteen but was not fully satisfied with its doctrines. One of his teachers referred him to Myōan Eisai (1141–1215), a founder of Rinzai Zen in Japan, and he entered Eisai's Kyoto temple Kennin-ji in or around 1217 to study under Eisai's disciple Myōzen (1184–1225). After six years, however, Dōgen resolved to go to China to pursue his training.

After visiting and studying at several temples for two years, Dōgen found the teacher he had been seeking in Ju-ching (1163–1228) of the Ts'ao-tung (Japanese: Sōtō) sect at the monastery on Mount T'ien-t'ung. In two months Dōgen achieved enlightenment, and two years later he was made Ju-ching's successor and returned to Japan.

Settling at first at Kennin-ji, Dōgen advocated a total focus upon meditation, writing Fukan Zazen-gi (A Universal Recommendation for Zazen) *in the year of his return. His reliance upon Zen, however, provoked animosity from monks of the Tendai sect, and he moved to a series of temples, finally settling in Kannon Dōri-in for the decade of 1233–1243. There he established a Monks' Training Hall in 1236, renamed the temple Kōshō Hōrin-ji, taught a number of important disciples, and wrote forty-four sections of* Shōbōgenzō.

In 1242 or 1243, Dōgen submitted a memorial to the Emperor advocating Zen Buddhism, but monks of rival sects were able to muster sentiments against him and he was forced to move. In 1244 he founded the temple later known as Eihei-ji in the mountains of northern Japan, where he continued training monk disciples while writing further sections of Shōbōgenzō *and other works, including this poem:*

Waga iho mo	My dwelling is in
Koshi no shirayama	the white mountains of Koshi—
fuyugomori	during the winter seclusion
kōri mo yuki mo	both ice and snow
kumo kakarikeri	hang down from the clouds

Becoming ill in 1252, Dōgen returned to Kyoto for medical treatment, but he died during the autumn of 1253 at the age of fifty-three.

Dōgen had a wide range of audiences, and his writings cover a broad spectrum. They range from basic instructions in meditation to extensive and detailed temple rules for monks, and also feature some of the most difficult and paradoxical yet deeply rewarding texts in Zen history.

In order to present the scope of Dōgen's work, the selections here begin with his instructions for zazen, continue with teachings to monks at his temple, and conclude with three of his most far-reaching essays from the Shōbōgenzō. Among these three essays, Actualizing the Fundamental Point *is better known as the* Genjō Kōan, *and it features Dōgen's most famous statement, "To study the Buddha way is to study the self. To study the self is to forget the self. To forget the self is to be actualized by myriad things."* The Time-Being (Uji) *is a rare Zen study of the complex question of time, in which Dōgen asks his followers to actualize all time as being, which can only be accomplished by vigorously abiding in each moment. The* Mountains and Waters Sutra (Sansui-kyō) *offers a Zen approach to understanding the environment, and it fully expresses the Japanese love of nature.*

A Universal Recommendation for Zazen (Fukan zazen-gi)

Now, when you trace the source of the Way, you find that it is universal and absolute. It is unnecessary to distinguish between "practice" and "enlightenment." The supreme teaching is free, so why study the means to attain it? The Way is, needless to say, very far from delusion. Why, then, be concerned about the means of eliminating the latter?

The Way is completely present where you are, so of what use is practice or enlightenment? However, if there is the slightest difference in the

From *Zen Master Dōgen*, by Yūhō Yokoi with Daizen Victoria © 1976. Reprinted by arrangement with Shambhala Publications Inc. Boston, MA. www.shambhala.com.

beginning between you and the Way, the result will be a greater separation than between heaven and earth. If the slightest dualistic thinking arises, you will lose your Buddha-mind. For example, some people are proud of their understanding, and think that they are richly endowed with the Buddha's Wisdom. They think that they have attained the Way, illuminated their minds, and gained the power to touch the heavens. They imagine that they are wandering about in the realm of enlightenment. But in fact they have almost lost the absolute Way, which is beyond enlightenment itself.

You should pay attention to the fact that even the Buddha Shakyamuni had to practice zazen for six years. It is also said that Bodhidharma had to do zazen at Shao-lin temple for nine years in order to transmit the Buddha-mind. Since these ancient sages were so diligent, how can present-day trainees do without the practice of zazen? You should stop pursuing words and letters and learn to withdraw and reflect on yourself. When you do so, your body and mind will naturally fall away, and your original Buddha-nature will appear. If you wish to realize the Buddha's Wisdom, you should begin training immediately.

Now, in doing zazen it is desirable to have a quiet room. You should be temperate in eating and drinking, forsaking all delusive relationships. Setting everything aside, think of neither good nor evil, right nor wrong. Thus, having stopped the various functions of your mind, give up even the idea of becoming a Buddha. This holds true not only for zazen but for all your daily actions.

Usually a thick square mat is put on the floor where you sit and a round cushion on top of that. You may sit in either the full or half lotus position. In the former, first put your right foot on your left thigh and then your left foot on your right thigh. In the latter, only put your left foot on the right thigh. Your clothing should be worn loosely but neatly. Next, put your right hand on your left foot and your left palm on the right palm, the tips of the thumbs lightly touching. Sit upright, leaning to neither left nor right, front nor back. Your ears should be on the same plane as your shoulders and your nose in line with your navel. Your tongue should be placed against the roof of your mouth and your lips and teeth closed firmly.

With your eyes kept continuously open, breathe quietly through your nostrils. Finally, having regulated your body and mind in this way, take a deep breath, sway your body to left and right, then sit firmly as a rock. Think of nonthinking. How is this done? By thinking beyond thinking and nonthinking. This is the very basis of zazen.

Zazen is not "step-by-step meditation." Rather it is simply the easy and pleasant practice of a Buddha, the realization of the Buddha's Wisdom. The Truth appears, there being no delusion. If you understand this, you are completely free, like a dragon that has obtained water or a tiger that reclines on a mountain. The supreme Law will then appear of itself, and you will be free of weariness and confusion. At the completion of zazen move your body slowly and stand up calmly. Do not move violently.

By virtue of zazen it is possible to transcend the difference between "common" and "sacred" and attain the ability to die while doing zazen or while standing up. Moreover, it is impossible for our discriminating mind to understand either how the Buddhas and patriarchs expressed the essence of Zen to their disciples with finger, pole, needle, or mallet or how they passed on enlightenment with a *hossu* [whisk], fist, staff, or shouts. Neither can this be understood through supernatural power or a dualistic view of practice and enlightenment. Zazen is a practice beyond the subjective and objective worlds, beyond discriminating thinking. Therefore, no distinction should be made between the clever and the stupid. To practice the Way single-heartedly is, in itself, enlightenment. There is no gap between practice and enlightenment or zazen and daily life.

The Buddhas and patriarchs, both in this world and that, in India and in China, have all preserved the Buddha-mind and enhanced Zen training. You should therefore devote yourself exclusively to and be completely absorbed in the practice of zazen. Although it is said that there are innumerable ways of understanding Buddhism, you should do zazen alone. There is no reason to forsake your own sitting place and make futile trips to other countries. If your first step is mistaken, you will stumble immediately.

You have already had the good fortune to be born with a precious [human] body, so do not waste your time meaninglessly. Now that you know what is the most important thing in Buddhism, how can you be satisfied with the transient world? Our bodies are like dew on the grass, and our lives like a flash of lightning, vanishing in a moment.

Earnest Zen trainees, do not be surprised by a real dragon or spend a long time rubbing only one part of an elephant. Exert yourself in the Way that points directly to your original [Buddha] nature. Respect those who have realized full knowledge and have nothing more to do. Become one with the Wisdom of the Buddhas and succeed to the enlightenment of the patriarchs. If you do zazen for some time, you will realize all this. The treasure house will then open of itself, and you will be able to enjoy it to your heart's content.

—Translation by Yūhō Yokoi

Excerpts from *Shōbōgenzō Zuimoki*

One day Dōgen instructed:

In the *Hsu kao-seng chuan,* there is a story about a monk in the assembly of a certain Zen Master. The monk always carried around with great reverence a golden image of the Buddha and other relics. Even when in the dormitory, he constantly burned incense to them and showed his respect with salutations and offerings.

One day the Zen Master said: "The Buddha image and relics that you are worshipping will be of no use to you later." The monk disagreed with him, but the Master continued: "This is the handiwork of demons. Throw them away." The monk grew indignant and started to leave, but the Zen Master called after him. "Open your box and look inside." When the enraged monk complied, he is said to have found a poisonous snake coiled within.

As I see it, relics should be reverenced, since they represent the Tathagata's image and his remaining bones. It is wrong, however, to expect enlightenment just by worshipping them. This is an error that delivers you into the hands of demons and poisonous snakes. The Buddha's teaching has established the merit of practicing reverence so that the images and relics offer the same blessings to men and devas as does the living Buddha. It is quite true that, if you revere and make offerings to the World of the Three Treasures, you eradicate your crimes, gain merit, remove the karma that leads to rebirth in the evil realms, and are rewarded with birth as man or deva. But it is a mistake to think that you can gain enlightenment in this way.

Since the true disciple follows the Buddha's teaching and seeks to attain the Buddha's rank directly, you must devote all your efforts to practice in accordance with these teachings. The true practice that accords with these teachings is concentrated zazen, the most essential element in the Zen monastery today. Think this over well.

Dōgen also said:

Although the precepts and the eating regulations should be maintained, you must not make the mistake of establishing them as of primary importance and of basing your practice on them; nor should they be considered a means to enlightenment. Since they suit the conduct of the Zen monk and the style of the true disciple, they are observed. To say that they are good, however, does not make them the most essential teaching. This does not

From *A Primer of Sōtō Zen: Dōgen's* Shōbōgenzō Zuimonki, by Dōgen and translated by Reihō Masunaga (Honolulu: University of Hawaii Press, 1971). Reprinted by permission of the publisher.

mean that you should break the precepts and become dissolute, but, if you attach to them, your view is wrong and you depart from the Way.

One day Dōgen instructed:

You should understand that a man who is born into a certain household and wants to enter the family occupation must first train himself in the family specialty. It is a mistake to strive for knowledge and training in an area outside your own specialty and competence.

Now, as men who have left your homes, if you are to enter the Buddha's house and become priests, you must learn thoroughly what you are supposed to do. To learn these things and to maintain the regulations mean to cast aside attachments to the Self and to conform to the teachings of the Zen Masters. The essential requisite is to abandon avarice. To do this, you must first free yourselves from egoism. To be free from egoism is to have a deep understanding of transiency. This is the primary consideration.

Most people in the world like to regard themselves as good and to have others think the same of them, but such a thing seldom happens. If, however, you gradually forsake attachment to the Self and follow the advice of your teacher, you will progress. You may say that you understand but still cannot give up certain things, and practice zazen while holding on to various attachments. If you take this attitude, you sink into delusion.

For a Zen monk the primary prerequisite for improvement is the practice of concentrated zazen. Without arguing about who is clever and who inept, who is wise and who foolish, just do zazen. You will then naturally improve.

Once, after a discussion of the doctrine, Dōgen instructed:

It is not good to overwhelm another person with argument even when he is wrong and you are right. Yet it is also not right to give up too easily, saying, "I am wrong," when you have every reason to believe that you yourself are right. The best way is to drop the argument naturally, without pressing the other person or falsely admitting that you yourself are wrong. If you don't listen to his arguments and don't let them bother you, he will do the same and not become angry. This is something to watch carefully.

In an evening talk Dōgen said:

The purpose of awakening to the old stories of the Patriarchs of Zen is to modify gradually what you have understood and thought up to now, under the guidance of a Zen Master. Even if the Buddha you have known up to now is endowed with the distinguishing marks, radiates light, and has, like Shakyamuni and Amida Buddha, the virtue of preaching sermons and bringing benefit to the people, you must believe it if the Zen Master tells you that the Buddha is a toad or an earthworm. You will have to give up the beliefs you have held up to now. But if you seek the Buddha's marks, his radiance, and the various virtues associated with him on the earthworm, you still have not modified your arbitrary views of the Buddha. Just recognize as the Buddha what you see now before your eyes. If you follow the words of the Zen Master and turn from deluded views and attachments, you will accord naturally with the Buddha Way.

Yet students today cling to their deluded views and hold on to their personal ideas, thinking that the Buddha is this thing or that thing. If these things differ from what they imagine, they deny that this can be and wander lost, looking for something similar to what their deluded ideas are. They make scarcely any progress along the Buddha Way. When told to let go of both hands and feet, after climbing to the top of a hundred-foot pole, and then to advance one step further without regard for their own bodies, they say: "It is only because I am alive today that I have the chance to study Buddhism." They are not really following their teacher. This must be understood thoroughly.

On another occasion Dōgen said:

Many people today think that the making of statues and building of pagodas cause Buddhism to prosper. This, too, is not so. No one gained the Way by erecting lofty buildings that have gleaming jewels and gold adornments. This merely is a good action that gives blessings by bringing lay treasures into the Buddhist world. Although small causes can have large effects, Buddhism does not prosper if monks engage in such activities. If you learn one phrase of the Buddha's teaching or practice zazen even for a moment in a thatched hut or even under a tree, Buddhism will truly flourish.

I am now trying to build a monastery and am asking people for contributions. While this requires much effort on my part, I cannot believe that it necessarily stimulates Buddhism. It is just that nowadays there is no one who wants to study Buddhism, and I have much time on my hands. Since there is no place now for them to study, I want to provide a place for students to practice zazen, should any deluded followers appear who might wish to establish a connection with Buddhism. If my plans do not work out, I will have no regrets. If I can put up just one pillar, I won't care if people see it later and think that I had a plan but was unable to carry it out.

One day a student asked: "I have spent months and years in earnest study, but I have yet to gain enlightenment. Many of the old Masters say that the Way does not depend on intelligence and cleverness and that there is no need for knowledge and talent. As I understand it, even though my capacity is inferior, I need not feel badly of myself. Are there any old sayings or cautionary words that I should know about?"

Dōgen replied: Yes, there are. True study of the Way does not rely on knowledge and genius or cleverness and brilliance. But it is a mistake to encourage people to be like blind men, deaf mutes, or imbeciles. Because study has no use for wide learning and high intelligence, even those with inferior capacities can participate. True study of the Way is an easy thing. But even in the monasteries of China, only one or two out of several hundred, or even a thousand, disciples under a great Zen Master actually gained true enlightenment. Therefore, old sayings and cautionary words are needed. As I see it now, it is a matter of gaining the desire to practice. A person who gives rise to a real desire and puts his utmost efforts into study under a teacher will surely gain enlightenment. Essentially, one must devote all attention to this effort and enter into practice with all due speed. More specifically, the following points must be kept in mind:

In the first place, there must be a keen and sincere desire to seek the Way. For example, someone who wishes to steal a precious jewel, to attack a formidable enemy, or to make the acquaintance of a beautiful woman must at all times watch intently for the opportunity, adjusting to changing events and shifting circumstances. Anything sought for with such intensity will surely be gained. If the desire to search for the Way becomes as intense as this, whether you concentrate on doing zazen alone, investigate a kōan by an old Master, interview a Zen teacher, or practice with sincere devotion, you will succeed no matter how high you must shoot or no matter how deep you must plumb. Without arousing this wholehearted will for the Buddha Way, how can anyone succeed in this most important task of cutting the endless round of birth and death? Those who have this drive, even if they have little knowledge or are of inferior capacity, even if they are stupid or evil, will without fail gain enlightenment.

Next, to arouse such a mind, one must be deeply aware of the impermanence of the world. This realization is not achieved by some temporary method of contemplation. It is not creating something out of nothing and then thinking about it. Impermanence is a fact before our eyes. Do not wait for the teachings from others, the words of the scriptures, and for the principles of enlightenment. We are born in the morning and die in the evening; the man we saw yesterday is no longer with us today. These are facts we see with our own eyes and hear with our own ears. You see and hear impermanence in terms of another person, but try weighing it with your own body. Even though you live to be seventy or eighty, you die in accordance with the inevitability of death. How will you ever come to terms with the worries, joys, intimacies, and conflicts that concern you in this life? With faith in

Buddhism, seek the true happiness of Nirvana. How can those who are old or who have passed the halfway mark in their lives relax in their studies when there is no way of telling how many years are left?

Even this is putting it too simply. Think of what might happen today, this very moment, in the ordinary world and the Buddhist world as well. Perhaps tonight, perhaps tomorrow, you will fall seriously ill; find your body racked with unendurable pain; die suddenly, cursed by some unknown demons; meet misfortune at the hands of robbers; or be slain by someone seeking vengeance. Life is indeed an uncertain thing. In this hateful world where death may come at any moment, it is absurd to plan your life, intrigue maliciously against others, and spend your time in fruitless pursuits.

Because impermanence is a fact of life, the Buddha spoke of it for the sake of all beings, and the Patriarchs preached of this alone. Even now in the lecture hall and in their instructions, Zen Masters dwell on the swiftness of impermanence and the vital matter of birth and death. I repeat, don't forget this truth. Think only of this very moment, and waste no time in turning your minds to the study of the Way. After this it is easy. It has nothing to do with the quality of your nature or the dullness or keenness of your capacity.

In a talk one evening Dōgen said:

Students must thoroughly consider the fact that they will eventually die. While you may not think about death directly, you must make sure not to waste time. Instead of spending time fruitlessly, use it for meaningful activities. If you wonder what the most important of all things is, it is to know the way in which the Buddhas and the Patriarchs conducted themselves. All else is of no use whatsoever.

On another occasion Dōgen instructed:

The student must above all separate himself from concepts of the Self. To separate from views of the Self means not to cling to this body. Even though you study deeply the sayings of the old Masters and practice zazen, remaining as immobile as stone or iron, you will never gain the Way of the Buddhas and the Patriarchs, even if you try for endless eons, unless you can free yourself from attachment to the body. No matter how well you say you know the true and provisional teachings or the esoteric and exoteric doctrines, as long as you possess a mind that clings to the body, you will be vainly counting others' treasures, without gaining even half a cent for yourself.

I ask only that you students sit quietly and examine with true insight the beginnings and end of this human body. The body, hair, and skin are the products of the union of our parents. When the breathing stops, the body is scattered amid mountains and fields and finally turns to earth and mud. Why then do you attach to this body?

Viewed from the Buddhist standpoint, the body is no more than the accumulation and dispersal of the eighteen realms of sense. Which realm should we pick out and identify as our body? While differences exist between Zen and other teachings, they agree in that, in the practice of the Way, emphasis is placed on the impermanence of the human body. Once you penetrate this truth, true Buddhism manifests itself clearly.

Dōgen instructed:

Students cannot gain enlightenment simply because they retain their preconceptions. Without knowing who taught them these things, they consider the mind to be thought and perceptions and do not believe it when they are told that the mind is plants and trees. They think of the Buddha as having marvelous distinguishing marks, with radiance shining from his body, and are shocked when they are told that he is tile and pebble. Such preconceptions were not taught them by their parents, but students come to believe them for no other reason than that they have heard about them from others over a long period of time. Therefore, when the Buddhas and the Patriarchs categorically state that the mind is plants and trees, revise your preconceptions and understand plants and trees as mind. If the Buddha is said to be tile and pebble, consider tile and pebble as the Buddha. If you change your basic preconceptions, you will be able to gain the Way.

Dōgen instructed:

There is a popular proverb: "Unless he behaves as though deaf and dumb, a man cannot become the head of a house." This means that a person who does not heed the slanders of others and who says nothing critical about their shortcomings will be able to accomplish his own work. Such a man deserves to become the head of a house. This may be only a popular proverb, but it applies to the conduct of Zen monks as well. How does one practice the Way without reacting to the scorn or hatred of others and without saying anything good or bad about them? Only those who have penetrated to the very bone and marrow are able to accomplish this.

On another occasion Dōgen said:

The basic point to understand in the study of the Way is that you must cast aside your deep-rooted attachments. If you rectify the body in terms of the four attitudes of dignity, the mind rectifies itself. If at first you uphold the precepts, the mind reforms itself. In China it is the custom among laymen to show their filial gratitude towards a deceased parent by assembling at the ancestral mausoleum and pretending to weep so earnestly that eventually real tears of grief would fall. Students of the Way, even though they do not have the mind that seeks the Way at the outset, eventually arouse this mind merely by a steadfast love and study of Buddhism.

Students who have been moved to study the Way should merely follow the rest of the assembly in their conduct. Don't try to learn the essential points and the examples from the past right away. It is best, however, that they be fully grasped before you go alone to practice in the mountains or conceal yourself within a city. If you practice by doing what the assembly does, you should be able to attain the Way. It is like riding in a boat without knowing how to row. If you leave everything up to a competent sailor, you will reach the other shore, irrespective of whether you know how to row or not. If you follow a good teacher and practice together with the assembly and have no concepts of the Self, you will naturally become a man of the Way.

Students, even if you gain enlightenment, do not stop practicing, thinking that you have attained the ultimate. The Buddha Way is endless. Once enlightened you must practice all the more.

Dōgen instructed:

Students today, when they listen to the teachings, try first to give the impression that they have understood well what they have heard, and they concern themselves with being able to give answers that are to the point. Thus, what they hear just passes through their ears. What this amounts to is that they lack the mind that seeks the Way, because they still possess egoistic views.

First of all, you must forget the Self. After listening carefully to what someone has to say, you should think about it quietly. If you find difficulties or have doubts about something, pursue them to the end. If you understand, you should offer your solutions to the Master again and again. To present what you understand at once shows that you have not listened to the teaching well.

Dōgen instructed:

The Buddhas and the Patriarchs were all at one time ordinary men. While in this common state, some were guilty of evil conduct and evil thought, some were dull and others foolish. Yet because they all reformed themselves, followed a good teacher, and practiced, they became Buddhas and Patriarchs. People nowadays must do the same. Don't demean yourself by saying that you are dull and stupid. If you don't arouse the determination to seek the Way in this life, when do you expect to be able to practice? If you force yourself to practice now, you will without fail gain the Way.

—Translation by Reihō Masunaga

Actualizing the Fundamental Point (Genjō Kōan)

1

As all things are buddha-dharma, there is delusion and realization, practice, and birth and death, and there are buddhas and sentient beings.

As the myriad things are without an abiding self, there is no delusion, no realization, no buddha, no sentient being, no birth and death.

The buddha way is, basically, leaping clear of the many and the one; thus there are birth and death, delusion and realization, sentient beings and buddhas.

Yet in attachment blossoms fall, and in aversion weeds spread.

2

To carry yourself forward and experience myriad things is delusion. That myriad things come forth and experience themselves is awakening.

Those who have great realization of delusion are buddhas; those who are greatly deluded about realization are sentient beings. Further, there are those who continue realizing beyond realization, who are in delusion throughout delusion.

When buddhas are truly buddhas they do not necessarily notice that they are buddhas. However, they are actualized buddhas, who go on actualizing buddhas.

3

When you see forms or hear sounds fully engaging body-and-mind, you grasp things directly. Unlike things and their reflections in the mirror, and unlike the moon and its reflection in the water, when one side is illuminated the other side is dark.

4

To study the buddha way is to study the self. To study the self is to forget the self. To forget the self is to be actualized by myriad things. When actualized by myriad things, your body and mind as well as the bodies and minds of others drop away. No trace of realization remains, and this no-trace continues endlessly.

5

When you first seek dharma, you imagine you are far away from its environs. But dharma is already correctly transmitted; you are immediately your original self.

6

When you ride in a boat and watch the shore, you might assume that the shore is moving. But when you keep your eyes closely on the boat, you can see that the boat moves. Similarly, if you examine myriad things with a confused body and mind, you might suppose that your mind and nature are permanent. When you practice intimately and return to where you are, it will be clear that nothing at all has unchanging self.

7

Firewood becomes ash, and it does not become firewood again. Yet, do not suppose that the ash is future and the firewood past. You should understand that firewood abides in the phenomenal expression of firewood, which fully includes past and future and is independent of past and future. Ash abides in the phenomenal expression of ash, which fully includes future and past. Just as firewood does not become firewood again after it is ash, you do not return to birth after death.

This being so, it is an established way in buddha-dharma to deny that birth turns into death. Accordingly, birth is understood as no-birth. It is an unshakeable teaching in Buddha's discourse that death does not turn into birth. Accordingly, death is understood as no-death.

Birth is an expression complete this moment. Death is an expression complete this moment. They are like winter and spring. You do not call winter the beginning of spring, nor summer the end of spring.

8

Enlightenment is like the moon reflected on the water. The moon does not get wet, nor is the water broken. Although its light is wide and great, the moon is reflected even in a puddle an inch wide. The whole moon and the entire sky are reflected in dewdrops on the grass, or even in one drop of water.

Enlightenment does not divide you, just as the moon does not break the water. You cannot hinder enlightenment, just as a drop of water does not hinder the moon in the sky.

The depth of the drop is the height of the moon. Each reflection, however long or short its duration, manifests the vastness of the dewdrop, and realizes the limitlessness of the moonlight in the sky.

9

When dharma does not fill your whole body and mind, you think it is already sufficient. When dharma fills your body and mind, you understand that something is missing.

For example, when you sail out in a boat to the middle of an ocean where no land is in sight, and view the four directions, the ocean looks circular, and does not look any other way. But the ocean is neither round nor square; its features are infinite in variety. It is like a palace. It is like a jewel. It only looks circular as far as you can see at that time. All things are like this.

Though there are many features in the dusty world and the world beyond conditions, you see and understand only what your eye of practice can reach. In order to learn the nature of the myriad things, you must know that although they may look round or square, the other features of oceans and mountains are infinite in variety; whole worlds are there. It is so not only around you, but also directly beneath your feet, or in a drop of water.

10

A fish swims in the ocean, and no matter how far it swims there is no end to the water. A bird flies in the sky, and no matter how far it flies there is no end to the air. However, the fish and the bird have never left their elements. When their activity is large their field is large. When their need is small their field is small. Thus, each of them totally covers its full range, and each of them totally experiences its realm. If the bird leaves the air it will die at once. If the fish leaves the water it will die at once.

Know that water is life and air is life. The bird is life and the fish is life. Life must be the bird and life must be the fish.

It is possible to illustrate this with more analogies. Practice, enlightenment, and people are like this.

11

Now if a bird or a fish tries to reach the end of its element before moving in it, this bird or this fish will not find its way or its place. When you find your place where you are, practice occurs, actualizing the fundamental point. When you find your way at this moment, practice occurs, actualizing the fundamental point; for the place, the way, is neither large nor small, neither yours nor others'. The place, the way, has not carried over from the past, and it is not merely arising now.

Accordingly, in the practice-enlightenment of the buddha way, meeting one thing is mastering it; doing one practice is practicing completely.

12

Here is the place; here the way unfolds. The boundary of realization is not distinct, for the realization comes forth simultaneously with the mastery of buddha-dharma.

Do not suppose that what you realize becomes your knowledge and is grasped by your consciousness. Although actualized immediately, the inconceivable may not be apparent. Its appearance is beyond your knowledge.

13

Zen master Pao-ch'e of Mt. Mayu was fanning himself. A monk approached and said, "Master, the nature of wind is permanent and there is no place it does not reach. Why, then, do you fan yourself?

"Although you understand that the nature of the wind is permanent," Pao-ch'e replied, "you do not understand the meaning of its reaching everywhere."

"What is the meaning of its reaching everywhere?" asked the monk again. The master just kept fanning himself. The monk bowed deeply.

The actualization of the buddha-dharma, the vital path of its correct transmission, is like this. If you say that you do not need to fan yourself because the nature of wind is permanent and you can have wind without fanning, you will understand neither permanence nor the nature of wind. The nature of wind is permanent; because of that, the wind of the buddha's house brings forth the gold of the earth and makes fragrant the cream of the long river.

> Written in mid-autumn, the first year of Tempuku [1233], and given to my lay student Kōshū Yō of Kyūshū Island. (Revised in) the fourth year of Kenchō [1252].

> —Translated by Robert Aitken and Kazuaki Tanahashi, and revised at the San Francisco Zen Center

The Time-Being (Uji)

1

An ancient buddha said:

> For the time being stand on top of the highest peak.
> For the time being proceed along the bottom of the deepest ocean.
> For the time being three heads and eight arms.
> For the time being an eight- or sixteen-foot body.
> For the time being a staff or whisk.
> For the time being a pillar or lantern.
> For the time being the sons of Chang and Li.
> For the time being the earth and sky.

"For the time being" here means time itself is being, and all being is time. A golden sixteen-foot body is time; because it is time, there is the radiant illumination of time. Study it as the twelve hours of the present. "Three heads

[Note: The "ancient Buddha" was Yueh-shan Wei-yen (745–828); "Chang and Li" are the Chinese equivalent of Tom, Dick, and Harry; twelve hours is the entire day, with one hour equal to two in a twenty-four-hour day; Ch'ing-yuan, Huang-po (Chapter 6), Chiang-hsi (Ma-tsu), Shih-t'ou (Chapter 5), Hung-tao, Ta-chi, Kuei-sheng, Shou-shan, and Lin-chi (Chapter 7) are major Zen Masters; Tathagata is the historical Buddha; the "Three Vehicles" and "Twelve Divisions" refer to all aspects of Buddhist doctrine.]

and eight arms" is time; because it is time, it is not separate from the twelve
hours of the present.

2

Even though you do not measure the hours of the day as long or short, far or
near, you still call it twelve hours. Because the signs of time's coming and going are obvious, people do not doubt it. Although they do not doubt it, they
do not understand it. Or when sentient beings doubt what they do not understand, their doubt is not firmly fixed. Because of that, their past doubts do not
necessarily coincide with the present doubt. Yet doubt itself is nothing but time.

3

The way the self arrays itself is the form of the entire world. See each thing
in this entire world as a moment of time.

Things do not hinder one another, just as moments do not hinder one
another. The way-seeking mind arises in this moment. A way-seeking moment arises in this mind. It is the same with practice and with attaining the
way. Thus the self setting itself out in array sees itself. This is the understanding that the self is time.

4

Know that in this way there are myriads of forms and hundreds of grasses
throughout the entire earth, and yet each grass and each form itself is the entire earth. The study of this is the beginning of practice.

When you are at this place, there is just one grass, there is just one form;
there is understanding of form and no-understanding of form; there is understanding of grass and no-understanding of grass. Since there is nothing
but just this moment, the time-being is all the time there is. Grass-being,
form-being are both time.

Each moment is all being, is the entire world. Reflect now whether any
being or any world is left out of the present moment.

5

Yet an ordinary person who does not understand buddha-dharma may hear
the words *the time-being* this way:

For a while I was three heads and eight arms. For a while I was an eight- or sixteen-foot body. This is like having crossed over rivers and climbed mountains. Even though the mountains and rivers still exist, I have already passed them and now reside in the jeweled palace and vermilion tower. Those mountains and rivers are as distant from me as heaven is from earth.

It is not that simple. At the time the mountains were climbed and the rivers crossed, you were present. Time is not separate from you, and as you are present, time does not go away.

As time is not marked by coming and going, the moment you climbed the mountains is the time-being right now. If time keeps coming and going, you are the time-being right now. This is the meaning of the time-being.

Does this time-being not swallow up the moment when you climbed the mountains and the moment when you resided in the jeweled palace and vermilion tower? Does it not spit them out?

6

Three heads and eight arms may be yesterday's time. The eight- or sixteen-foot body may be today's time. Yet yesterday and today are both in the moment when you directly enter the mountains and see thousands and myriads of peaks. Yesterday's time and today's time do not go away.

Three heads and eight arms move forward as your time-being. It looks as if they are far away, but they are here and now. The eight- or sixteen-foot body moves forward as your time-being. It looks as if it is nearby, but it is exactly here. Thus, a pine tree is time, bamboo is time.

7

Do not think that time merely flies away. Do not see flying away as the only function of time. If time merely flies away, you would be separated from time. The reason you do not clearly understand the time-being is that you think of time only as passing.

In essence, all things in the entire world are linked with one another as moments. Because all moments are the time-being, they are your time-being.

8

The time-being has the quality of flowing. So-called today flows into to-morrow, today flows into yesterday, yesterday flows into today. And today flows into today, tomorrow flows into tomorrow.

Because flowing is a quality of time, moments of past and present do not overlap or line up side by side. Ch'ing-yuan is time, Huang-po is time, Chiang-hsi is time, Shih-t'ou is time, because self and other are already time. Practice-enlightenment is time. Being splattered with mud and getting wet with water is also time.

9

Although the views of an ordinary person and the causes and conditions of those views are what the ordinary person sees, they are not necessarily the ordinary person's truth. The truth merely manifests itself for the time being as an ordinary person. Because you think your time or your being is not truth, you believe that the sixteen-foot golden body is not you.

However, your attempts to escape from being the sixteen-foot golden body are nothing but bits and pieces of the time-being. Those who have not yet confirmed this should look into it deeply. The hours of Horse and Sheep, which are arrayed in the world now, are actualized by ascendings and de-scendings of the time-being at each moment. The rat is time, the tiger is time, sentient beings are time, buddhas are time.

10

At this time you enlighten the entire world with three heads and eight arms, you enlighten the entire world with the sixteen-foot golden body. To fully actualize the entire world with the entire world is called thorough practice.

To fully actualize the golden body to arouse the way-seeking mind, prac-tice, attain enlightenment, and enter nirvana is nothing but being, is noth-ing but time.

11

Just actualize all time as all being; there is nothing extra. A so-called "extra being" is thoroughly an extra being. Thus, the time-being half-actualized is half of the time-being completely actualized, and a moment that seems to be missed is also completely being. In the same way, even the moment before or after the moment that appears to be missed is also complete-in-itself the time-being. Vigorously abiding in each moment is the time-being. Do not mistakenly confuse it as nonbeing. Do not forcefully assert it as being.

12

You may suppose that time is only passing away, and not understand that time never arrives. Although understanding itself is time, understanding does not depend on its own arrival.

People only see time's coming and going, and do not thoroughly understand that the time-being abides in each moment. This being so, when can they penetrate the barrier? Even if people recognized the time-being in each moment, who could give expression to this recognition? Even if they could give expression to this recognition for a long time, who could stop looking for the realization of the original face?

According to ordinary people's view of the time-being, even enlightenment and nirvana as the time-being would be merely aspects of coming and going.

13

The time-being is entirely actualized without being caught up in nets or cages. Deva kings and heavenly beings appearing right and left are the time-being of your complete effort right now. The time-being of all beings throughout the world in water and on land is just the actualization of your complete effort right now. All beings of all kinds in the visible and invisible realms are the time-being actualized by your complete effort, flowing due to your complete effort.

Closely examine this flowing; without your complete effort right now, nothing would be actualized, nothing would flow.

14

Do not think flowing is like wind and rain moving from east to west. The entire world is not unchangeable, is not immovable. It flows.

Flowing is like spring. Spring with all its numerous aspects is called flowing. When spring flows there is nothing outside of spring. Study this in detail.

Spring invariably flows through spring. Although flowing itself is not spring, flowing occurs throughout spring. Thus, flowing is completed at just this moment of spring. Examine this thoroughly, coming and going.

In your study of flowing, if you imagine the objective to be outside yourself and that you flow and move through hundreds and thousands of worlds, for hundreds, thousands, and myriads of eons, you have not devotedly studied the buddha way.

15

Great Master Hung-tao of Mt. Yao [Yao-shan], instructed by Great Master Shih-t'ou Wu-chi, once went to study with Zen Master Ta-chi of Chiang-hsi.

Yao-shan asked, "I am familiar with the teaching of the Three Vehicles and Twelve Divisions. But what is the meaning of Bodhidharma coming from the west?"

Zen Master Ta-chi replied:

> For the time being have him raise his eyebrows and wink.
> For the time being do not have him raise his eyebrows and wink.
> For the time being to have him raise his eyebrows and wink is right.
> For the time being to have him raise his eyebrows and wink is not right.

Hearing these words, Yao-shan experienced great enlightenment and said to Ta-chi, "When I was studying with Shih-t'ou, it was like a mosquito trying to bite an iron bull."

What Ta-chi said is not the same as other people's words. The "eyebrows" and "eyes" are mountains and oceans, because mountains and oceans are eyebrows and eyes. To "have him raise the eyebrows" is to see the mountains. To "have him wink" is to understand the oceans. The "right" answer belongs to him, and he is activated by your having him raise the eyebrows and wink. "Not right" does not mean not having him raise the eyebrows and wink. Not to have him raise the eyebrows and wink does not mean not right. These are all equally the time-being.

Mountains are time. Oceans are time. If they were not time, there would be no mountains or oceans. Do not think that mountains and oceans here and now are not time. If time is annihilated, mountains and oceans are annihilated. As time is not annihilated, mountains and oceans are not annihilated.

This being so, the morning star appears, the Tathagata appears, the eye appears, and raising a flower appears. Each is time. If it were not time, it could not be thus.

16

Zen Master Kuei-sheng of She Prefecture is the heir of Shou-shan, a dharma descendant of Lin-chi. One day he taught the assembly:

> For the time being mind arrives, but words do not.
> For the time being words arrive, but mind does not.
> For the time being both mind and words arrive.
> For the time being neither mind nor words arrive.

Both mind and words are the time-being. Both arriving and not-arriving are the time-being. When the moment of arriving has not appeared, the moment of not-arriving is here. Mind is a donkey, words are a horse. Having-already-arrived is words and not-having-left is mind. Arriving is not "coming," not-arriving is not "not yet."

17

The time-being is like this. Arriving is overwhelmed by arriving, but not by not-arriving. Not-arriving is overwhelmed by not-arriving, but not by arriving. Mind overwhelms mind and sees mind, words overwhelm words and see words. Overwhelming overwhelms overwhelming and sees overwhelming. Overwhelming is nothing but overwhelming. This is time.

As overwhelming is caused by you, there is no overwhelming that is separate from you. Thus you go out and meet someone. Someone meets someone. You meet yourself. Going out meets going out. If these are not the actualization of time, they cannot be thus.

18

Mind is the moment of actualizing the fundamental point; words are the moment of going beyond, unlocking the barrier. Arriving is the moment of casting off the body; not-arriving is the moment of being one with just this, while being free from just this. In this way you must endeavor to actualize the time-being.

19

The old masters have thus uttered these words, but is there nothing further to say?

> Mind and words arriving "part-way" are the time-being.
> Mind and words not arriving "part-way" are the time-being.

In this manner, you should examine the time-being.

> To have him raise the eyebrows and wink is "half" the time-being.
> To have him raise the eyebrows and wink is the time-being "missed."
> Not to have him raise the eyebrows and wink is "half" the time-being.
> Not to have him raise the eyebrows and wink is the time-being "missed."

Thus, to study thoroughly, coming and going, and to study thoroughly, arriving and not-arriving, is the time-being of this moment.

> On the first day of winter, first year of Ninji [1240], this was written at Kōshō Hōrin Monastery.

> —Translation by Dan Welch and Kazuaki Tanahashi

Mountains and Waters Sutra (Sansui-kyō)

1

Mountains and waters right now are the actualization of the ancient Buddha way. Each, abiding in its phenomenal expression, realizes completeness. Because mountains and waters have been active since before the Empty Eon, they are alive at this moment. Because they have been the self since before form arose they are emancipation-realization.

2

Because mountains are high and broad, the way of riding the clouds is always reached in the mountains; the inconceivable power of soaring in the wind comes freely from the mountains.

3

Priest Tao-kai of Mt. Furong said to the assembly, "The green mountains are always walking; a stone woman gives birth to a child at night."

Mountains do not lack the qualities of mountains. Therefore they always abide in ease and always walk. You should examine in detail this quality of the mountains' walking.

Mountains' walking is just like human walking. Accordingly, do not doubt mountains' walking even though it does not look the same as human walking. The Buddha ancestors' words point to walking. This is fundamental understanding. You should penetrate these words.

4

Because green mountains walk, they are permanent. Although they walk more swiftly than the wind, someone in the mountains does not realize or understand it. "In the mountains" means the blossoming of the entire world. People outside the mountains do not realize or understand the mountains walking. Those without eyes to see mountains cannot realize, understand, see, or hear this as it is.

If you doubt mountains' walking, you do not know your own walking; it is not that you do not walk, but that you do not know or understand your own walking. Since you do know your own walking, you should fully know the green mountains' walking.

Green mountains are neither sentient nor insentient. You are neither sentient nor insentient. At this moment, you cannot doubt the green mountains' walking.

5

You should study the green mountains, using numerous worlds as your standards. You should clearly examine the green mountains' walking and your own walking. You should also examine walking backward and backward walking and investigate the fact that walking forward and backward has never stopped since the very moment before form arose, since the time of the King of the Empty Eon.

If walking stops, buddha ancestors do not appear. If walking ends, the buddha-dharma cannot reach the present. Walking forward does not cease; walking backward does not cease. Walking forward does not obstruct walking backward. Walking backward does not obstruct walking forward. This is called the mountains' flow and the flowing mountains.

6

Green mountains master walking and eastern mountains master traveling on water. Accordingly, these activities are a mountain's practice. Keeping its own form, without changing body and mind, a mountain always practices in every place.

Don't slander by saying that a green mountain cannot walk and an eastern mountain cannot travel on water. When your understanding is shallow, you doubt the phrase, "Green mountains are walking." When your learning is immature, you are shocked by the words "flowing mountains." Without fully understanding even the words "flowing water," you drown in small views and narrow understanding.

Yet the characteristics of mountains manifest their form and life-force. There is walking, there is flowing, and there is a moment when a mountain gives birth to a mountain child. Because mountains are buddha ancestors, buddha ancestors appear in this way.

Even if you see mountains as grass, trees, earth, rocks, or walls, do not take this seriously or worry about it, it is not complete realization. Even if there is a moment when you view mountains as the seven treasures shining, this is not returning to the source. Even if you understand mountains as the realm where all buddhas practice, this understanding is not something to be attached to. Even if you have the highest understanding of mountains as all buddhas' inconceivable qualities, the truth is not only this. These are conditioned views. This is not the understanding of buddha ancestors, but just looking through a bamboo tube at a corner of the sky.

Turning an object and turning the mind is rejected by the great sage. Explaining the mind and explaining true nature is not agreeable to buddha ancestors. Seeing into mind and seeing into true nature is the activity of people outside the way. Set words and phrases are not the words of liberation. There is something free from all of these understandings: "Green mountains are always walking," and "Eastern mountains travel on water." You should study this in detail.

7

"A stone woman gives birth to a child at night" means that the moment when a barren woman gives birth to a child is called "night."

There are male stones, female stones, and nonmale nonfemale stones. They are placed in the sky and in the earth and are called heavenly stones and earthly stones. These are explained in the ordinary world, but not many people actually know about it.

You should understand the meaning of giving birth to a child. At the moment of giving birth to a child, is the mother separate from the child? You should study not only that you become a mother when your child is born, but also that you become a child. This is the actualization of giving birth in practice-realization. You should study and investigate this thoroughly.

8

Great Master Yun-men said, "Eastern mountains travel on water." The reason these words were brought forth is that all mountains are eastern mountains, and all eastern mountains travel on water. Because of this, Nine Mountains, Mt. Sumeru, and other mountains appear and have practice-realization. These are called "Eastern mountains." But could Yun-men penetrate the skin, flesh, bones, and marrow of the eastern mountains and their vital practice-realization?

9

Now in Great Sung China there are careless fellows who form groups; they cannot be set straight by the few true masters. They say that the statement, "The eastern mountains travel on water," or Nan-ch'uan's story of a sickle, is illogical; what they mean is that any words having to do with logical thought are not buddha ancestors' Zen stories, and that only illogical stories are buddha ancestors' expressions. In this way they consider Huang-po's staff and Lin-chi's shout as beyond logic and unconcerned with thought; they regard these as great enlightenments that precede the arising of form.

"Ancient masters used expedient phrases, which are beyond understanding, to slash entangled vines." People who say this have never seen a true master and they have no eye of understanding. They are immature, foolish fellows not even worth discussing. In China these last two or three hundred years, there have been many groups of bald-headed rascals. What a pity! The great road of buddha ancestors is crumbling. People who hold this view are not even as good as listeners of the Small Vehicles and are more foolish than those outside the way. They are neither lay people nor monks, neither human nor heavenly beings. They are more stupid than animals who learn the buddha way.

The illogical stories mentioned by you bald-headed fellows are only illogical for you, not for buddha ancestors. Even though you do not understand, you should not neglect studying the buddha ancestors' path of understanding. Even if it is beyond understanding in the end, your present understanding is off the mark.

I have personally seen and heard many people like this in Sung China. How sad that they do not know about the phrases of logical thought, or penetrating logical thought in the phrases and stories! When I laughed at them in China, they had no response and remained silent. Their idea about illogical words is only a distorted view. Even if there is no teacher to show you the original truth, your belief in spontaneous enlightenment is heretical.

10

You should know that "eastern mountains traveling on water" is the bones and marrow of the buddha ancestors. All waters appear at the foot of the eastern mountains. Accordingly, all mountains ride on clouds and walk in the sky. Above all waters are all mountains. Walking beyond and walking within are both done on water. All mountains walk with their toes on all waters and splash there. Thus in walking there are seven paths vertical and eight paths horizontal. This is practice-realization.

11

Water is neither strong nor weak, neither wet nor dry, neither moving nor still, neither cold nor hot, neither existent nor nonexistent, neither deluded nor enlightened. When water solidifies, it is harder than a diamond. Who can crack it? When water melts, it is gentler than milk. Who can destroy it? Do not doubt that these are the characteristics water manifests. You should reflect on the moment when you see the water of the ten directions as the water of the ten directions. This is not just studying the moment when human and heavenly beings see water; this is studying the moment when water sees water. Because water has practice-realization of water, water speaks of water. This is a complete understanding. You should go forward and backward and leap beyond the vital path where other fathoms other.

12

All beings do not see mountains and waters in the same way. Some beings see water as a jeweled ornament, but they do not regard jeweled ornaments as water. What in the human realm corresponds to their water? We only see their jeweled ornaments as water.

Some beings see water as wondrous blossoms, but they do not use blossoms as water. Hungry ghosts see water as raging fire or pus and blood. Dragons see water as a palace or a pavilion. Some beings see water as the seven treasures or a wish-granting jewel. Some beings see water as a forest or a wall. Some see it as the dharma nature of pure liberation, the true human body, or as the form of body and essence of mind. Human beings see water as water. Water is seen as dead or alive depending on causes and conditions.

Thus the views of all beings are not the same. You should question this matter now. Are there many ways to see one thing, or is it a mistake to see many forms as one thing? You should pursue this beyond the limit of pursuit. Accordingly, endeavors in practice-realization of the way are not limited to one or two kinds. The ultimate realm has one thousand kinds and ten thousand ways.

When we think about the meaning of this, it seems that there is water for various beings but there is no original water—there is no water common to all types of beings. But water for these various kinds of beings does not depend on mind or body, does not arise from actions, does not depend on self or other. Water's freedom depends only on water.

Therefore, water is not just earth, water, fire, wind, space, or consciousness. Water is not blue, yellow, red, white, or black. Water is not forms, sounds, smells, tastes, touchables, or mind-objects. But water as earth, water, fire, wind, and space realizes itself.

For this reason, it is difficult to say who is creating this land and palace right now or how such things are being created. To say that the world is resting on the wheel of space or on the wheel of wind is not the truth of the self or the truth of others. Such a statement is based only on a small view. People speak this way because they think that it must be impossible to exist without having a place on which to rest.

13

Buddha said, "All things are ultimately liberated. There is nowhere that they abide." You should know that even though all things are liberated and not tied to anything, they abide in their own phenomenal expression. However, when most human beings see water they only see that it flows unceasingly. This is a limited human view; there are actually many kinds of flowing. Water flows on the earth, in the sky, upward, and downward. It can flow around a single curve or into many bottomless abysses. When it rises it becomes clouds. When it descends it forms abysses.

14

Wen-tzu said, "The path of water is such that when it rises to the sky, it becomes raindrops; when it falls to the ground, it becomes rivers." Even a secular person can speak this way. You who call yourselves descendants of buddha ancestors should feel ashamed of being more ignorant than an ordinary person. The path of water is not noticed by water, but is realized by water. It is not unnoticed by water, but is realized by water.

"When it rises to the sky, it becomes raindrops" means that water rises to the heavens and skies everywhere and forms raindrops. Raindrops vary according to the different worlds. To say that there are places water does not reach is the teaching of the listeners of the Small Vehicles or the mistaken teaching of people outside the way. Water exists inside fire and inside mind, thought, and ideas. Water also exists within the wisdom of realizing buddha nature.

"When it falls to the ground, it becomes rivers" means that when water reaches the ground it turns into rivers. The essence of the rivers becomes wise people. Now ordinary fools and mediocre people think that water is always in rivers or oceans, but this is not so. Rivers and oceans exist in water. Accordingly, even where there is not a river or an ocean, there is water. It is just that when water falls down to the ground, it manifests the characteristics of rivers and oceans.

Also do not think that where water forms rivers or oceans there is no world and there is no buddha land. Even in a drop of water innumerable buddha lands appear. Therefore it is not a question of whether there is only water in the buddha land or a buddha land in water. The existence of water is not concerned with past, future, present, or the phenomenal world. Yet water is actualization of the fundamental point. Where buddha ancestors reach, water never fails to appear. Because of this, buddha ancestors always take up water and make it their body and mind, make it their thought.

In this way, the words "Water does not rise" are not found in scriptures inside or outside of Buddhism. The path of water runs upward and downward and in all directions. However, one Buddhist sutra does say, "Fire and air go upward, earth and water go downward." This "upward" and "downward" require examination. You should examine them from the Buddhist point of view. Although you use the word "downward" to describe the direction earth and water go, earth and water do not actually go downward. In the same way, the direction fire and air go is called "upward."

The phenomenal world does not actually exist in terms of up, down, or the cardinal directions. It is tentatively designated according to the directions in which the four great elements, five great elements, or six great elements go. The Heaven of No Thought should not be regarded as upward nor the Avichi Hell as downward. The Avichi Hell is the entire phenomenal world; the Heaven of No Thought is the entire phenomenal world.

16

Now when dragons and fish see water as a palace, it is just like human beings seeing a palace. They do not think it flows. If an outsider tells them, "What you see as a palace is running water," the dragons and fish will be astonished, just as we are when we hear the words, "Mountains flow." Nevertheless, there may be some dragons and fish who understand that the columns and pillars of palaces and pavilions are flowing water.

You should reflect and consider the meaning of this. If you do not learn to be free from your superficial views, you will not be free from the body and mind of an ordinary person. Then you will not understand the land of buddha ancestors, or even the land or the palace of ordinary people.

Now human beings well know as water what is in the ocean and what is in the river, but they do not know what dragons and fish see as water and use as water. Do not foolishly suppose that what we see as water is used as water by all other beings. You who study with buddhas should not be limited to human views when you are studying water. You should study how you view the water used by buddha ancestors. You should study whether there is water or no water in the house of buddha ancestors.

17

Mountains have been the abode of great sages from the limitless past to the limitless present. Wise people and sages all have mountains as their inner chamber, as their body and mind. Because of wise people and sages, mountains appear. You may think that in mountains many wise people and great sages are assembled. But after entering the mountains, not a single person meets another. There is just the activity of the mountains. There is no trace of anyone having entered the mountains.

When you see mountains from the ordinary world, and when you meet mountains while in mountains, the mountains' head and eye are viewed quite differently. Your idea or view of mountains not flowing is not the same as the view of dragons and fish. Human and heavenly beings have attained a position concerning their own worlds which other beings either doubt or do not doubt.

You should not just remain bewildered and skeptical when you hear the words, "Mountains flow"; but together with buddha ancestors you should study these words. When you take one view you see mountains flowing, and when you take another view, mountains are not flowing. One time mountains are flowing, another time they are not flowing. If you do not fully understand this, you do not understand the true dharma wheel of the Tathagata.

An ancient buddha said, "If you do not wish to incur the cause for Unceasing Hell, do not slander the true dharma wheel of the Tathagata. You should carve these words on your skin, flesh, bones, and marrow; on your body, mind, and environs; on emptiness and on form. They are already carved on trees and rocks, on fields and villages."

18

Although mountains belong to the nation, mountains belong to people who love them. When mountains love their master, such a virtuous sage or wise person enters the mountains. Since mountains belong to the sages and wise people living there, trees and rocks become abundant and birds and animals are inspired. This is so because the sages and wise people extend their virtue. You should know it as a fact that mountains are fond of wise people and sages. Many rulers have visited mountains to pay homage to wise people or to ask for instructions from great sages. These have been important events in the past and present. At such times these rulers treat the sages as teachers, disregarding the protocol of the usual world. The imperial power has no authority over the wise people in the mountains. Mountains are apart from the human world. At the time the Yellow Emperor visited Mt. K'ung-tung to pay homage to Kuang-ch'eng, he walked on his knees, touched his forehead to the ground, and asked for instruction.

When Shakyamuni Buddha left his father's palace and entered the mountains, his father the king did not resent the mountains, nor was he suspicious of those who taught the prince in the mountains. The twelve years of Shakyamuni Buddha's practice of the way were mostly spent in the mountains, and his attainment of the way occurred in the mountains.

Thus even his father, a wheel-turning king, did not wield authority in the mountains.

You should know that mountains are not the realm of human beings nor the realm of heavenly beings. Do not view mountains from the scale of human thought. If you do not judge mountains' flowing by the human understanding of flowing, you will not doubt mountains' flowing and not-flowing.

19

On the other hand, from ancient times wise people and sages have often lived near water. When they live near water they catch fish, catch human beings, and catch the way. For long these have been genuine activities in water. Furthermore there is catching the self, catching catching, being caught by catching, and being caught by the way.

Priest Te-ch'eng abruptly left Mt. Yao and lived on the river. There he produced a successor, the wise sage of the Hua-t'ing. Is this not catching a fish, catching a person, catching water, or catching the self? The disciple seeing Te-ch'eng is Te-ch'eng. Te-ch'eng guiding his disciple is his disciple.

20

It is not only that there is water in the world, but there is a world in water. It is not just in water. There is also a world of sentient beings in clouds. There is a world of sentient beings in the air. There is a world of sentient beings in fire. There is a world of sentient beings on earth. There is a world of sentient beings in the phenomenal world. There is a world of sentient beings in a blade of grass. There is a world of sentient beings in one staff. Wherever there is a world of sentient beings, there is a world of buddha ancestors. You should thoroughly examine the meaning of this.

21

Therefore water is the true dragon's palace. It is not flowing downward. To consider water as only flowing is to slander water with the word "flowing." This would be the same as insisting that water does not flow. Water is only the true thusness of water. Water is water's complete virtue; it is not flowing. When you investigate the flowing of a handful of water and the not-flowing of it, full mastery of all things is immediately present.

22

There are mountains hidden in treasures. There are mountains hidden in swamps. There are mountains hidden in the sky. There are mountains hidden in mountains. There are mountains hidden in hiddenness. This is complete understanding.

An ancient buddha said, "Mountains are mountains, waters are waters." These words do not mean mountains are mountains; they mean mountains are mountains.

Therefore investigate mountains thoroughly. When you investigate mountains thoroughly, this is the work of the mountains.

Such mountains and waters of themselves become wise persons and sages.

At the hour of the Rat, eighteenth day, tenth month, first
year of Ninji [1240], this was taught to the assembly at
Kannondori Kōshō Hōrin Monastery.

—Translation by Arnold Kotler and Kazuaki Tanahashi

18

The Awakening of

Mugai Nyodai (died 1298)

(complete)

Mugai Nyodai, often known by her secular name of Chiyono, was one of the first Japanese women to receive transmission in a Zen lineage, in her case from the visiting Chinese Master Wu-hsueh Tsu-yuan. She went on to become a distinguished Zen Master, founding several convents in Kyoto including Keiai-ji, the leading women's Zen monastery in Japan's medieval period.

This story of Mugai's enlightenment, possibly used as a Dharma talk to instruct and inspire young nuns, emphasizes that despite her high-ranking birth, she began her Zen life as a servant, much like the Sixth Patriarch Hui-neng. The gradual empowerment of a woman from a humble position no doubt had particular resonance in Japan, and Mugai became venerated in Buddhist convents and monasteries for many centuries and also appeared in every kind of publication from gazetteers and diaries to kōan collections. The text contains some contradictory passages, which suggests that it was a compilation of earlier stories.

The Enlightenment of Chiyono

In the village of Hiromi in the Mugi district of Minō province there were three nuns who built a Zen temple and devoted themselves to practicing the Buddhist way. Together with other nuns who came from all parts, and, on some occasions, with numerous lay disciples, they assembled for communal Zen meditation and practice.

"The Enlightenment of Mugai Nyodai," translated by Anne Dutton. © Anne Dutton. Reprinted by permission of the translator.

At that time there was a servant woman about twenty-four or twenty-five years of age who had been employed at the convent for many years. Her name was Chiyono. She was said to be the daughter of a high-ranking family. Everyone knew her. When the aspiration to attain enlightenment developed in her, straightaway she left her parents' home and came to this convent, taking a position as a servant, cutting firewood and carrying water.

Chiyono observed the monastic women practicing Zen meditation. Without noticing it herself, she held their words and teachings in high esteem. She used to peek at the nuns through the gaps in the curtains that hung in the doorway, and then go back to her room and imitate them by sitting facing the wall—but without any benefit.

One day, Chiyono approached a young nun. "Please tell me the essential principles of practicing zazen," she pleaded.

The nun answered her by saying, "Your practice is simply to serve the nuns of this temple as well as possible, without giving any thought to physical hardship or uttering a word of complaint. This is your zazen."

Chiyono thought to herself, "This is grievous! I make my way in the world as a lowly, menial person, living in pain and suffering. If I continue like this, I will suffer in the next life also. Time will pass, but when will there be a chance for me to attain salvation? What evil past has led to these karmic consequences?" Her grieving was endless.

One evening, concealed by the waning moon, she ventured near the meditation hall and looked inside. There she observed aspirants for enlightenment sitting in meditation with the nuns—laymen as well as laywomen, both old and young. Casting away utterly the concerns of the world, they were immersed in their practice of zazen. It was truly an impressive sight.

"Even girls too young to know the difference between right and wrong are in there practicing the difficult exercises of a monastic renunciant. Their desire to slip the confines of this world of delusion is very great. Admonishing themselves to try harder, they sit all night in single-minded silence without falling asleep. How can I who lack such impressive qualities ever be like them? These are all laypeople who amuse themselves by night and day and have no understanding of things—and yet they all sit there on the mats, throwing away any thought of the world, never laying their heads down on a pillow. Their bodies are emaciated, their spirits are exhausted and yet they pay no attention to whether their lives are endangered. They possess a truly profound aspiration. How aptly they are called 'disciples of the Buddha,'" thought Chiyono to herself as she wept.

Now, one of the nuns at the convent was an elderly woman who was deeply compassionate by nature. One day Chiyono approached her and said, "I have a desire to practice zazen but I am of humble birth. I cannot read or write. I am not very smart. If I set an intention, is it possible I too might attain the way of the Buddha even though I have no skills?"

The elderly nun answered her, saying, "This is wonderful, my dear! In fact, what is there to attain? In Buddhism there is no distinction between a man and a woman, between a layperson and a renunciant. Also there is no separation between noble and humble, between old and young. There is only this—each person must hold fast to his or her aspiration and proceed along the way of the Bodhisattva. There is no higher way than this.

"You must not theorize about the words or teachings of the Buddhas and masters. According to the scriptures the goal is to attain Buddhahood yourself. These teachings say that zazen means 'to seek the Buddha in your own heart.' According to the ancient worthies, the teachings of the sutras are like a finger pointing to the moon. The words of the patriarch are like a key that opens a gate. If one looks directly at the moon, there is no need for a finger. If the gate has been opened, there is no use for a key. A priest who is familiar with ten million scriptures uses not a single character word in zazen. Great learning and vast knowledge are only impediments to entering the gate of the dharma. They lead to philosophizing and words. If you know your own mind, what teachings about the scripture do you need? In entering the Way we must rely on our bodies [alone].

"Furthermore, those who would practice zazen should cultivate a heart of great compassion with the intention of saving all sentient beings. Do not seek enlightenment for yourself alone. Go to a quiet place, sit in lotus posture, and place one hand on top of the other. Without leaning to either side, bring your ears into alignment with your shoulders. Open your eyes only halfway and fix your attention on the tip of your nose. Rest your tongue on the roof of your mouth. Throw away your body and your life. Looking from the inside, your self has no mind. Forget also about your connections with others. Looking from the outside, there is no mind anywhere to be found. If random thoughts should occur to you unexpectedly, let them go straight away. Do not follow them. This is the essential technique of zazen. Believe this and stick to it, waiting faithfully." The kindly nun explained all this in great detail.

Chiyono received these teachings with faith and made a prostration in front of the nun to express her happiness. "When I first began to practice zazen, the various things I had seen and heard in the past kept coming up in my mind. When I tried to stop them, they only increased. This teaching that I have just heard shows me that when random thoughts occur in my mind, I should let them exhaust themselves. I should not make an effort to try to stop my thoughts."

"Yes," the nun responded. "Otherwise it would be like using blood to wash out blood stains. According to an ancient teacher, 'Sudden [enlightenment] is the medicine that cures our endless sickness.'"

Chiyono spoke, "If I carry on with this practice, commendable results will surely appear of their own accord. Surely, I will see Buddha nature clearly and truly achieve Buddhahood in an instant."

The nun intoned in a strong voice, "You have just now understood that all sentient beings have already attained Buddhahood. The world of life and death and the world of nirvana are like a dream."

Chiyono then said, "I have heard that the Buddha emits rays of light from a tuft of white hair between his eyebrows, illuminating all ten directions. Gazing at them is like looking at the palm of your hand. Can I point to my lowly self and say that I have Buddha nature or am I deluding myself?"

The nun replied, "Listen carefully. The teachers of the past have said that people are complete as they are. Each one is perfected; not even the width of one eyebrow hair separates them from this perfection. All sentient beings fully possess the wisdom and virtues of the Buddha. But because they are overcome by delusive thoughts and attachments, they cannot manifest this."

Chiyono asked, "What are these delusive thoughts?"

The nun replied, "The fact that you adhere to the thoughts that you produce conceals your essential Buddha nature. This is why we speak of 'delusive thoughts.' It's like taking gold and making a helmet or a pair of shoes out of it, calling what you use to cover your head a 'helmet' and what you put on your feet 'shoes.' Even though you use different names for the products, gold is still gold. What you put on your head is not exalted. The things you put on your feet are not lowly. If you apply this metaphor to Buddhism, the gold symbolizes Buddha—that is, realizing your essential nature. Those who are misguided about their essential nature are what we call sentient beings. If we say someone is a Buddha, their essential nature does not increase. If we call them a sentient being, their essential nature does not diminish. Buddha or sentient being—people take the point of view that these are two different things because of delusive thoughts. If you don't fall into delusive patterns of thinking, there is no Buddha and also no sentient being. There is only one essential nature, just as there is only one complete world although we refer to the world of the ten directions.

"The Buddha once said, 'When you get away from all conditions, then you will see the Buddha.' He also said, 'You must throw away the dharma.' What is this so-called dharma? If you really want to know your true nature you must orient yourself towards the source of delusive thoughts and get to the bottom of it. When you hear a voice, do not focus on the thing that you are hearing but, instead, return to the source of your own hearing. If you practice in this way with all things you will definitely clarify your true nature."

Chiyono then asked, "What is the mind that fathoms the source of things?"

The nun answered, "The question you have just now asked me—this is an instance of your thinking. Turn to the stage where that thought has not yet arisen. Encourage yourself fiercely. Not mixing in even a trace of thought—this is what we call fathoming the source."

Chiyono then said, "Does that mean that no matter what we do, as we go about our daily life, we should not observe things but rather turn towards the source of our perceptions and unceasingly try to fathom it?"

The nun said, "Yes, this is called zazen."

Chiyono said, "What I have heard brings me great happiness. It is not possible for me to practice seated meditation night and day since I am always fetching logs and carrying water and my duties are many. But if it is as I have heard, there is nothing that is impossible to accomplish in those twelve hours. Encountering the source of my perceptions both to my right and to my left, according to the time and according to the circumstances, how could I neglect my duties? With this practice as my companion, I have only to go about my daily life. If I wake practicing and go to bed practicing, what hindrance can there be?" With this she joyfully departed.

The nun called out her name as she walked away. Chiyono answered and turned around. The nun said, "Your aspiration to practice is clearly very deep and unchanging."

Chiyono replied, "When it comes to practice, I've never been concerned about destroying my body or losing my life. I've never even questioned it. If it is as you say, I must not diverge from practicing the totality of the Buddhist teaching even for a little while. All actions are a form of practice. Why be negligent?"

The nun said, "Just now when I called out 'Chiyono,' why did you adhere to the sound of my voice? You should have just listened to it and returned directly to the source of the perception. Never forget: Birth and death are the great matter. All things pass swiftly away. Do not wait—with each in-breath, with each out-breath, rely on your practice at all times. When something is in your way, you must not grieve or linger over it, even though you may have regrets later. Hold to this firmly."

After receiving this lesson, Chiyono sighed and fell silent. She had not gone very far before the nun again called out her name. Chiyono turned her head slightly but did not allow her ears to become attached to the nun's voice, returning directly to the source of her perception. In this manner she continued her practice, day after day, month after month. Some days she returned home and forgot to eat. Sometimes she went to fetch water and forgot to transfer it into a bucket. Sometimes she went to collect firewood and forgot that she was in a steep valley. Sometimes she went all day without eating or speaking or went all night without lying down. Although she had eyes she didn't see and although she had ears she didn't hear. Her movements were like a wooden person. The assembly of nuns at the temple began to talk about her, saying that realization was near at hand.

The elderly nun heard the talk and secretly went and stood outside her bedroom. Behind a bamboo screen with her hair piled high on her head, Chiyono sat facing the wall. She looked accustomed to sitting, like a mature practitioner. She sat having called up the world of great truth in which all delusions have been abandoned. Turning her consciousness around and looking back on herself, she practiced the most important thing according to the conditions of the moment, guarding her practice without ceasing. Her body was that of a woman who truly displayed the grit of an adept. Even in ancient times such a person was rare. Those who lack such urgency of purpose are shameful.

The nun then asked her, "What place is it that you face?" Chiyono looked back at her then turned back around and sat facing the wall again like a tree. The nun asked her again, "What?! What?!" This time she did not turn her head. Like that, she lost herself in zazen.

In the eighth lunar month of the following year, on the evening of the fifteenth, the full moon was shining. Taking advantage of the cloudless night sky, she went to draw some water from the well. As she did, the bottom of her bucket suddenly gave way and the reflection of the moon vanished with the water. When she saw this she instantly attained great realization. Carrying the bucket, she returned to the temple.

Previously, she had called the elderly nun who had been her guide and said, "My sickness is incurable and I will die during the night. I want to shave my head and die [that way]. Will you permit this?" The nun shaved her head.

Furthermore, the elderly nun had heard Wu-hsueh say, "Chiyono may have lowly status but her character is not that of an ordinary woman. Her aspiration is very deep—it far exceeds that of others." She decided Wu-hsueh was right.

When she went to look for herself, Chiyono made a standing bow and said, "You have taught me with great kindness and compassion. As a result, during the third watch of the night, the one moon of self has illuminated the thousand gates of the dharma." When she finished speaking, she made three prostrations in front of her teacher and then stood as befitting her place.

The nun said, "You have attained the great death, the one, in fact, that enlivens us. From now on, you will study with Wu-hsueh—you must go and see him.

After this Chiyono was known as Abbess Nyodai. When people came to her with their questions, she would invariably answer, "The Buddha whose face is the moon." She met with Wu-hsueh and received transmission, becoming his dharma successor. Her dharma name was Mujaku Nyodai. She was the financial patron of the temple of Rokuon-ji in the Kitayama district of Kyoto in the province of Yamashiro, now called Kinkaku-ji.

Chiyono's enlightenment poem:

> With this and that I contrived
> And then the bottom fell out of the bucket.
> Where water does not collect,
> The moon does not dwell.

—Translation by Anne Dutton

Figure 11. Sculptural Portrait of Musō Soseki (detail)

19

Musō Soseki (1275–1351)

Selected Poems

One of the leading Zen Masters of the fourteenth century, Musō Soseki was the teacher of everyone from emperors and military leaders to Zen monk pupils and everyday people. Born in Ise, he was a descendant of Emperor Uda and might have been expected to hold a high position in society, but his mother died when he was only three years old, and he is said to have turned to Buddhism the following year. At first he studied Esoteric Buddhism of the Shingon sect; he was ordained as a monk at the great temple of Tōdai-ji in Nara when he was seventeen.

Within a few years, however, Musō became critical of the established Buddhism of his day, and in 1399 he began to study Zen with the visiting Chinese Master I-shang I-ning (1244–1317) at Kenchō-ji in Kamakura. Although Musō progressed well in his training, he decided to seclude himself in northern Japan for a few years, but then returned to Kamakura for further study with Kōhō Kennichi (1241–1316). Musō attained satori in 1305 while at a hermitage in the countryside. Reaching for a wall in the dark, he realized it was not there; giving a great laugh, he reached enlightenment.

Three years later Kōhō gave Musō Dharma transmission. But Musō declined a request from the Shogun to stay at Kenchō-ji and departed again to live in seclusion for nearly twenty years. Finally, in 1325, he accepted the summons of Emperor Go-Daigo to become abbot of Nanzen-ji in Kyoto. The following year Musō returned to Kamakura, but he came back to Nanzen-ji in 1334 when the temple was named first among the Gozan ("five mountains") monasteries of Japanese Zen. This came at a time when Go-Daigo was leading an ill-fated rebellion against Shogunal rule, but when the Emperor fled to Yoshino in 1336, Musō remained in Kyoto at the request of the Shogunate. It is clear that somehow he managed to maintain good relations with both sides of the political conflict, and his influence upon the Zen world of his day was enormous, with 13,145 recorded pupils.

In 1339 Musō converted the temple Saihō-ji from Pure Land Buddhism to Zen, and in the process reworked the temple garden into one of the most celebrated and oft-copied of all Zen gardens. It features a pond in the form of the character for heart-mind (kokoro 心), an area of flat stones for meditating upon, a "dry waterfall" of vertical stones, a splendid grove of bamboo, and more than one hundred varieties of moss—for which Saihō-ji is popularly known as the Moss Temple.

During his years of solitude in the mountains, Musō wrote a series of poems that express his profound unity with nature. He is also the author of a prose work called "Dream Conversations," a series of written replies to questions from the Shogun about Buddhism. In all his writings, he expressed his depth of spirit in clear and direct language.

Snow Valley

Each drifting snowflake
        falls nowhere
                but here and now
Under the settling flowers of ice
        the water is flowing
                bright and clear
The cold stream
        splashes out
                the Buddha's words
startling
        the stone tortoise
                from its sleep

People's Abuse

People's abuse
        has melted what was golden
                and it has gone from the world
Fortune and misfortune
        both belong to the land
                of dreams
Don't look back
        to this world
                your old hole in the cellar

From *Sun at Midnight: Poems and Sermons,* by Musō Soseki and translated by W. S. Merwin and Soiku Shigematsu (San Francisco: North Point Press, 1989). © 1989 by W. S. Merwin, The Wylie Agency. Reprinted by permission of The Wylie Agency.

From the beginning
        the flying birds have left
                no footprints on the blue sky

Old Hut

A handful of thatch
        has sheltered its master's head
                since before time began
Now some new students
        are gathering to wait
                outside the gate
Don't say
        there's nothing
                new at all
Year after year
        in this garden
                the trees blossom

Green Mountains

Green mountains
        have turned yellow
                so many times
The troubles and worries
        of the world of things
                no longer bother me
One grain of dust in the eye
        will render the Three Worlds
                too small to see
When the mind is still
        the floor where I sit
                is endless space

Time for a Walk

Time for a walk
        in the world outside
                and a look at who I am

Originally I had no cares
    and I am seeking
        nothing special
Even for my guests
    I have nothing
        to offer
Except these white stones
    and this clear
        spring water

Truth Hall

First the outer gate
    then the inner gate
        under the high roof the low roof
Deep within
    there is no argument
        to be heard
Each of you be sure
    to find the deepest truth
        in yourself
and say "Maitreya
    Buddha of the future
        —no more, thank you!"

Incomparable Verse Valley

The sounds of the stream
    splash out
        the Buddha's sermon
Don't say
    that the deepest meaning
        comes only from one's mouth
Day and night
    eighty thousand poems
        arise one after the other
and in fact
    not a single word
        has ever been spoken

No Word Hut

I left my locked mouth
        hanging
                on the wall
With the brushwood
        door shut tight
                I delight in my own freedom
Inside
        my secret talk resounds
                like thunder
Even the bare
        posts and the lamps
                can't pretend they don't hear it

The Peak of the Held-up Flower

On Vulture Peak
        once the Buddha
                held up a flower
It has been multiplied
        into a thousand plants
                one of them is on this mountain
Look: the fragrant seedlings
        have been handed all the way down
                to the present
No one knows
        how many spring winds are blowing
                in the timeless world

Temple of Eternal Light

The mountain range
        the stones in the water
                all are strange and rare
The beautiful landscape
        as we know
                belongs to those who are like it
The upper worlds
        the lower worlds
                originally are one thing

There is not a bit of dust
        there is only this still and full
                perfect enlightenment

Toki-no-ge **(Satori Poem)**

Year after year
        I dug in the earth
                looking for the blue of heaven
only to feel
        the pile of dirt
                choking me
until once in the dead of night
        I tripped on a broken brick
                and kicked it into the air
and saw that without a thought
        I had smashed the bones
                of the empty sky

Beyond Light

The clear mirror
        and its stand
                have been broken
There is no dust
        in the eyes
                of the blind donkey
Dark
        dark everywhere
                the appearance of subtle Zen
Let it be
        The garden lantern
                opens its mouth laughing

Hut in Harmony

When the master
        without a word
                raises his eyebrows

The posts and rafters
     the cross beams and roof tree
         begin to smile
There is another place
    for conversing
        heart to heart
The full moon
    and the breeze
        at the half-open window

—Translations by W. S. Merwin and Soiku Shigematsu

20

T'aego (1301–1382)

Collected Sayings (excerpts)

T'aego was born in the southern part of Korea and became a monk at the age of thirteen. During his later teens he visited several Zen Masters, and throughout his twenties he worked on the kōan, "The ten thousand dharmas return to the one; where does the one return?" At age thirty-three he had a breakthrough and then worked on the Mu *kōan. When he was thirty-seven he had a final enlightenment experience, which he expressed in this poem:*

> The solid doors shatter.
> Clear wind blows through
> From beginningless time.

T'aego settled down to teach on Samgak Mountain, near modern Seoul, and attracted many students. When he was forty-seven he traveled to China and sought out the eminent Zen Master Shih-wu, an eighteenth-generation Dharma descendant of Lin-chi. Shih-wu confirmed T'aego's enlightenment. T'aego was then invited by the Mongol Emperor to address the nobility at the Eternal Peace Zen Temple in the capital. When T'aego returned to Korea he became a confidant of the king. As National Teacher he used his political power to unify the Nine Mountain Zen sects of Korea, which dated back to the eighth century, into one school, the Chogye order, which remains the dominant school of Buddhism in Korea to this day. He carried on a prolific correspondence with people from all walks of life and trained a large number of monks. Almost all of the current Zen lineages in Korea lead back to T'aego.

The first two of the five selections here are formal talks T'aego gave to the imperial court in China and to the Korean nobility, respectively. Like other forms of Buddhism, Zen schools and teachers in China, Korea, and Japan often had close relationships with the governing powers and were sometimes called upon to make public appearances. These talks are excellent examples of the stance a Zen Master might take on such occasions. They also illustrate the general style and various aspects of a formal Dharma speech.

T'aego's teaching words were collected by Kim Chung-hyon around 1356, and this record was followed by Chong Mong-ju, the writer of this collection, in 1388.

1. Public and Private

When T'aego occupied the abbot's seat at Yung-ning Temple [in Beijing], he brandished his staff and said: "Here is the great furnace and bellows for melting down buddhas and patriarchs, the hammer and tongs for forging birth and death. Those who confront its point lose their courage. Don't be surprised that I have no face."

He brandished the staff again and said: "All the hundreds of thousands of buddhas disintegrate right here."

Again he brandished the staff; then he held it up and said: "This is it. When the whale drinks the ocean dry, it reveals the coral branches."

T'aego held up the robe [emblematic] of succession and said: "This piece of cowhide is the symbol that the blood-line of the buddhas and patriarchs has not been broken off. Old Shakyamuni could not use it up in thirty-nine years [of teaching] at more than three hundred assemblies. At the end, at the assembly on Spirit Peak, he entrusted it to Mahakasyapa, the golden-hued ascetic, and said: 'Pass it on from generation to generation, until the last age, and do not let it be cut off.' Obviously, obviously."

T'aego held up the golden Dharma-robe and said: "Why has this golden monk's robe come from the lord's palace today? Haven't you read [in the *Benevolent King Sutra*] that this Dharma has been entrusted to the monarch and the great ministers?"

He held up the robe [emblematic] of the succession and said: "This one is a private matter intimately transmitted from father to son."

He held up the golden robe and said: "This one is a public matter bestowed by the royal house. The private is not equal to the public: the public comes before the private."

Then he put on the golden robe, lifted up one corner of it, and called to the assembly: "Do you see this one? Not only am I glad to receive it and wear it humbly, but it has already wrapped up numberless buddhas and patriarchs."

From *A Buddha from Korea: The Zen Teachings of T'aego,* by J. C. Cleary © 1988. Reprinted by arrangement with Shambhala Publications Inc., Boston, MA. www.shambhala.com.

T'aego gave a shout and held up the robe [emblematic] of succession and said: "Does everyone clearly witness this? This is something evil transmitted from [my teacher to me on] Mount Hsia-wu."

Then he put it on, pointed to the teacher's seat, and said: "The one road on top of Vairocana's head is very clear. Does everyone see where the road begins?"

Then T'aego climbed the stairs saying, "One, two, three, four, five."

He ascended to the teacher's seat carrying incense and said: "This incense has no coming or going; it mysteriously pervades past, present, and future. It is not inside or outside; it penetrates all directions. I salute the august personage of the present emperor of the great Yuan dynasty, the lord of the world. May he live for ten thousand years, for ten thousand times ten thousand years. I humbly hope that his golden orb will enjoy sovereignty over the three thousand worlds, that his jade leaves will be fragrant for a million million springs." Then T'aego held up the incense and said: "This incense is clean and pure. It contains myriad virtues. It is serene and at ease, and secures thousands of blessing. I respectfully wish that all the queen mother's family will preserve their good health and tranquility, and live as long as heaven. May the glory of this dragon's progeny know an eternal spring, and never grow old, enjoying the happiness of being the mother of the monarch."

Then he lifted the incense and said: "As I hold up this incense, heaven is high and earth deep. If I put it down, the ocean is deep and the rivers are pure. I respectfully wish that the crown prince may live a thousand years, a thousand years, and another thousand years. May he traverse jade realms for a thousand years of happiness and serve the Heavenly Visage [of the emperor] with filial piety for ten thousand years of joy."

Then T'aego held up a stick of incense he had inside his robe and said: "The buddhas and patriarchs do not know this incense, and ghosts and spirits cannot fathom it. It was not born of heaven and earth, nor was it gained spontaneously. In the past, while traveling on foot in Korea, I came to a patron's garden, and under a shadowless tree, I encountered this thing with no edges or seams or place to get a grip. I came to a ten-thousand-fathom cliff, and let go with my whole body. There was no breath of life at all, when suddenly I came to life again, floating at ease. Nevertheless, people doubted me, and I thought there would be no one to give clear proof. The more I hid it, the stronger it became; the more I wanted to hide it, the more it was evident. My evil repute and stinking smell filled the world, and today I obey the imperial command [to become abbot here], and hold it up before you.

"In front of this assembly of gods and humans, I burn [this incense] in the brazier. I offer it up to [my former teacher], Master Shih-wu, who formerly dwelled at Fu-yuan P'u-hui Zen Temple in West Che circuit, and who has retired to a hut on the peak of Mount Hsia-wu. I offer it to him to repay his kindness in attesting [to my enlightenment] holiness. The emperor asked: 'Who is the one facing me now?' Bodhidharma said: 'I don't know.'

"This is the model of the first communication of the message of Zen in the eastern lands. Today the king of our country has invited me, a minor monk, to talk about the vehicle of the Zen school. I salute His Imperial Majesty, Her Imperial Majesty, the Imperial Crown Prince above, the great assembly of humans and devas in between, and the officials and commoners below, for bestowing the great gift of the Dharma. I have not said a word, and Their Majesties have not asked a word. Has it been the same as or different from the questions and answers between Emperor Wu and Bodhidharma? If you can tell, I'll allow you one eye. If you cannot tell, listen to a verse:

> The high ancient's voice is closest
> Too bad the season is spring when the blossoms fall
> I urge you to drain another cup of wine
> At the gate where the sun rises in the west,
> There are no old acquaintances.

7. Making the Nation Great

On the fifteenth day of the first month of 1357 [in Kaesong, the Korean capital], T'aego went up to the teaching hall at the Temple for the Protection of the Military in the royal palace. After dedicating the incense, T'aego took the seat and held up the rescript [summoning him there] and said:

"The samadhis of the buddhas—the buddhas do not know them. Our present monarch protects and upholds the Buddha Dharma. The samadhis are all right here: who can truly master them?

"Let me trouble the duty distributor to read out [the rescript] for you."

When the rescript had been read aloud, T'aego picked up the whisk and said: "Is there anyone who is truly worthy of the vehicle of the school that has come down from antiquity? All the scriptures of the twelve-part canon of the five teachings and three vehicles are just piss left behind by an old barbarian. The buddhas and patriarchs were just guys talking about a dream in a dream. If you discuss them by making up reasons, you bury the vehicle of the school. If you discuss them in terms of conventional truth, you are turning your back on the former sages. This way won't do, otherwise won't do, won't do also won't do. If you are a legitimate patchrobed monk, you can see it beyond all the permutations of affirmation and denial."

After answering questions, T'aego held up his staff horizontally and said: "All the buddhas of past, present, and future are Thus. All the generations of enlightened teachers are Thus. If it were not for our monarch's invitation, I would never explain fully this way.

"If the monarch and his high ministers can believe like this at this point, they will attract the protection of the buddhas and bring down the blessings of the devas. The monarch of the realm will live forever, with the warp and woof of cultural refinement and military might to assist his kingly enterprise of civilizing [the people]. The worthy ministers and high officials will extend their lives and their tenure in office. The transformative influence will reach the common people, so that worthy people will be found everywhere. All supernatural threats will dissipate even before they become manifest. Treason and rebellion will keep out of sight. Heaven and Earth will work their transformations even more, sun and moon will be even brighter, mountains and rivers will be even more solid, and the altars of earth and grain [emblematic of state and society] will flourish again. With timely rain and timely sunshine, the hundred grains will grow and the myriads of common people will be happy. Lucky unicorns and phoenixes resplendent with many colors will vie to offer auspicious signs in response [to your virtuous rule].

"If you are this way, then you are acting in accord with the sayings of the worthy sages of previous dynasties. If you believe in Buddha and submit to Heaven, then naturally you will succeed in making the nation great.

"Directed down, words get long: leave it to the staff! Again I have explained it clearly for the King, the Princess, the Queen, the Great Ministers, Generals, and Inner and Outer Officials."

T'aego brandished the staff once, held it up, and said: "Since this staff has no consciousness, how could there be right and wrong? I ask Your Majesty and the Great Ministers to collect your minds well and listen. Don't let it leak away."

He brandished the staff again and said: "If you're stuck in thinking what to do, you won't accomplish the noble task."

He brandished the staff again and said: "[Those in power who act] with complete public-spirited fairness without any private biases are protected and remembered by Heaven."

He brandished the staff again and said: "If they honor Buddha and stand in awe of Heaven, everyone will be safe and secure."

He brandished the staff again and said: "If they act contrary to this, [the consequences will be so dire that] though I have a mouth, it is hard to speak about it."

He brandished the staff again and said: "If the sage lord has a fit of anger, it thunders the same through millions of people's hearts." Then T'aego brandished the staff one more time and put it across his shoulder.

[The end of the scene was not recorded.]

[Later in the same session] T'aego again held up his staff and said: "In the old days on Sosol Mountain, I did not explain anything to people at all. Today in Locana Hall again there is nothing for me to say to people. I have received the benevolence of the state to no purpose: I lack the virtue to repay it in the least.

"I just keep busy like this mixing socially with idle spirits and wild demons, phantasmagorical ghosts and monsters. All I hear are schemes for gain, which engender false thoughts and erroneous conceptions. As they make such calculations about the fickle, evanescent world, people's attempts to deal with it do not allow them a moment's rest. Isn't this caused by past deeds?"

T'aego brandished his staff and said: "This phony! Why is he rebuking himself?" [Noting the occasion] T'aego said: "I have been invited to the royal palace and have ascended on high to this jewel seat. In the assembly of humans and devas, it is good to ask about the Path and good to ask about Zen. This is the ideal pattern, but in fact it is not so.

"This month the cold has already retreated and the morning sun shines victorious. This is our Great Lord ascending to the Bright Hall. There is no place that his flying intellect and swift illumination do not reach.

"To spread good order and employ humane considerations is the great policy of those who act as kings. When there are major events for the nation, they should rely on the power of the Buddha Dharma to secure themselves from false moves. Thus they must first set right their dealings with the Buddha Dharma. They must reward those who have the Path and act as patrons of Buddhist monasteries, leading their congregations in scrupulous practice, and bringing blessings on the families of the land. This is the way the Former Kings carried out the Dharma. This is the starting point for Kingly Government.

"The reason to leave home for the Path is not to seek fame or profit; it is not to make plans for a place to stay, clothes to wear, or food to eat; it is not to seek people's respect and acclaim. [Leavers of home] gladly keep discipline; they wear poor clothes and eat poor food; they hide away in the mountain valleys and have no expectations for their present bodies: this can be called the conduct of those who leave home to study the Path. People today are not only self-seeking, they take advantage of the power of others for their seeking. I cannot do anything about them."

T'aego brandished his staff and said: "Tigers do not eat animals with stripes, for fear of injuring their own kind."

T'aego also said: "Among the common people, there are indeed those loyal to the lord and filial to their parents, those who possess talent and virtue. Though they may be abandoned among the weeds, they still have concerns for the trend of the times, concerns for the nation, and are intent on saving the world and its people. Although I am stupid and unworthy, because I could not bear to be silent in the face of so many concerns, I have been introduced in the highest circles [as a Zen teacher].

"If [those in power] rewarded the worthy and the good and punished the wicked and the deceitful, who would not be loyal? Who would not be filial? Who would be without the Path? Who wouldn't study? Who wouldn't cultivate his own virtue?

"Nevertheless, if there is anyone here with the strength to uproot mountains and the energy to top the world, let him come forward and fight along with me. Let us sacrifice our bodies for the nation, and accomplish the great enterprise. This is not only for great nobles. If there are no such people here, then the old monk T'aego goes off to serve in the border forts by himself with a single horse and spear.

"But tell me, though I do go off, what is the one phrase that accomplishes the great enterprise?" After a long silence, T'aego said: "Holding the peerless sword crosswise, the true imperative whole: in the universe of Great Peace, cutting down stubborn stupidity." Then he brandished his staff twice.

8. Returning Home to Three Corners Mountain

When he reached the temple gate, T'aego said: "I never left this gate in the old days and I am not entering it today. Nor is there any place within it to stay. Where will all of you go to see where I wander at play?" He brandished the staff.

After a long silence, T'aego said: "On the northern ridge, idle flowers red as brocade. In front of the mountain stream, flowing water green as indigo-plants."

9. Entry into Phoenix Cliff Zen Temple on Mount Huiyang

When he reached the temple gate, T'aego said: "All the buddhas of the past, present and future all come in and go out through this gate. But tell me, today am I going out or coming in? I am neither going out nor coming in: what is the principle of this?" He brandished the staff three times.

10. Entry into Precious Forest Zen Temple on Mount Kaji

When he arrived at the temple gate, T'aego said: "Old Shakyamuni said, 'I entrust this Dharma gate of mine to the rulers of states and their great ministers.' These are true words! Today I have come with a large group: we started out from Mount Huiyang and finally we have ended up before the gate of Mount Kaji, over three hundred miles away. We were on the road fourteen days. We proceeded south day after day and encountered no trouble on the road. Wherever we went it was the universal gate of perfect penetration: the way opened before us, all thanks to the protection and aid and benevolent power of the King and his ministers."

T'aego called out to the great assembly: "We have arrived, but how can we advance and repay such profound benevolence from above?" He brandished his staff and said: "The sound of the rushing stream is most intimate. The colors of the mountains are like it too."

At the buddha shrine T'aego said: "The ancient buddha Chao-chou said, 'I don't like to hear even the word *buddha*.' I am not this way. I don't like the one who doesn't like it. In the old days I was you, today you are me." Then he lit incense and bowed in homage.

—Translations by J. C. Cleary

Figure 12. Bokusai Shōtō (died 1492), *Portrait of Ikkyū* (detail)

21

Ikkyū Sōjun (1394–1481)

Selected Poems in

Chinese and Japanese

Ikkyū Sōjun was the most iconoclastic and unusual Zen Master in Japanese history. In his own unique manner, he battled what he considered corrupt and deluded Zen teachings during a time when Zen had reached its high point of governmental and social esteem. According to Ikkyū, that was exactly the problem; too much success had led to a weakening of the standards, and so he spent much of his life trying to revive the great Zen traditions of the past.

Reputed to be the son of Emperor Gokomatsu (1377–1432) and a low-ranking court lady, Ikkyū was sent to the temple Ankoku-ji in Kyoto at the age of five. As well as training in Zen, he learned Chinese classical prose and poetry, and was able to compose poetry in Chinese by the age of twelve. At the age of sixteen he became a Zen pupil of Kenō Sōi (died 1415) for five years, then at his teacher's death he left Kyoto to study with Kasō Sōdon (1352–1428) on the shores of Lake Biwa. Although part of the Daitoku-ji lineage, Kasō had become disillusioned with the temple's close ties with the governmental and social establishment, and so he set up a strict training center in the small town of Katata.

Ikkyū had a major enlightenment experience at the age of twenty-six when, while meditating in a small boat on Lake Biwa, he heard the sudden cawing of a crow. He thereupon settled in the commercial town of Sakai where he startled onlookers by such behavior as waving a wooden sword to illustrate the toothless nature of establishment Zen, and frequenting wineshops. Famously, on one New Year's Day he brandished a human skull to remind holiday-makers of the impermanence of life.

Over the following decades Ikkyū moved around the country, decrying nonauthentic Zen and exerting a strong influence upon many artists, including painters, poets, and tea masters. His own calligraphy and paintings

*are full of nervous energy and fierce spirit, often defying the traditions of the
past to express his own Zen mind.*

*The civil wars of the 1450s and 1460s were devastating to Kyoto, and
when Ikkyū was asked to become abbot and rebuild Daitoku-ji in 1474, he
could not refuse despite his previous incendiary comments on former abbots.
He was able to raise funds successfully for the restoration of the temple, but he
shocked the populace with his fervent love affair in his seventies with a blind
young singer named Mori. He celebrated this affair with erotic Zen poetry, a
form that had never before existed.*

*There are many portraits of Ikkyū, several of which are like no other
Buddhist portraits but perfectly convey his eccentric and vibrant personality.
Ikkyū's own works cover a variety of formats and media both formal and
informal, including a touching Buddhist memorial to a dead sparrow. He is
perhaps best known for his "Crazy Cloud Anthology" of more than one
thousand Chinese-style poems, as well as his prose-poetry "Skeletons" about
the transience of life.*

*It was difficult to choose which of Ikkyū's works to include here, but a
selection of Chinese and Japanese poetry seems most appropriate. His poems in
Chinese quatrains reflect the main themes of his life: iconoclastic Zen; his free
existence before he was finally persuaded to become abbot of Daitoku-ji; and
the love he found late in his life for the blind singer Mori.*

Deluded and Enlightened

No beginning and no end to my single mind,
No achievement of Buddha-nature in this original mind;
Innate Buddhahood? Just the Buddha's wild talk—
Innate delusion is mankind's original mind.

Shakyamuni's Ascetic Practice
(for Jasoku's Painting of Shakyamuni)

Six years hunger and cold piercing his bones,
Ascetic discipline was the Buddha's mysterious principle;
Those of you who believe you are just like Shakyamuni
Are only rice-bags in monks' robes.

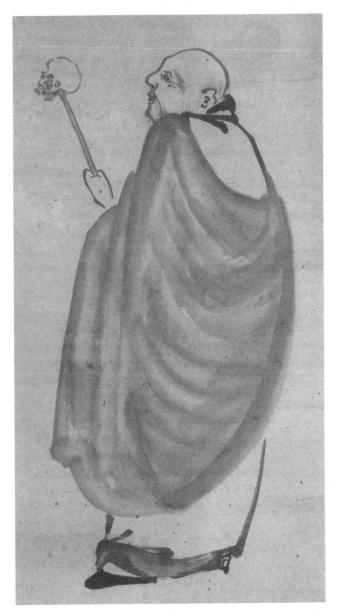

Figure 13. Suiō Genro (1716–1789), *Ikkyū* **(detail)**

Ikkyū's New Year's greeting:
Your body is near death,
Be careful, be careful!

Praising Lin-chi

Katsu! Katsu! Katsu! Katsu! Katsu!
In each moment he gives life or death
With his glowing demonic eyes
Shining and blazing like the sun and moon.

For a Monk Who Burned His Books

Under the trees, over the rocks, in a reed hut
Poems, prose, sacred writings gathered together—
You can burn the volumes in your bag,
But can you forget the books in your belly?

Straw Coat and Hat

Woodcutters and fishermen have everything they need;
What use have I for the carved chairs and wooden floors
    of Zen?
With straw sandals and a bamboo staff, I roam three thousand
    worlds,
Dwelling in water, subsisting on wind for twenty years.

Praising Myself

A storm-crazed madman stirring up a crazy storm,
Coming and going from brothel to wineshop—
Which of you patch-robe monks can be right here
As I paint north, paint south, paint east and west?

On Monks in Training

Pain within pleasure—Ikkyū's training monks;
One after another, frogs fighting for honor at the bottom of the
    well.
From dawn to dusk puzzling over the words of the Masters,
Right and wrong, him and me, a lifetime of complaining.

At a Brothel

Beautiful women—clouds and rain at the deep river of love;
The brothel girl and the old Zen monk sing in the pavilion.
I am inspired by the joining of our lips,
And do not believe I am casting my body and mind into the flames.

Untitled

A belly swollen full of hell,
Unending eons of passions,
Wildfires burning without end—
But flowering grasses are born again in the spring wind.

Lady Mori Rides a Cart

The blind girl often rides a phoenix cart on spring outings;
When I feel depressed she is good consolation for my sadness.
Even though people mock and despise us,
I love to see Mori, so beautiful and elegant.

Summoning My Hand to Create Mori's Hand

My hand—how does it resemble Mori's hand?
The lord of self-confidence and the master of elegance.
When I am sick, she cures the jade stem,
And my followers will rejoice at our meeting.

The Secret Skill of Great Peace

Natural strangeness—the secret skill;
Yesterday's wisdom is today's foolishness.
In this world of brightness and shade, trust only in change,
And, just once, bow to the full moon.

*[In contrast to his Chinese quatrains, which are often complex and difficult,
Ikkyū's poems in the classical Japanese* waka *style of 5-7-5-7-7 syllables are
very simple and direct, no doubt intended for the general public rather than
monks in training.]*

Between the rainy path
and the path without rain
　　a person can rest—
if it rains, it rains
if the wind blows, it blows

Originally nonexistent
your long-ago self
　　will go nowhere at death—
for there's nowhere to go
and nothing at all

Speaking when questioned
silent when not questioned
　　Bodhidharma—
was there anything at all
within his mind?

Empty at the beginning
empty at the end
　　mind—
when it is born and when it dies
ultimate emptiness

What kind of thing
is mind
　　cannot be said—
painted in ink
the sound of wind in the pines

Just as it was
when you were born
　　mind—
without any prayers
becomes Buddha

If you ask
all night long
　　the way of Buddha—
the search will
enter your own mind

If it rains, it rains
if it doesn't rain, it doesn't—
    but even if
it doesn't rain
our sleeves will be wet

Viewing cherry blossoms
their color and aroma
    fall with the blossoms—
yet mindlessly
they come again with spring

Buddhism
is shaving the kettle,
    the whiskers on the stone,
the sound that comes
from painted bamboo

My home
has no pillars
    and no roof—
but the rain does not wet it
and the wind does not blow on it

When it blows
this mountain wind
    is fierce—
and when it doesn't blow
it doesn't blow

In the well not yet dug
on the water not yet gathered
    there are ripples—
the man without a shadow
scoops it up

As for mind,
because there is no such thing
    as mind,
with what enlightenment
can it be enlightened?

The crescent moon
becomes full and wanes
        until nothing is left—
But there it is again
the moon at dawn

In this world
we eat, we shit
        we sleep and we wake up—
and after all that
all we have to do is die

Being born
and then dying
        is the law of life—
Buddha, Bodhidharma,
the cat and the cradle.

Coming alone into the world
and leaving it alone
        is also illusion—
I can teach you the way
not to come and not to leave

No matter what it is
everything is just part of
        this world of falsehoods—
even death itself
is not reality

Without dying
and without going anywhere
        I will be here—
But don't ask questions
because I won't answer

Since Ikkyū
does not consider his body
        as his body
city dwellings and mountain huts
are the same place to live

If I say "it exists"
people all think it exists—
    although it answers
perhaps it does not exist
the mountain echo

If I say "it doesn't exist"
people all think it doesn't exist
    although it answers—
perhaps it does exist
the mountain echo

Right now
there is no cloud
    hanging over the mind
and no mountain
for the moon to hide behind

Is and *Is Not*
weigh down the fisherman
    on the ocean of life and death—
heave them off the boat
Is and *Is Not* disappear

Become a Buddha?
The mind can't do it
    the body can't do it—
only what can't become a Buddha
becomes a Buddha

As for Buddha
searching
    outside the mind
is just illusion
within illusion

When I reflect
there is no otherness
    between anyone and myself—
outside the mind
there is no other mind

The original body
must return to
        its original place
so why search for
a Buddha we don't need?

    Even when I say
"nothing much to it"
    I have already lied—
there's nothing more to say
Bodhidharma Ikkyū

—Translations by Stephen Addiss

Figure 14. Kim Myong-guk (1600–after 1662), *Bodhidharma*

22

So Sahn (1520–1604)

The Mirror of Zen (excerpts)

So Sahn Hyu Jeong (also known as Sosan Taesa) was born in northern Korea during a period when Buddhism was oppressed by the government. He was a precocious child and studied for the civil service examination while still quite young. During a vacation sightseeing in the mountains and wandering from one Buddhist temple to another, an old monk asked him if he wanted to pass the examination of the empty mind. When So Sahn asked him what that was, the old monk blinked and asked him, "Do you understand?" He then gave So Sahn several dozen Buddhist scriptures and sent him off to study with Zen Master Yonggwang. After three years of scriptural study So Sahn began to feel confined by name and form and at a dead end with words until one evening, returning from drawing water, he "turned his head and saw his original home." He then devoted himself to Zen meditation and practiced in a number of temples and hermitages.

In 1545 Queen Munjong became regent for her son and set in motion a Buddhist revival. In 1552 So Sahn passed the newly instituted advanced monk examinations and soon became head of both the Doctrinal and Zen schools in Korea. He resigned both positions after three years and wandered through the Diamond Mountains until finally settling at Myohang Mountain in northwest Korea (hence his name So Sahn, "Western Mountain"), where he spent the rest of his life. He taught more than a thousand students, seventy of whom became distinguished monks. He produced a large number of poems, letters, biographies, and a teaching manual called The Mirror of Zen. *His reputation both as a monk and man of letters spread, and he enjoyed the special favor of the king. When in 1592 the Japanese invaded Korea, the king, rallying all the military support he could, appealed to So Sahn to organize a force of monks. So Sahn assembled an army of five thousand monks and helped to repel the invaders. Popular stories ascribed supernatural powers to So Sahn and his monks in battle, and he became a beloved figure and national hero. He retired shortly thereafter, and died in 1604 after inscribing a death poem on the back of a portrait:*

Eighty years past, this is a portrait of me.
Eighty years later, I will be this portrait.

So Sahn's influence on Korean Zen through his own teaching and his lineage has been profound. His Mirror of Zen *has been basic to the training of Korean monks and nuns for the last four hundred years. It has eighty-six sections, some extremely short, some quite long. We present nineteen of these sections, including the first and the last, all but one in its entirety. According to tradition, So Sahn wrote this work poring over a huge number of Buddhist texts, extracting what he considered to be their essence, and then presenting what he had extracted, followed by commentary. The commentaries themselves may be followed by further text: a* gatha *(a short poem), or another prose section called "capping word." So Sahn's commentary is sometimes straightforward ("The word Buddha refers to Shakyamuni Buddha"), but more often it points directly to our original nature, either in So Sahn's own language or through quotes by and stories about other Zen Masters. Rhetorical strategies and levels of discourse are quite varied, and the subject matter ranges widely. Particularly important historically are his sections on* kong-an *(Japanese:* kōan*) practice, on ethics and precepts, on studying sutras, and on Pure Land practice.*

In Korea, a distinction is often made between hwa-du *(Chinese:* hua-t'ou *or "great question," often the heart of a* kong-an*) and* kong-an *practice. At times So Sahn seems to honor this distinction, at times he does not. Some of his commentary derives from earlier Chinese and Korean sources such as Ta-hui (see Chapter 14) and Chinul (see Chapter 16).*

To So Sahn, precepts are absolutely essential, the root without which practice cannot flourish. Given the origins of this text and his own background, he clearly supports sutra study, but only with a base of strong practice and deep experience—he is scathing about what are often called "dead words."

Pure Land Buddhism, whose practice includes chanting to Amita (Japanese: Amida) Buddha hoping for rebirth in the Western Pure Land, is often seen as antithetical to Zen. Hakuin in particular (see Chapter 24) cautioned about trying to combine Pure Land practice with Zen. So Sahn includes this sort of criticism, but he is also sympathetic to the idea that "paradise and Amita Buddha . . . really do exist." This reflects the syncretism of Korean Zen, which is able to incorporate a wide variety of sincere practices as a means toward awakening.

1

There is only one thing, from the very beginning, infinitely bright and mysterious by nature.

It was never born, and it never dies. It cannot be described or given a name.

Commentary

What is this "one thing"?
An eminent teacher wrote,

> Even before the ancient Buddhas were born,
> One thing was already perfectly complete.
> Even Shakyamuni Buddha could not understand it.
> How could he transmit it to Mahakasyapa?

There is one "thing" that is never born, and never dies. For this reason it cannot be named in any way, or expressed, or depicted.

The Sixth Patriarch of Zen once addressed the assembly thus: "I have something that has no name and no form: Do any of you see it?" Zen Master Shen-hui immediately replied, "It is the essence of all Buddhas, and also my buddha-nature." Due to this answer, Shen-hui cannot be considered a legitimate heir and descendant of the Sixth Patriarch.

Zen Master Nan-yueh came from Mount Seung Sahn [Chinese: Hsi-shan] to see the Sixth Patriarch, who asked, "What is it that comes here like this?" Nan-yueh was completely stuck, and could not answer anything. After eight years of practice, he finally attained enlightenment and said, "If you even call this a 'thing,' it is not correct." This answer is why Nan-yueh thus became the premier Dharma heir and successor of the Sixth Patriarch.

Gatha

> *The sages of the three great teachings*
> *Can be found in this phrase:*
> *Who dares express it must be careful*
> *Your eyebrows may fall out!*

2

The appearance of all Buddhas and Patriarchs in this world can be likened to waves arising suddenly on a windless ocean.

Commentary

The word *Buddha* refers to Shakyamuni Buddha, and *Patriarch* refers to the Venerable Mahakasyapa. Their coming into the world means that, out of great kindness and great compassion, they appeared in order to save all sentient beings from suffering.

In view of "the one thing," however, everyone's original nature is already complete, just as it is. Why have we come to depend on others, always wanting to dress up this simple matter with more powder and rouge? Therefore their coming into this world can be viewed in just the same way you would if waves were to somehow arise on a sea without wind. This is the reason why the *Maha Sunyata Sutra* says, "Words on a page are demon-karma, names and forms are demon-karma, and even the Buddha's own speech is demon-karma."

All of this is just to say that when you correctly attain your original nature, both Buddha and Patriarchs are no longer of any use to you.

Gatha

Light fades away in heaven and earth,
When the sun and moon grow dark.

3

Yet, dharma has many depths of meaning, and people have different capacities to receive it. Therefore it is necessary to adopt different kinds of skillful means.

Commentary

Dharma refers to the one thing, and *people* refers to all sentient beings. Dharma has two aspects: it never changes, and yet it also follows conditions, cause and effect. People also have two kinds of capacity: they always have the ability to awaken to themselves in an instant, while there is the constant need to refine themselves through gradual practices as well. Therefore it is necessary to adopt different kinds of skillful means employing words and speech. There is an old adage that goes, "According to official policy, even giving so much as a needle tip as a bribe is strictly prohibited. Yet in actual reality, horse-drawn carts laden up with bribes endlessly come and go."

Sentient beings' original nature is already complete, but they do not open their wisdom eye, and thus, of their own free will, fall into the cycle of rebirth [*samsara*]. Without the gleaming sword of Wisdom transcending worldly matters, who could cut through the heavy veil of ignorance? Owing to the Buddha's great kindness and compassion, we are enabled to cross the ocean of suffering and arrive on the other side. Were we to sacrifice our life as many times as there are sands in the Ganges River, it would still be difficult to repay even the tiniest portion of this debt.

All of this demonstrates how much we should truly appreciate the blessings of the Buddha and the Patriarchs and redouble our efforts anew to attain our original nature.

Gatha

The king mounts the royal throne.
An old man in the countryside sings a song.

4

You may call it "mind," or "Buddha," or "sentient being." Yet you should neither become attached to the names nor make distinctions or understanding. The essence of things is just-like-this. If even one thought appears, that is already a mistake.

Commentary

Sutra teachings rely on words such as these three names ("mind," "Buddha," "sentient being") to express the one thing. Zen meditation teaches that you must not become attached to any words or speech.

Picking it up or putting it down. Creating or destroying. These are the actions of a Free Person who is without any hindrance.

The selection above demonstrates how Buddhas and Patriarchs have freely used myriad expedient means to convey their teachings.

Gatha

It's like sweet rain falling after a long drought;
Like encountering an old friend in a faraway, foreign land.

6

If you become attached to words and speech, then even the Buddha's silently raising a flower or Mahakasyapa's wordless smile will be only another trace of the sutras. However, when you attain the truth within your own mind, even all the base chatter or elegant speech of the mundane world become nothing less than this same "special transmission outside the sutras."

Commentary

Dharma has no name, and so it cannot be grasped through words. It has no form, and so it cannot be understood through thinking. The instant you open your mouth to speak it, you have already departed from your original mind. When you lose this original mind, then even the story of the Buddha silently lifting a flower overhead and Mahakasyapa wordlessly smiling is, in the end, no better than dead speech to you.

If you attain the truth within your own mind, then even the senseless chitchat in the streets and markets are like the Dharma speech of a great teacher, and even a chirping bird or the wail of an animal express truth. For this very reason, when Zen Master Pao-chi heard the crying of bitter mourning, he awakened to his own mind and danced joyfully. And Zen Master Pao-shou was suddenly enlightened to his true nature by the sight of a street fight!

This teaching expresses the depth and shallowness of the Zen meditation and scriptural traditions, respectively.

Gatha

A precious gem shining in the palm of your hand.
Playfully roll and rub it here and there.

7

I would like to say just one thing:
Cutting off all thinking, forgetting all conditions
While sitting here with nothing to do—
Yet spring comes, and grass grows all by itself.

Commentary

To cut off all thinking and let go of all conditions, all cause and effect—this is already attaining the truth within your own mind. You can then be called a true man of the way who has nothing left to accomplish! How wonderful! Such a one is completely unfettered and from moment to moment does not make anything: when hungry, he eats; when tired, he sleeps. He wanders freely among the clear streams and blue mountains. He mingles easily and without hindrance in the busy ports and alehouses. The ebb and flow of time does not concern him, and yet spring comes and the green grass grows, as it always has.

The essential point here is that whenever thinking arises, one should instead reflect inwardly on our own true mind's light.

Gatha

I wondered if there be
Such a person,

Anywhere.
But he's already here.

9

In all of the sutras expounded by the Buddha, he first draws distinctions between various kinds of Dharmas, and then only later explains the principle of emptiness. The Zen meditation tradition handed down from the Patriarchs teaches, however, that when all traces of thinking are cut off, the principle of emptiness appears clearly, of itself, as the very origin of mind.

Commentary

The Buddha is a teacher for all generations, so his teaching on the principle of emptiness is as complete and meticulous as is possible to communicate. On the other hand, Patriarchs awaken others to liberation directly, so their teachings are primarily focused on attaining sudden enlightenment. The term "traces" refers to the Patriarch's words, and "thinking" refers to the thinking of the student.

Gatha

Contort your body as you may, and yet still
You cannot bend your arm backward at the elbow.

13

You should hold the *kong-an* with total determination, like a hen nesting on her brood, like a cat hunting a mouse, like a hungry man thinking of food, like a thirsty man thinking of water, and like a child longing for its mother. Only if you practice with this kind of mind are you sure to penetrate your Great Doubt.

Commentary

The Patriarchs left 1,700 *kong-ans,* such as "A dog has no Buddha-nature," "the pine tree in the courtyard," "three pounds of flax," and "dry shit-stick." A hen nests on her brood, always keeping them warm. When a cat chases a mouse, its mind and eyes never wander from the object of its hunt, no matter what. A starving man has but one object: food; a man with throat parched from thirst conceives of but one goal: get water. A child who has been left alone for a long time by its mother only longs to see her again.

All of these focused efforts come only from the deepest mind, and are not artificial. It is a kind of intense sincerity. Without such a deeply straightforward striving mind, it is impossible to attain enlightenment.

16

When you raise your *hwa-du,* your *kong-an* or Great Doubt, never attempt to figure out some correct answer, nor pursue it with thought. And do not just wait around until you become awakened. If you arrive at the place where thought cannot enter, your mind will have nowhere to go. It will be for you like an old rat that has entered the trap made of an ox horn: there is no way for retreat, and seemingly no way forward, either. It would be complete delusion to calculate this and that, to wander here and there following the karma of life and death, and to run about in fear and confusion. These days, people do not know that this is a sickness, and keep falling in and out of this sickness over and over and over again.

Commentary

There are ten sicknesses to avoid in *hwa-du* practice: trying to figure out the *kong-an* using discriminative thought; seizing on the master's wordless teaching gestures, such as raising his eye-brows or winking; allowing yourself to get caught by words and speech; searching for proofs or evidence in the *kong-an;* miming the shout or sudden-expression of some master as if it were your own thing; abandoning everything by falling into emptiness; attempting to distinguish between conditions of existence or nonexistence; thinking in terms of absolute nothingness; knowing things in terms of logical reasoning; and impatiently expecting awakening.

You must completely avoid these ten sicknesses! Instead, firmly holding the Great Doubt inspired by the *kong-an,* and keeping your mind clear, pour all of your energy into the question "What is this?"

17

This matter of *hwa-du* practice can be likened to a mosquito biting an iron bull. The mosquito does not try to figure out, "Do I do it this way, or that?" Its needlelike mouth pressed firmly on the impenetrable, it risks body and life, in one moment penetrating through with its whole being.

Commentary

This teaching recalls the point made earlier about the "live word." It is restated here in order to protect those who look deeply into the live word from regressing in their practice. An eminent teacher said, "Those who practice Zen must penetrate thoroughly the gate of the Patriarchs. In other words, to attain profound enlightenment, simply cut off the mind-road!"

25

And yet even though you have broken through the appearance of even a single thought, you must still find a keen-eyed master to check whether you have attained a correct insight.

Commentary

It is extremely difficult to attain enlightenment. So you should be very careful, even humble about any sense of attainment. The Dharma is like the vast sea: the farther you dive, the deeper it is. Only the truly foolish would allow themselves to be satisfied with some small attainment. Even experiencing some sort of breakthrough, you must still meet a keen-eyed master to have your insight verified: failing to do this, even the rarefied taste of *manda* [refined exotic Indian milk] may well turn into venom.

38

Practicing Zen meditation while remaining immersed in sexual concerns is like cooking sand for a meal. Practicing Zen meditation while yet not avoiding killing any living thing is like a person who plugs his own ears and then shouts something important to himself. Practicing Zen meditation with a mind that would steal is like trying to fill a leaky bowl. And a liar who practices Zen meditation is a person who would try to use feces for incense. Even for the one who has much wisdom, such failings can only lead you to the way of demons.

Commentary

This illuminates the most basic guidelines for our practice. It encompasses the traditional threefold practice (precepts, meditation, wisdom) through which we can cut off the karmic out-flows (sensual craving, desire for becoming, attachment to false views, ignorance). In the Hinayana tradition, precepts are used to receive the Dharma and also help us to live by it. In a manner of speaking, these are the "outer nature of the precepts," and keeping them is an end in itself. Mahayana students use precepts to seek their mind, cutting off "mind" at its root.

Therefore, in the Hinayana, precepts protect the Dharma by teaching us not to violate it with the actions of our body, while the Mahayana emphasizes keeping "mind precepts" so that we do not stray from the Dharma through the arising of our thinking mind. Lust blots out our pure nature. Killing living beings cuts off our innately compassionate mind. Taking things not given cuts off our good fortune, merit, and virtue. Lying cuts off the truth of things as they are. For though you have already attained some insight and may even possess the six supernatural powers, you will fall onto the path of demons and be forever denied access to these teachings of perfect enlightenment unless you abstain from killing, stealing, lustful attachment, and deception.

These four precepts are the foundation for all of the precepts. They are explained here at such great length to prevent you from violating them even in thought. Not following after the thinking-mind is what is meant by "precepts" [*sila*]. Not giving rise to thinking, but keeping a mind before thinking arises is what is known as "meditation" [*samadhi*]. And not being guided into action by foolish thought is what is known as "wisdom" [*prajna*].

Put another way, precepts capture the thief—our deluded mind, our defiled mind; meditation ties up the thief; and wisdom kills the thief. Only a strong, uncracked bowl made from the precepts can contain the pure, clear water of meditation, reflecting wisdom like the moon on its surface.

This threefold practice is the foundation for all the countless dharmas. It has been explained here specifically to prevent all of the karmic outflows. Had the Buddha, who enunciated this threefold practice, been reckless in his teaching? Or perhaps even Bodhidharma, who reiterated it, should be accused of telling lies?

39

People lacking in virtue do not rely on the Buddha's precepts, nor do they maintain vigilance over the three kinds of karma (karma of thought, speech, and action). Such people lead a lazy and dissolute life, looking down on others and provoking quarrels.

Commentary

Once you break the precepts—even in your mind—then every imaginable misdeed will appear as well.

Capping Word

Those who practice the Dharma should always keep in mind that, in an instant, legions of karmic demons can spread like a flash fire. Their intent is to distort and taint these teachings on how to find a correct way and correct life. It is especially true during this period of the decline of the Dharma.

40

If you do not abide by the precepts, in your next rebirth you will not even be able to receive the body of a mangy fox. How, then, can you even imagine attaining the fruit of pure wisdom by living like this?

Commentary

You should abide by the precepts as if, by doing so, you were serving the Buddha himself. Then it is as if the Buddha were constantly with you. Take as models the monk who endured being tied and bound with living grasses by thieves, and the monk who refused to report the goose that swallowed a priceless gem, preferring instead to absorb the blame and scorn of others who believed that he had absconded with the jewel, rather than see the goose be killed to have the gem removed.

41

To get out of the cycle of life and death, it is absolutely essential that you first cut off your desires and lusting.

Commentary

Attachment is the root cause of our endless transmigration through birth and death. Is it not enough to see that the lust that our parents kindled in each other was the condition that produced our own bodies? The Buddha said about this, "You will never shake off the dust of defilement and delusion if you do not cut off the lusting mind." He also taught, "Once you let yourself get tangled up in sensual desires, you are soon dragged to the gate of error." "Burning with desire" and "burning passion" are terms we use often in everyday life; they show that constant desire and lusting are to our mind as flame is to dry wood.

45

Some people may be under the impression that we practice dharma in order to attain Nirvana.

But this is a mistake. Mind is originally calm and perfectly clear, just as it is. Attaining this realization is true "Nirvana," or salvation. That is why it is taught, "All dharmas are originally marked by Nirvana."

Commentary

Your eyes cannot see your own eyes. So it would be false to say that you can see your own eyes. This explains why, when challenged to explain the principle of nonduality, Manjusri Bodhisattva resorted to conceptual thinking, but the layman Vimalakirti answered the same question by remaining silent.

[Note: Vimalakirti was a Buddhist layman who debated successfully with the Bodhisattva Manjusri.]

52

Merely chanting with the lips is nothing more than recitation of the Buddha's name. Chanting with a one-pointed mind is true chanting. Just mouthing the words without mindfulness, absorbed in habitual thinking, will do no real good for your practice.

Commentary

The six-worded dharma practice of chanting "namu amita bul" [Chinese: *namo amito fo;* Japanese: *namu amida butsu*] can be a shortcut road for cutting through the cycle of transmigration. But when you chant this, you must remain focused one-pointedly on the realm of the Buddha, reciting the Buddha's name clearly and without clinging to any passing thoughts. When your mindfulness accords with the sound produced by your lips, completely cutting off all thinking, this can truly be called "chanting."

Capping Word

The Fifth Patriarch once said, "It is better to keep your true, original mind than to contemplate the Buddhas of the ten directions." The Six Patriarch said, "If you only contemplate other Buddhas, you will never break free from life and death. You should keep your buddha-mind as it is in order to arrive on the other shore." And he taught further, "Buddha originates in your own nature. There is no need to seek outside yourself." He also said, "Ignorant people chant in the hope of being born in the Pure Land, or Land of Utmost Bliss, but true practitioners only focus instead on clearing their own mind." Also, "The Buddha does not save sentient beings. Rather, sentient beings save themselves the instant they awaken to their true mind." These eminent teachers pointed directly to our original mind, without depending on skillful means: there is no other teaching than this.

And yet, however direct and effective such teaching may be, we must also be able to say that paradise and Amita Buddha with his forty-eight vows really do exist. Therefore it is taught that one who recites Amita Buddha's name even ten times will attain rebirth in a lotus flower, thus escaping the cycle of birth and death. This teaching has been given by all the Buddhas in the three divisions of time, all bodhisattvas of the ten directions vow to attain such a rebirth, too. The stories of those who have been reborn this way—either in the past or in the present—have been faithfully handed down to us. So it is hoped that no practitioners hold to mistaken views, and simply practice hard.

53

When you hear sutras being chanted—either by your own voice or by other people—you are cultivating affinity for the teachings and practice. It is a Way that leads to a joyful mind and great spiritual merit. This body is no more stable than a bubble: it will soon disappear. But any efforts made for the sake of truth will never die.

Commentary

These words point to truly wise study: It is like one who ingests a priceless diamond; this is something greater than just receiving and holding the seven other most precious gems. Zen Master Yung-ming said, "Even if you hear the Dharma teachings, though you may not necessarily have complete faith in their meaning, nevertheless a seed has been planted that will eventually result in your becoming a buddha. And then even if you study these teachings yet still fail to attain their true meaning; you have nevertheless made enough merit that you cannot fail to be reborn as a human or *deva* [heavenly spirit]."

86

> The sacred radiance of our original nature never darkens.
> It has shined forth since beginningless time.
> Do you wish to enter the gate that leads to this?
> Simply do not give rise to conceptual thinking.

Commentary

When we say, "The sacred radiance of our original nature never darkens," it is in direct reference to the very first line of this text: "There is only one thing, from the very beginning, infinitely bright and mysterious by nature." The verse "It has shined forth since beginningless time" also completes the phrase "It was never born, and it never dies." And the teaching "Simply do not give rise to conceptual thinking" completes the phrase from [section] 4, "You should neither become attached to the names nor make distinctions or understanding." Having a gate implies clearly that there is a way through that both ordinary people and experienced practitioners can enter. For exactly this reason Venerable Shen-hui once said that "true knowledge" is entered "through the mysterious gate of not-knowing," quoting Lao-tzu.

So the entire teaching of this text began with the statement that "It cannot be described, or given a name" and ends here with the exhortation, "Simply do not give rise to conceptual thinking." This cuts off all entangling views in a single phrase: simply don't know.

Our whole text begins and ends by pointing to the nature of knowing, of what is true knowledge. And in between we have cited all kinds of virtues and practices. Intellectual, conceptual, word-based knowledge and knowing are a potent threat to realizing the Buddha's dharma. So this is why we cannot fail to return to this point of "What is true knowledge?" here at the conclusion. And for this same reason, Master Shen-hui, though he practiced with the Sixth Patriarch before the latter established a thriving community on Chogye Mountain, cannot be regarded as a legitimate holder of the Chogye lineage that succeeds to this day. It was precisely his reliance on intellectual views and mere conceptual understanding of the Dharma that cut him off from the Patriarchal lineage.

Gatha

All of this effort, spent
Setting out the teachings in such detail.
And yet wouldn't this, too,
Cause our founder Bodhidharma to laugh out loud?
But is there any other choice?
HO!!!
The bright moon now shining down;
Mountains and rivers are calm and still.
Laughing at this whole enterprise, even at myself,
Also startles heaven and earth!
Ha ha ha ha ha !!

—Translation by Boep Joeng and Hyon Gak

Figure 15. Sculptural Portrait of Bankei (detail)

23

Bankei Yōtaku (1622–1693)

The Ryūmon-ji Sermons (excerpts)

As the new Tokugawa Shogunate took control of Japan at the start of the
seventeenth century, major changes began to take place in many aspects of
Japanese life, including religion. As the century progressed, instead of relying
on Zen Masters as advisors, teachers, and even leaders of trade delegations to
China, the Shoguns began to turn to Neo-Confucian scholars for advice and
appointed them teachers in the major schools and academies. As a result, the
powerful influence that Zen had been exerting on many aspects of Japanese
life, including the arts, began to fade, although it never completely
disappeared.

Faced with less social influence during a time when Japan was becoming
increasingly mercantile, what were Zen Masters to do? Some were determined
to maintain their ties with the governmental and cultural elite; monks
and abbots at major urban monasteries such as Daitoku-ji in Kyoto
utilized activities such as the tea ceremony to interact with high-ranking
administrators, leading samurai, and court nobles. Other Zen Masters
retreated to rural and mountain areas to cultivate their own spiritual lives,
training a few followers who were willing to opt out of the new, rigidly
controlled social order in which the populace was divided into samurai,
farmers, artisans, and merchants.

A third choice for Zen Masters, however, was to reemphasize their
connections with everyday people. Chief among these populists in the
seventeenth century was Bankei Yōtaku, who lived his life completely
according to his own wishes and beliefs. His father died when he was very
young, which may have increased his willfulness; for example, at the age of
eleven he refused to attend calligraphy lessons, although he was later to
become an outstanding Zen calligrapher. In his Confucian schooling, he was
not content to memorize texts like the other students, but he continually
questioned his teachers about the meanings of the phrases. Being told that
Buddhist monks might help him, he first studied Esoteric and then Pure
Land Buddhism, but at the age of sixteen he switched to Rinzai (Chinese:
Lin-chi) Zen.

*After three years of Zen training, Bankei went on pilgrimage for four
years but still did not achieve enlightenment. Being told he could never find
satori outside his own mind, he shut himself up in a small hut, determined
to meditate until he awakened to his self-nature. According to his later
autobiographical writings, he sat until his buttocks festered, and he seems also
to have contracted tuberculosis. One day he spat out a mass of black phlegm,
and as he watched it drip down the wall in front of him, he finally came to
the realization that "all things are perfectly resolved in the unborn."*

*This was the first of several enlightenment experiences, but Bankei's teacher
suggested he visit other Zen Masters for further training and verification.
Hearing of eminent Chinese Zen Masters coming to Nagasaki, in 1651 he
went there to train under Tao Che-yuan (Japanese: Dōshagen, 1559–1662),
with whom he communicated primarily by writing in Chinese, since neither
fluently spoke the other's language. At first, Tao Che-yuan informed him that
although he had penetrated to his inner self, he still needed to clarify the
teachings, but after another awakening experience, he certified Bankei's
enlightenment.*

*Bankei then set out for another period of traveling and study, becoming active
at no fewer than forty temples, finally settling at Ryūmon-ji in Harada. There he
not only taught a large number of monk and nun followers but also reached out
to the general public with a series of well-attended semiannual public meetings.
The record of one of these meetings was kept by one of his disciples, and it shows
how Bankei stressed the direct experience of Zen through what he called "the
Unborn." Avoiding any complex language or concepts, he used everyday
experiences, including some from his own life. His teachings reached thousands
of people directly, and many more through the publication of both his sermons
and his straightforward responses to questions from people from all walks of life.*

The Dharma Talks of Zen Master Bankei

In the third year of Genroku [1690], at the time of the great winter retreat
at the Ryūmon-ji held under Zen master Butchi Kosai Bankei, founder of
the temple, the attendance roster listed 1,683 priests. They came from all
the different sects: from the two Zen schools, Soto and Rinzai, and also from

"The Ryūmon-ji Sermons," from *The Unborn: The Life and Teaching of Zen Master
Bankei, 1622–1693*, translated by Norman Waddell. Translation copyright © 1984
by Norman Waddell. Reprinted by permission of North Point Press, a division of
Farrar, Straus and Giroux LLC.

the Shingon, Tendai, Jodo, Jodo-shin, and Nichiren sects. Masters and novices alike and priests of every kind and rank gathered in a great assembly around the Dharma seat. The master might very well have been taken for the Buddha himself; as the teacher of his age and the master of all people and devas throughout the universe.

When the master came and ascended to the Dharma seat, he spoke the following words to the assembled audience of priests and laity.

I was still a young man when I came to discover the principle of the Unborn and its relation to thought. I began to tell others about it. What we call a "thought" is something that has already fallen one or more removes from the living reality of the Unborn. If you priests would just live in the Unborn, there wouldn't be anything for me to tell you about it, and you wouldn't be here listening to me. But because of the unbornness and marvelous illuminative power inherent in the Buddha-mind, it readily reflects all things that come along and transforms itself into them, thus turning the Buddha-mind into thought. I'm going to tell those in the lay audience all about this now. As I do, I want the priests to listen along too.

Not a single one of you people at this meeting is unenlightened. Right now, you're all sitting before me as Buddhas. Each of you received the Buddha-mind from your mothers when you were born, and nothing else. This inherited Buddha-mind is beyond any doubt unborn, with a marvelously bright illuminative wisdom. In the Unborn, all things are perfectly resolved. I can give you proof that they are. While you're facing me listening to me speak like this, if a crow cawed, or a sparrow chirped, or some other sound occurred somewhere behind you, you would have no difficulty knowing it was a crow or a sparrow, or whatever, even without giving a thought to listening to it, because you were listening by means of the Unborn.

Figure 16. Bankei Yōtaku, *Fusho (Unborn)*

If anyone confirms that this unborn, illuminative wisdom is in fact the Buddha-mind and straight away lives, as he is, in the Buddha-mind, he becomes at that moment a living Tathagata, and he remains one for infinite kalpas in the future. Once he has confirmed it, he lives from then on in the mind of all the Buddhas, which is the reason the sect I belong to has sometimes been called the "Buddha-mind" sect.

While you face this way listening to me now, if a sparrow chirps behind you, you don't mistake it for a crow; you don't mistake the sound of a bell for that of a drum, or hear a man's voice and take it for a woman's, or take an adult's voice for a child's. You hear and distinguish those different sounds, without making a single mistake, by virtue of the marvelous working of illuminative wisdom. This is the proof that the Buddha-mind is unborn and wonderfully illuminating.

None of you could say that you heard the sounds because you had made up your minds to hear them beforehand. If you did, you wouldn't be telling the truth. All of you are looking this way intent upon hearing me. You're concentrating singlemindedly on listening. There's no thought in any of your minds to hear the sounds or noises that might occur behind you. You are able to hear and distinguish sounds when they do occur without consciously intending to hear them because you're listening by means of the unborn Buddha-mind.

When people are firmly convinced that the Buddha-mind is unborn and wonderfully illuminating and live in it, they're living Buddhas and living Tathagatas from then on. "Buddha," too, is just a name, arising after the fact. It's only the skin and shell. When you say "Buddha," you're already two or more removes from the place of the Unborn. A man of the Unborn is one who dwells at the source of all the Buddhas. The Unborn is the origin of all and the beginning of all. There is no source apart from the Unborn and no beginning that is before the Unborn. So being unborn means dwelling at the very source of all Buddhas.

If you live in the Unborn, then, there's no longer any need to speak about "non-extinction," or "undying." It would be a waste of time. So I always talk about the "Unborn," never about the "Undying." There can be no death for what was never born, so if it is unborn, it is obviously undying. There's no need to say it, is there? You can find the expression "unborn, undying" here and there in the Buddha's sutras and in the recorded sayings of the Zen masters. But there was never, until now, any proof or confirmation given of the Unborn. People have just known the words "unborn, undying." No one before has ever really understood this matter of the Unborn by confirming it to the marrow of his bones. I first realized how everything is perfectly resolved by means of the Unborn when I was twenty-six years old, and since then, for the past forty years, I've been telling people about nothing else. I'm the first one to do this by giving the actual proof of the Unborn, by showing that the Unborn is the Buddha-mind and that it is always without a shadow of doubt marvelously bright and illuminating. None of the priests or other people here at this meeting today can say that they have heard of anyone who has done this before me. I'm the first.

When you are unborn, you're at the source of all things. The unborn Buddha-mind is where the Buddhas of the past all attained their realization and where future Buddhas will all attain theirs. Although we're now in the Dharma's latter days, if a single person lives in the Unborn, the right Dharma flourishes in the world. There's no doubt about it.

Upon confirming yourself in the Unborn, you acquire the ability to see from the place of that confirmation straight into the hearts of others. The name the Zen school is sometimes given, the "Clear-eyed" sect, stems from this. There, at that place of confirmation, the Buddha's Dharma is fully achieved. Once the eye that can see others as they are opens in you, you can regard yourself as having fully achieved the Dharma, because wherever you are becomes a place of total realization. When you reach that place, no matter who you are, you are the true successor to my Dharma.

A certain priest has said, "All you do is repeat the same things day after day. You ought to give your listeners a change. Their minds will be more receptive if you throw in some stories about the Zen masters of the past."

Dull-witted as I am, I think if I put my mind to it, I could probably remember a couple of anecdotes to tell people. But that would be like feeding them poison. I don't want to do that.

I never cite the Buddha's words or the words of Zen patriarchs when I teach. All I do is comment directly on people themselves. That takes care of everything. I don't have to quote other people. So you won't find me saying anything about either the "Buddha Dharma" or the "Zen Dharma." I don't have to, when I can clear everything up for you by commenting directly on you and your personal concerns right here and now. I've no reason to preach about "Buddhism" or "Zen." Despite the fact that you arrived in this world with nothing but an unborn Buddha-mind, your partiality for yourselves now makes you want to have things move in your own way. You lose your temper, become contentious, and then you think, "I haven't lost my temper. That fellow won't listen to me. By being so unreasonable he has made me lose it." And so you fix belligerently on his words and end up transforming the valuable Buddha-mind into a fighting spirit. By stewing over this unimportant matter, making the thoughts churn over and over in your mind, you may finally get your way, but then you fail in your ignorance to realize that it was meaningless for you to concern yourself over such a matter. As ignorance causes you to become an animal, what you've done is to leave the vitally important Buddha-mind and make yourself inwardly a first-class animal.

You're all intelligent people here. It's only your ignorance of the Buddha-mind that makes you go on transforming it into a hungry ghost, fighting spirit, or animal. You turn it into this and into that, into all manner of things, and then you become those things. Once you have, once you've become an animal, for example, then even when the truth is spoken to you, it doesn't get through to you. Or, supposing it does; since you didn't retain it even when you were a human being, you certainly won't have the intelligence as an animal to keep it in your mind. So you go from one hell or animal existence to the next or spend countless lifetimes as a hungry ghost. You pass through lives and existences one after another in this way in constant darkness, transmigrating endlessly and suffering untold torment, for thousands of lives and through endless kalpas of time, and during it all, you have no opportunity whatever to rid yourself of the burden of your evil karma. This happens to everyone when, through a single thought, they let the Buddha-mind slip away from them. So you can see that it's a very serious matter indeed.

Therefore, you must thoroughly understand about not transforming the Buddha-mind into other things. As I told you before, not a single one of you in attendance here today is an unenlightened person. You're a gathering of unborn Buddha-minds. If anyone thinks, "No, I'm not. I'm not enlightened," I want him to step forward. Tell me: What is it that makes a person unenlightened?

In fact, there are no unenlightened people here. Nonetheless, when you get up and begin to file out of the hall, you might bump into someone in front of you as you cross over the threshold. Or someone behind you might run into you and knock you down. When you go home, your husband, son, daughter-in-law, servant, or someone else may say or do something that displeases you. If something like that happens, and you grasp onto it and begin to fret over it, sending the blood to your head, raising up your horns, and falling into illusion because of your self-partiality, the Buddha-mind turns willy-nilly into a fighting spirit. Until you transform it, you live just as you are in the unborn Buddha-mind; you aren't deluded or unenlightened. The moment you do turn it into something else, you become an ignorant, deluded person. All illusions work the same way. By getting upset and favoring yourself you turn your Buddha-mind into a fighting spirit—and fall into a deluded existence of your own making.

So whatever anyone else may do or say, whatever happens, leave things as they are. Don't worry yourself over them and don't side with yourself. Just stay as you are, right in the Buddha-mind, and don't change it into anything else. If you do that, illusions don't occur and you live constantly in the un-born mind. You're a living, breathing, firmly established Buddha. Don't you see? You have an incalculable treasure right at hand.

You must understand about the marvelous illumination of the unborn mind. Once you have been to a certain place, you don't forget it, even after years have passed. It's easy for you to remember it. You don't always have to be keeping it consciously in mind. If someone else goes to that same place, the two of you will be able to talk about it, though you may be miles distant from it at the time. No matter where you are when you talk about it, it makes no difference; your accounts will still be in agreement.

While you're walking down a road, if you happen to encounter a crowd of people approaching from the opposite direction, none of you gives a thought to avoiding the others, yet you don't run into one another. You aren't pushed down or walked over. You thread your way through them by weav-ing this way and that, dodging and passing on, making no conscious deci-sions in this, yet you're able to continue along unhampered just the same. Now in the same way, the marvelous illumination of the unborn Buddha-mind deals perfectly with every possible situation.

Suppose that the idea to step aside and make way for the others should arise spontaneously in your mind before you actually moved aside—that too would be due to the working of the Buddha-mind's illuminative wisdom. You may step aside to the right or to the left because you have made up your mind to do that, but still, the movement of your feet, one step after another, doesn't occur because you think to do it. When you're walking along natu-rally, you're walking in the harmony of the Unborn. Your self-partiality is at the root of all your illusions. There aren't any illusions when you don't have this preference for yourself. If the men sitting next to you start quarreling, it may be easy for you to tell which of the disputants is in the right and which in the wrong, because you're not involved yourself. You are a bystander, so you can keep a cool head. But what if you do have a part in it? Then you take your own side and oppose the other fellow. As you fight with one an-other, you transform your Buddha-minds into fighting spirits.

Or again, because of the Buddha-mind's wonderful illuminative wisdom, such things as you have done and experienced in the past cannot fail to be reflected in it. If you fix onto those images as they reflect, you are unwit-tingly creating illusion. The thoughts do not already exist at the place where those images are reflecting; they are caused by your past experiences and occur when things you have seen and heard in the past are reflected on the Buddha-mind. But thoughts originally have no real substance. So if they are reflected, you should just let them be reflected, and let them arise when they arise. Don't have any thought to stop them. If they stop, let them stop. Don't pay any attention to them. Leave them alone. Then illusions won't appear. And since there are no illusions when you don't take note of the reflecting images, while the images may be reflected in the mind, it's just the same as if they weren't. A thousand thoughts may arise, yet it's just as though they hadn't. They won't give you a bit of trouble. You won't have any thoughts to clear from your mind—not a single thought to cut off.

Bankei spoke to the assembly on the first day of the twelfth month: At my temples, every moment, day and night, is the fixed and appointed time for practice. I don't do as they do elsewhere and tell you that the period of practice begins at such and such a time. Everyone doesn't start dashing around making a great fuss.

There was once a monk in my temple who had been dozing off. Another monk saw him and really laid into him with a stick. I reprimanded him: "Why hit him when he's enjoying a pleasant nap? Do you think he leaves the Buddha-mind and goes somewhere else when he sleeps?" Now I don't urge people to sleep around here. But once they are asleep, you're making a serious mistake if you hit them. Nothing like that is allowed to happen here any more. We don't go out of our way to urge people to take naps. Yet neither do we hit them nor scold them for it if they do. We don't scold them or praise them for sleeping, any more than we scold them or praise them for not sleeping.

If you stay awake, you stay awake. If you sleep, you sleep. When you sleep, you sleep in the same Buddha-mind you were awake in. When you're awake, you're awake in the same Buddha-mind you were sleeping in. You sleep in the Buddha-mind while you sleep and are up and about in the Buddha-mind while you're up and about. That way, you always stay in the Buddha-mind. You're never apart from it for an instant.

You're wrong if you think that people become something different when they fall asleep. If they were in the Buddha-mind only during their waking hours and changed into something else when they went to sleep, that wouldn't be the true Buddhist Dharma. It would mean that they were always in a state of transmigration.

All of you people here are working hard to become Buddhas. That's the reason you want to scold and beat the ones who fall asleep. But it isn't right. You each received one thing from your mother when you were born—the unborn Buddha-mind. Nothing else. Rather than try to become a Buddha, when you just stay constantly in the unborn mind, sleeping in it when you sleep, up and about in it when you're awake, you're a living Buddha in your everyday life—at all times. There's not a moment when you're not a Buddha. Since you're always a Buddha, there's no other Buddha in addition to that for you to become. Instead of trying to become a Buddha, then, a much easier and shorter way is just to *be* a Buddha.

The unborn Buddha-mind deals freely and spontaneously with anything that presents itself to it. But if something should happen to make you change the Buddha-mind into thought, then you run into trouble and lose that freedom. Let me give you an example. Suppose a woman is engaged in sewing something. A friend enters the room and begins speaking to her. As long as she listens to her friend and sews in the Unborn, she has no trouble doing both. But if she gives her attention to her friend's words and a thought arises in her mind as she thinks about what to reply, her hands stop sewing; if she turns her attention to her sewing and thinks about that, she fails to catch everything her friend is saying, and the conversation does not proceed smoothly. In either case, her Buddha-mind has slipped from the place of the Unborn. She has transformed it into thought. As her thoughts fix upon one thing, they're blank to all others, depriving her mind of its freedom.

What I call the "Unborn" is the Buddha-mind. This Buddha-mind is unborn, with a marvelous virtue of illuminative wisdom. In the Unborn all things fall right into place and remain in perfect harmony. When everything you do is done according to the Unborn, the eye that sees others as they are opens in you, and you know in your own mind that everyone you see is a living Buddha. That's the reason why once you live in the Unborn you never fall back into your old ways, just like that old woman of Sanuki. Once you know the great worth of the Buddha-mind, you can't leave it for illusion again. But as long as you're ignorant of its great value, you will continue to create illusions for yourself in whatever you do, insignificant things included, and you will live as an unenlightened person.

I notice that there are many ladies here today. Compared with men, you women tend to get excited rather easily. Even unimportant things are enough to upset you and turn your unborn Buddha-mind into a fighting spirit, ignorant animal, or craving hungry ghost, submerging you in illusion and causing you to transmigrate into many different forms. You should pay particular attention to everything I say.

In the houses with domestic help, servant boys and girls are employed in large numbers. Some among them are bound to be careless with things. Occasionally, treasured dishes or other articles are broken. Perhaps it is something not even worth mentioning, but in any case, you let the blood rush to your head. You lash out and scold the offender angrily. But no matter how prized the dish or teabowl may have been, it wasn't broken deliberately. It was an accident, and now there's nothing that can be done about it. Just the same, you fly into a rage and let the defilements from your self-centered passions transform the precious Buddha-mind given when you were born into a fighting spirit. You can always buy another teacup. Tea tastes the same any-way, whether from an ordinary Imari teacup or from a priceless Korean teabowl. You can drink it just as well from either one. But a temper, once lost, can't easily be undone.

Now if you really understand what I've been saying about the teabowl, you should know, without my having to tell you about them one by one, that it's the same for everything else. Whatever happens; just don't turn your Buddha-minds into fighting spirits by worrying over it. Don't change them into ignorance or let your self-centered thoughts turn them into hungry ghosts. Then you'll automatically be living in the unborn Buddha-mind. You won't have any choice in the matter. Once you know the Buddha-mind's great value, there's no way you can avoid dwelling in the Unborn even if you don't want to. I want to make you know how vitally important it is for you not to change your Buddha-minds into the three poisons, so you will have to listen to me attentively and then be very careful that you don't transform your Buddha-minds into something else.

Telling people about the Unborn like this, they sometimes assume it's a teach-ing I came up with all by myself. But that's mistaken. If you look through the sutras and other Buddhist records, you'll find that the Unborn was preached in the past in various ways. The patriarchs of the Zen school mentioned it. It was heard from the golden mouth of Shakyamuni himself. Even children have known of it. But it's always the words "unborn, undying" which you find. There's never any verification given to show just what this "unborn, undying" really is. I am the first to teach people by giving them proof of the Unborn. It's understandable, then, that those who don't know this should make the mistake of thinking that I thought the words up myself.

As a young man striving to realize the Buddha-mind, I tried my hand at kōan study. I had interviews with Zen teachers and engaged in Zen dialogues with them in Chinese. I worked very diligently at it. But it is better for us Japa-nese to use the common language we speak every day when we ask questions having to do with the Way. Since we aren't very good at Chinese, when we have to use it for such questions and answers, we have trouble expressing ourselves fully and saying just what we want to. But if we use our own every-day language and speak just the way we normally do, there's nothing at all we can't ask about. Instead of straining around worrying about how to ask something in Chinese, we should ask our questions in a language we can use easily, free of the burdens and constraints of a foreign language. Of course, if we couldn't attain realization unless we used Chinese, I would be the first to say use it. But the fact is that we can ask about the Way, and attain it, without any trouble at all by using our own language. It's wrong for us to have to ask questions in a language we have difficulty using. You must remember this, and whenever you have something to ask me, feel no hesitation. I don't care what it is, ask it just the way you want to, in your own words, and I'll help you clear it up. Since you're able to resolve things in that way, what could be as useful to you and convenient to use as the ordinary Japanese you speak every day?

People generally have the wrong idea about living and dying at will. They think it means that someone decides on one day that he will die on the next, or that he predicts the day and month in the following year when he is to die and then does indeed die a natural death on that date, or they think it means the ability to extend one's lifetime so many days or months. Such are the notions many people have. I myself won't say that there aren't examples of living and dying at will; obviously, in a sense, such people do live and die very much at will. But since their ability is the result of training and practice, it's sometimes seen even in those whose religious eye has not yet been opened. Even some nonreligious people may know when they're going to die. But in such cases, since their religious eye is not opened, they don't have the slightest idea of its real meaning.

A man of the Unborn is beyond living and dying [Samsara]. What I mean by that is: Someone who is unborn is also undying, so he is beyond both birth and death. What I call living and dying at will is when someone dies without being troubled by life and death, the continuous succession of birth-death, birth-death that is samsaric existence. Moreover, living and dying is taking place at every instant throughout the twenty-four hours of the day; dying does not occur only once in your life when you cease breathing. When you're living without being concerned about life or death, you're always living in such a way that whenever death does come, even right now, at this moment, it's no great matter. Now that's what I call "living and dying at will." It means living confirmed in your unborn Buddha-mind. To make a declaration that you'll die at a certain time on a certain fixed day and to have that on your mind—can you imagine how confining and unfree that would be?

Here, I always urge people simply to live in the unborn Buddha-mind. I don't try to make anyone do anything else. We haven't any special rules. But since everyone got together and decided that they wanted to spend six hours each day (for a period of twelve sticks of incense) doing zazen, I let them do as they wish. That amount of time has been set aside for zazen. But the unborn Buddha-mind has no connection with those sticks of incense. It's just being at home in the Buddha-mind, not straying into illusion, and not seeking enlightenment beyond that. Just sit in the Buddha-mind, stand in the Buddha-mind, sleep in the Buddha-mind, awake in the Buddha-mind, do everything in the Buddha-mind—then, you'll be functioning as a living Buddha in all that you do in your daily life. There's nothing further.

Now, in zazen, it's a matter of the Buddha-mind sitting at rest. It's the Buddha-mind doing continuous zazen. Zazen isn't limited to the time you sit. That's why, around here, if people have something to do while they're sitting, they're free to get up and do it. It's up to them, whatever they've a mind to do. Some of them will do *kinhin* [walking meditation] for one stick of incense. But they can't just continue walking, so then they sit down and for another stick of incense they do zazen. They can't be sleeping all the time so they get up. They can't talk constantly, so they stop talking and do some zazen. They aren't bound by any set rules.

My religion has nothing to do with either "self-power" or "other-power." It's beyond them both. My proof is this: While you face me and listen to me say this, if somewhere a sparrow chirps, or a crow caws, or a manor woman says something, or the wind rustles the leaves, though you sit there without any intent to listen, you will hear and distinguish each sound. Because it isn't your self that's doing the listening, it isn't self-power. On the other hand, it wouldn't do you any good if you had someone else hear and distinguish the sounds for you. So it isn't other-power. That's the reason why I can say that my teaching has nothing to do with self-power or other-power and is beyond them both. When you're listening like this in the Unborn, each and every sound is heard as it occurs. And all other things as well, in just the same way, are perfectly well taken care of in the Unborn. Anyone who lives his life in the Unborn, whoever he may be, will find this to be true. No one who lives in the Unborn is concerned with self or other. He's beyond them both.

I went around the country wasting time and energy on ascetic practices, all because I wanted to discover my Buddha-mind. I ended up bringing on serious illness instead. I've been confined to sickbeds for long periods, so I've learned all about sickness at first hand. Everyone who is born into this world and receives bodily form is therefore bound to experience illness. But if you become confirmed in the unborn Buddha-mind, you aren't troubled by the suffering that normally accompanies illness. Illness and suffering are differentiated: The illness is illness, the suffering is suffering. Now the way it works is this. Being originally unborn, the Buddha-mind has no concern with either pain or joy. Since being unborn means that it is completely detached from thought, and since it is through the arising of thoughts that you experience both pain and joy, so long as the Buddha-mind remains as it is in its original unbornness, unworried by and unattached to the illness, it doesn't experience suffering. But if a thought arises from the ground of the Unborn and you start to worry about your illness, you create suffering for yourself; you change your Buddha-mind into suffering. It can't be helped. The sufferings of hell itself are no different.

Now suppose someone is suffering because he worries anxiously about his illness. The illness may at some point begin to improve, yet because he worries, over and above the original illness, about the medicine being wrong or about the physician being inept, he changes the Buddha-mind into various painful thoughts, until the disease in his mind becomes a more serious affliction than the original illness. While the turmoil of thoughts crowd through his mind as he attempts to escape from his illness, the original illness may gradually continue to improve and he may regain his health. But now he suffers because he's plagued by the troubled thoughts churning in his mind, which have grown and intensified in the course of his illness and recovery.

But even though I say this, if someone who is down with an illness or undergoing any other kind of suffering were to say that he doesn't suffer, he would have to be called a liar. He's ignorant of the way in which the marvelous wisdom of the Buddha-mind works. If he pledged on his honor that he was positively not suffering, it would only mean that his suffering was taking the form of not suffering. There is no way such a person could be free from suffering. Since the working of illuminative wisdom is intrinsic to the Buddha-mind, by which it knows and perfectly differentiates not only suffering but all other things as well, when the sickness comes, the Buddha-mind remains free of any involvement or concern with pain or suffering. But, even then, since you will inevitably think about your sickness, it's best at such times to give yourself up to the sickness, and to moan when there is pain. Then, all the time, both when you're sick and when you're well, you'll be living in the unborn Buddha-mind. But you ought to be aware that when thought becomes involved in your suffering, the Buddha-mind is changed into the thought of sickness or the thought of suffering, quite apart from the sickness or suffering itself, and you will suffer because of that.

The unborn Buddha-mind is originally free from all thought, so long as a person is ignorant of the Buddha-mind's unbornness and suffers because he has changed it into thought, no matter how loudly he may deny his suffering, his denial—the notion that "I'm not suffering"—is only a determination he has created out of thought. He couldn't possibly be detached from suffering. He may think that he's not suffering, but inasmuch as he hasn't confirmed himself in the unborn Buddha-mind that is detached from birth and death, that very birth and death is the cause of his suffering.

The working of your bright, illuminating Buddha-mind is as different from an ordinary mirror as a cloud is from mud. Kyoto, Osaka, Edo, Sendai, Nagasaki, or wherever, once you've been and seen a place, even after many years pass and you're at an entirely different location, if someone else who has been there comes and talks to you about it, your conversation will go along in perfect agreement. Moreover, while a mirror is able only to illuminate and show objects a yard or two away at most, the working of the Buddha-mind's resplendent clarity is such that you can see and recognize a man over a block away; you can see a towering mountain peak fifty leagues distant, even behind rows of hills, and your Buddha-mind can tell that it's Mount Fuji, or Mount Kongo, or some other mountain. So while the Buddha-mind is often compared to a mirror, how vastly different its brightness really is! Even the sun and moon light up only the earth and the heavens. The marvelous brightness of the Buddha-mind, by means of words, is able to enlighten people and deliver them from their illusions one by one. And when someone hears these words, and understands and affirms them, he will know for himself that the Buddha-mind's wonderful brightness surpasses even the brightness of the sun and moon. What an incalculable treasure your Buddha-mind is!

A monk said to Bankei: I was born with a short temper. It's always flaring up. My master has remonstrated with me time and again, but that hasn't done any good. I know I should do something about it, but as I was born with a bad temper, I'm unable to rid myself of it no matter how hard I try. Is there anything I can do to correct it? This time, I'm hoping that with your teaching, I'll be able to cure myself. Then, when I go back home, I'd be able to face my master again, and of course I will benefit by it for the rest of my life. Please, tell me what to do.

Bankei: That's an interesting inheritance you have. Is your temper here now? Bring it out here. I'll cure it for you.

Monk: I'm not angry now. My temper comes on unexpectedly, when something provokes me.

Bankei: You weren't born with it then. You create it yourself, when some pretext or other happens to appear. Where would your temper be at such times if you didn't cause it? You work yourself into a temper because of your partiality for yourself, opposing others in order to have your own way. Then you unjustly accuse your parents of having burdened you with a short temper. What an extremely unfilial son you are!

Each person receives the Buddha-mind from his parents when he's born. His illusion is something he produces all alone, by being partial to himself. It's foolish to think that it's inherent. When you don't produce your temper, where is it? All illusions are the same; as long as you don't produce them, they cease to exist. That's what everyone fails to realize. There they are, creating from their own selfish desires and deluded mental habits something that isn't inherent, but thinking it is. On account of this, they're unable to avoid being deluded in whatever they do.

You certainly must cherish your illusions dearly, for you to change the Buddha-mind into them just so you can be deluded. If you only knew the great value of the Buddha-mind, there's no way you could ever be deluded again, not even if you wanted to be. Fix this clearly in your head: When you are not deluded, you are a Buddha, and that means you are enlightened. There is no other way for you to become a Buddha. So draw close and listen carefully and be sure that you understand what I say.

You create your outbursts of temper when the organs of your six senses [vision, hearing, smell, taste, touch, and faculty of mind] are stimulated by some external condition and incite you to oppose other people because you desire to assert your own preciously held ideas. When you have no attachment to self, there are no illusions. Have that perfectly clear.

All your parents gave you when you were born was a Buddha-mind. Nothing else. What have you done with it? From the time you were a tiny baby you've watched and listened to people losing their tempers around you. You've been schooled in this, until you too have become habituated to irascibility. So now you indulge in frequent fits of anger. But it's foolish to think that's inherent. Right now, if you realize you've been mistaken and don't allow your temper to arise any more, you'll have no temper to worry about. Instead of trying to correct it, don't produce it in the first place. That's the quickest way, don't you agree? Trying to do something about it after it occurs is very troublesome and futile besides. Don't get angry to begin with, then there's no need to cure anything. There's nothing left to cure.

Once you've realized this and you stop creating that temper of yours, you'll find that you won't have any other illusions either, not even if you want to, for you'll be living constantly in the unborn Buddha-mind. There is nothing else.

Since everything is in perfect harmony if you live and work in the unborn mind of the Buddhas, my school is also known as the "Buddha-mind" sect. Live in the Buddha-mind and you're a living Buddha from that moment on. This is the priceless thing "directly pointed to." I want you to trust completely in what I've been telling you. Do just as I've said. To start with, try to stay in the Unborn for thirty days. Once you've accustomed yourself to that, then you'll find it's impossible to live apart from the Unborn. It will come naturally to you then, and even if you don't want to, even if you grow tired of it, there'll still be no way you can avoid living in the Unborn and doing an admirable job of it too. Everything you do will be according to the Unborn. You'll be a living Buddha.

You should all listen to my words as if you were newly born this very day. If something's on your mind, if you have any preconception, you can't really take in what I say. But if you listen as if you were a newborn child, it'll be like hearing me for the first time. Since then there's nothing in your mind, you can take it right in, grasp it even from a single word, and fully realize the Buddha's Dharma.

A laywoman from Izumo, who had come to the retreat because she had heard of Bankei and his teaching, asked: According to what you say, all we have to do is simply remain effortlessly in the Buddha-mind. Don't you think that teaching is too lightweight?

Bankei: Lightweight? You set no store by the Buddha-mind. You get angry and turn it into a fighting spirit. You give vent to selfish desires and change it into a hungry ghost or do something foolish and convert it into an animal. You deludedly turn the Buddha-mind into all sorts of different things—that's lightweight, not my teaching. Nothing is of more gravity, and nothing more praiseworthy, than living in the Buddha-mind. So you may think when I tell you to live in the Buddha-mind that it is lightweight, but believe me, it's just because it has such weight that you are unable to do it.

This, however, might give you the idea that living in the Buddha-mind is a very difficult business. But isn't it true that if you listen carefully to my teaching, understand it well, and live in the Buddha-mind, then, simply and easily, without doing any hard work, you're a living Buddha this very day?

You decided after hearing what I said that dwelling effortlessly in the Buddha-mind was an easy matter. But in fact it's not easy, so you go on transforming it into a fighting spirit, a hungry ghost, or animal. You get angry, even over trifles. When you do, you create the cause of rebirth as a fighting spirit. So though you may not be aware of it, you're spending your existence as a human being creating a fighting spirit of the first order. And sure enough, if you work earnestly at it, you'll not only be a fighting spirit during your lifetime, you'll fall into such an existence after you die as well, have no doubt about it. On account of self-interest, you toil away to turn the Buddha-mind into greed and desire. Since that's the cause of rebirth as a denizen of the realm of hungry ghosts, you're unknowingly paving the *way* for rebirth into that realm. You're readying yourself for a postmortem fall into a hungry ghost existence. It's a foregone conclusion; you'll surely end up there.

Owing to selfish thoughts and aims, you dwell on one thought after another, fretting senselessly over things that can get you nowhere. Continuing on like that, unable to stop, you turn the Buddha-mind into ignorance. Ignorance causes you to be reborn as an animal. It's clear even now while you're alive and busily creating the cause of such a wretched fate that when you die you'll enter that existence.

I see people unaware of this, dedicating their lives to carefully fashioning the very causes of their rebirth into the three evil realms. It's pitiful. They're reserving seats for the passage. But when you don't change your Buddha-mind into a fighting spirit, hungry ghost, or animal, you can't avoid dwelling naturally in the Buddha-mind. It's obvious, isn't it?

The laywoman: Yes, of course. It's true! I have no words to thank you.

A monk: To live in the Buddha-mind as you say would mean to live in a state of unknowing, to be insensible.

Bankei: What if someone came up behind you without your knowing it and suddenly poked you in the back with a gimlet? Would you feel pain?

The monk: Of course I would.

Bankei: Then you're not unknowing or insensible, are you? If you were, it wouldn't hurt. You feel it because you're not insensible. You never have been. Have confidence in me. Live in the unborn Buddha-mind.

A monk: You tell people to dwell in the Unborn, but it seems to me that would mean remaining totally indifferent to things.

Bankei: While you face me there listening innocently to what I say, suppose someone should come up behind you and touch a firebrand to your back. Would it feel hot?

The monk: Of course it would.

Bankei: In that case, you aren't indifferent. How could someone who feels heat be indifferent? You feel it because you aren't indifferent. You have no difficulty telling what is hot and what is cold, without having to give rise to a thought to make such a distinction. The very fact that you ask that question about being indifferent or not shows that you're not indifferent. You have no trouble telling by yourself whether you're indifferent or not—that's because you're not indifferent. So you see, the Buddha-mind with its illuminating wisdom is capable of discriminating things with a miraculous efficiency. It is anything but indifferent. How could any human being, who is able to think, be indifferent? A man who was really indifferent wouldn't be engaged in thinking. I can assure you that you are not indifferent and that you never have been.

Another monk (who had been listening to this): If that's true, what about all the old kōans? Are they useless and unnecessary?

Bankei: When worthy Zen masters of the past dealt with those who came to them, every word and every movement was appropriate to the moment. It was a matter of responding to their students and their questions face to face. They had no other purpose in mind. Now there's no way for me to tell you whether that was necessary, or helpful, or not. If everyone just stays in the Buddha-mind, that's all they have to do—that takes care of everything. Why do you want to go and think up other things to do? There's no need to. Just dwell in the Unborn. You're eager to make this extra work for yourself—but all you're doing is creating illusion. Stop doing that. Stay in the Unborn. The Unborn and its marvelous illumination are perfectly realized in the Buddha-mind.

During the retreat, a large number of women from the provinces of Tamba, Tango, Izumo, and Mino came to see Bankei. Some were mourning the death of a parent. Others were grieving inconsolably for the loss of a child. They came hoping to lessen the pain of their bereavement by meeting with Bankei. He spoke to them as follows:

The sorrow of a parent who loses his child, of a child who loses his father or his mother, is the same the world over. The karma that binds together parent and child is deep. When death takes one from the other, sorrow is only natural. And yet the dead won't come back no matter how great your sorrow may be. Should you spend your lives in unbroken sadness grieving foolishly over something you can't possibly change? Have you ever heard of anyone who was successful in restoring the dead to life because of the intensity of his sorrow? Of course you haven't. Since there's no way for the dead to return, don't give any more time to grief. Cease it right now. Use the time instead to do some zazen, recite a sutra, or offer some flowers and incense for them. That will be a real demonstration of your filial devotion or parental love.

—Translation by Norman Waddell

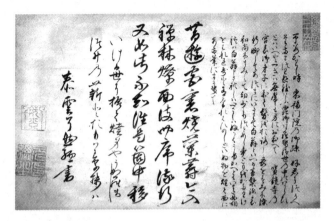

Figure 17. Ryōnen Gensō (1646–1711), *Autobiographical Poems*

Ryōnen was one of the outstanding female Zen Masters of the seventeenth century. She first trained in the women's monastery Hōkyō-ji but was stymied in her attempt to study further with a male Master of the Ōbaku (Chinese: Huang-po) sect in Japan. She tells her own story in this calligraphy, with a prose introduction and then poems in Chinese and Japanese. Haku-ō was so impressed with her dedication that he allowed her into his temple, of which she later became the abbot.

When I was young I served Yoshino-kimi, the granddaughter of the Empress Tofukumon-in, who was a disciple of the imperial temple Hōkyō-ji. Recently she passed away; although I know that is the law of nature, the transience of the world struck me deeply and I became a nun. I cut my hair, dyed my robes black, and went on pilgrimage to Edo [Tokyo]. There I had an audience with the monk Haku-ō of the Ōbaku sect. I recounted to him such things as my deep devotion to Buddhism since childhood, but Haku-ō replied that although he could see my sincere intentions, I could not escape my womanly appearance. Therefore I heated up an iron and held it against my face, and then wrote as my brush led me:

> Formerly to amuse myself at court I would burn orchid incense;
> Now to enter the Zen life I burn my own face.
> The four seasons pass by like this,
> But who am I amidst the change?

> In this living world
> the body I give up and burn
> would be wretched
> if I thought of myself
> as anything but firewood.

Figure 18. Hakuin Ekaku, *Self-Portrait* (detail)

24

Hakuin Ekaku (1684–1786)

Autobiographical Writings (excerpts)

and *Song of Meditation* (complete)

Widely regarded as the most important Zen Master of the past five hundred years, Hakuin revived the Japanese Rinzai (Chinese: Lin-chi) tradition in two ways. First, he taught a large number of monk followers through strict training and deep insight, and second, he reached out to people at all levels of society through sermons, letters, commentaries, poems, songs, paintings, and calligraphy. Examples of Hakuin's brushwork are scattered through this sourcebook; they display his ability to relate to both Zen and non-Zen audiences with his teachings, which often contain a sprinkling of humor.

For his direct followers, Hakuin was adamant that they not cling to anything, including famous Buddhist texts. For example, he wrote a commentary on the Heart Sutra *that seems anything but respectful. Regarding the lines "form is emptiness, emptiness is form," Hakuin wrote, "Rubbish! A useless collection of junk. Don't be trying to teach apes to climb trees. These goods have been gathering dust on the shelves for two thousand years." Similarly, for "form is nothing but emptiness, emptiness is nothing but form," he wrote, "A nice hot kettle of stew. He ruins it by dropping a couple of rat turds in. It's no good pushing delicacies at a man with a full belly" (trans. Norman Waddell,* Zen Words for the Heart). *Such commentary on this revered text may seem strange, but as Lin-chi would say, if you meet the* Heart Sutra, *kill the* Heart Sutra. *It is also worth bearing in mind that in some modes of Zen discourse, invective can constitute high praise.*

Hakuin respected all forms of Buddhism, and for followers of the Pure Land tradition he often wrote out the mantra namu amida butsu *("I entrust myself to Amida Buddha") as large-scale calligraphy. However, he did not want Zen pupils pursuing outer-directed practices and insisted that they focus on delving deep into themselves to discover their own Buddha-nature. Quoting another monk that "Adding Pure Land to Zen is like fixing wings on a tiger," he insisted that Zen should not borrow teachings from other schools: "Once you*

have awakened, your own mind is Buddha." According to his many significant
followers, he was rigorous in his training methods, which were to transform the
Rinzai tradition in succeeding generations through the use of a developed series
of kōans.

In teaching monks and especially his lay followers, Hakuin often used his
own life as an example, and his autobiographical writings follow the traditions
of Hui-neng and Bankei in providing a direct and personal record of Zen
experience. Here is the story of his youth and first enlightenment from his
Oretegama, *a title that refers to Hakuin's favorite tea kettle.*

Autobiographical Writings

When I was seven or eight years old my mother took me to a temple for
the first time and we listened to a sermon on the hells as described in the
Mo-ho chih-kuan. The priest dwelt eloquently on the torments of the Hells
of Wailing, Searing Heat, Incessant Suffering, and the Red Lotus. So vivid
was the priest's description that it sent shivers down the spines of both monks
and laymen and made their hair stand on end in terror. Returning home, I
took stock of the deeds of my short life and felt that there was but little hope
for me. I did not know which way to turn and I was gooseflesh all over. In
secret I took up the chapter on Kannon from the *Lotus Sutra* and the *dharani* on Great Compassion and recited them day and night.

One day when I was taking a bath with my mother, she asked that the
water be made hotter and had the maid add wood to the fire. Gradually my
skin began to prickle with the heat and the iron bath-cauldron began to rum-
ble. Suddenly I recalled the descriptions of the hells that I had heard and I
let out a cry of terror that resounded through the neighborhood.

From this time on I determined to myself that I would leave home to become a monk. To this my parents would not consent, yet I went constantly
to the temple to recite the sutras and to study the works of Confucianism.
At fifteen I left home to become a monk and at that time I vowed to myself:
"Even if I should die I will not cease my efforts to gain the power of one
whom fire will not burn and water will not drown." Day and night I recited
the sutras and made obeisance to the Buddhas, but I noticed that when I

From *The Zen Master Hakuin: Selected Writings,* translated by Philip B. Yampolsky
(New York: Columbia University Press, 1971). Reprinted by permission of the publisher.

was ill or taking acupuncture or *moxa* [burning herbs] treatment, the pain I felt was just as it had been before. I was greatly depressed and said to myself: "I became a monk against my parents' wishes and have yet to make the slightest progress. I have heard that the *Lotus* is the king of all sutras, venerated even by ghosts and spirits. People who are suffering in the lower worlds, when they rely on others in their efforts to be saved, always ask that the *Lotus Sutra* be recited for them. When one considers that recitation by others can save a person from suffering, how much more effective must be recitation by oneself! There must indeed be profound and mysterious doctrines in this sutra."

Thereupon I picked up the *Lotus Sutra* and in my study of it found that, other than the passages that explain that there is only One Vehicle and that all phenomena are in the state of Nirvana, the text was concerned with parables relating to cause and effect. If this *Sutra* had all these virtues, then surely the six Confucian classics and the books of all the other schools must be equally effective. Why should this particular sutra be so highly esteemed? My hopes were completely dashed. At this time I was sixteen years of age.

When I was nineteen I happened to read the *Wu-chi cheng-tsung tsan* [biographies of famous monks] in which the story of how the Master Yen-t'ou was killed by bandits and how his cries at the time resounded for over three *li* is described. I wondered why such an enlightened monk was unable to escape the swords of thieves. If such a thing could happen to a man who was like a unicorn or phoenix among monks, a dragon in the sea of Buddhism, how was I to escape the staves of the demons of hell after I died? What use was there in studying Zen? What a fraud Buddhism! How I regretted that I had cast myself into this band of strange and evil men. What was I to do now? So great was my distress that for three days I could not eat and for a long time my faith in Buddhism was completely lost. Statues of the Buddha and the sacred scriptures looked like mud and dirt to me. It seemed much better to read lay works, to amuse myself with poetry and prose, and thus to a small degree to alleviate my distress.

When I was twenty-two I went to the province of Wakasa, and while attending lectures on the *Hsu-t'ang lu,* I gained an awakening. Later, when I was in the province of Iyo I read the *Fo-tsu san-chin* and achieved an intense awakening. I concentrated night and day on the *Mu* kōan without a moment's rest, but to my great disappointment I was unable to achieve a pure and uninvolved state of undistracted meditation. Equally disappointing to me was the fact that I could not achieve the state where waking and sleeping are the same.

The spring of my twenty-fourth year found me in the monk's quarters of the Eigan-ji in Echigo, pursuing my strenuous studies. Night and day I did not sleep; I forgot both to eat and rest. Suddenly a great doubt manifested itself before me. It was as though I were frozen solid in the midst of an ice sheet extending tens of thousands of miles. A purity filled my breast and I could neither go forward nor retreat. To all intents and purposes I was out of my mind and the *Mu* alone remained. Although I sat in the Lecture Hall and listened to the Master's lecture, it was as though I were hearing a discussion from a distance outside the hall. At times it felt as though I were floating through the air.

This state lasted for several days. Then I chanced to hear the sound of the temple bell and I was suddenly transformed. It was as if a sheet of ice had been smashed or a jade tower had fallen with a crash. Suddenly I returned to my senses. I felt then that I had achieved the status of Yen-t'ou, who through the three periods of time encountered not the slightest loss [although he had been murdered by bandits]. All my former doubts vanished as though ice had melted away. In a loud voice I called: "Wonderful, wonderful. There is no cycle of birth and death through which one must pass. There is no enlightenment one must seek. The seventeen hundred kōans handed down from the past have not the slightest value whatsoever." My pride soared up like a majestic mountain, my arrogance surged forward like the tide. Smugly I thought to myself: "In the past two or three hundred years no one could have accomplished such a marvelous breakthrough as this."

Shouldering my glorious enlightenment, I set out at once for Shinano. Calling on Master Shoju, I told of my experience and presented him with a verse. The Master, holding my verse up in his left hand, said to me: "This verse is what you have learned from study. Now show me what your intuition has to say," and he held out his right hand.

I replied: "If there were something intuitive that I could show you, I'd vomit it out," and I made a gagging sound.

The Master said: "How do you understand Chao-chou's *Mu?*"

I replied: "What sort of place does *Mu* have that one can attach arms and legs to it?"

The Master twisted my nose with his fingers and said: "Here's someplace to attach arms and legs." I was nonplussed and the Master gave a hearty laugh. "You poor hole-dwelling devil!" he cried. I paid him no attention and he continued: "Do you think somehow that you have sufficient understanding?"

I answered: "What do you think is missing?"

Then the Master began to discuss the kōan that tells of Nan-ch'üan's death. I clapped my hands over my ears and started out of the room. The Master called after me: "Hey, monk!" and when I turned to him he added:

Figure 19. Hakuin Ekaku, *Mu*

"You poor hole-dwelling devil!" From then on, almost every time he saw me, the Master called me a "poor hole-dwelling devil."

One evening the Master sat cooling himself on the veranda. Again I brought him a verse I had written. "Delusions and fancies," the Master said. I shouted his words back at him in a loud voice, whereupon the Master seized me and rained twenty or thirty blows with his fists on me, and then pushed me off the veranda.

This was on the fourth day of the fifth month after a long spell of rain. I lay stretched out in the mud as though dead, scarcely breathing and almost unconscious. I could not move; meanwhile the Master sat on the veranda roaring with laughter. After a short while I regained consciousness, got up, and bowed to the Master. My body was bathed in perspiration. The Master called out to me in a loud voice: "You poor hole-dwelling devil!"

After this I devoted myself to an intensive study of the kōan on the death of Nan-ch'üan, not pausing to sleep or eat. One day I had a kind of awakening and went to the Master's room to test my understanding, but he would not approve it. All he did was call me a "poor hole-dwelling devil."

I began to think that I had better leave and go somewhere else. One day when I had gone to town to beg for food I encountered a madman who tried to beat me with a broom. Unexpectedly I found that I had penetrated the kōan on the death of Nan-ch'üan. Then the other kōans that had puzzled me, Su-shan's Memorial Tower and Ta-hui's verse on the Roundness of the Lotus Leaf, fell into place of themselves and I penetrated them all. After I returned to the temple I spoke of the understanding I had gained. The Master neither approved nor denied what I said, but only laughed pleasantly. But from this time on he stopped calling me a "poor hole-dwelling devil." Later I experienced enlightenment two or three times, accompanied by a great feeling of joy. At times there are words to express such experiences, but to my regret at other times there are none. It was as though I were walking about in the shadow cast by a lantern. I returned then and attended on my old teacher Nyōka, who had fallen ill.

One day I read in the verse given by Hsi-keng to his disciple Nampō as they were parting, the passage: "As we go to part a tall bamboo stands by the gate; its leaves stir the clear breeze for you in farewell." I was overcome with a great joy, as though a dark path had suddenly been illumined. Unconsciously I cried aloud: "Today for the first time I have entered into the *samadhi* of words." I arose and bowed in reverence.

After this I set out on a pilgrimage. One day when I was passing through southern Ise, I ran into a downpour and the waters reached to my knees. Suddenly I gained an even deeper understanding of the verse on the Roundness of the Lotus Leaf by Ta-hui. I was unable to contain my joy. I lost all awareness of my body, fell headlong into the waters, and forgot completely to get up again. My bundles and clothing were soaked through. Fortunately a passer-by, seeing my predicament, helped me to get up. I roared with laughter and everyone there thought I was mad. That winter, when I was sitting at night in the monk's hall at Shinoda in Izumi, I gained an enlightenment from the sound of snow falling. The next year, while practicing walking meditation at the monk's hall of the Reisho-in in Mino, I suddenly had an enlightenment experience greater than any I had had before, and was overcome by a great surge of joy.

I came to this dilapidated temple when I was thirty-two. One night in a dream my mother came and presented me with a purple robe made of silk. When I lifted it, both sleeves seemed very heavy, and on examining them I found an old mirror, five or six inches in diameter, in each sleeve. The reflection from the mirror in the right sleeve penetrated to my heart and vital organs. My own mind, mountains and rivers, the great earth seemed serene and bottomless. The mirror in the left sleeve, however, gave off no reflection whatsoever. Its surface was like that of a new pan that had yet to be touched by flames. But suddenly I became aware that the luster of the mirror from the left sleeve was innumerable times brighter than the other. After this, when I looked at all things, it was as though I were seeing my own face. For the first time I understood the meaning of the saying, "The Tathagata sees the Buddha-nature within his eye."

Later I happened to read the *Pi-yen-lu [Blue Cliff Record]* again, and my understanding of it differed completely from what it had been before. One night, some time after, I took up the *Lotus Sutra*. Suddenly I penetrated to the perfect, true, ultimate meaning of the *Lotus*. The doubts I had held initially were destroyed and I became aware that the understanding I had obtained up to then was greatly in error. Unconsciously I uttered a great cry and burst into tears.

—Translation by Philip B. Yampolsky

While Hakuin's first enlightenment came from penetrating the Mu *kōan, for lay followers he invented the second most celebrated of meditation questions, "What is the sound of one hand?" If they broke through this barrier, he painted for them an abbot's staff (which over the years began to resemble a dragon) with an inscription certifying that on such-and-such a date, this [named] person broke through the kōan on the sound of one hand. A number of these dragon-staff paintings still survive, testifying to Hakuin's continued work with lay followers even when more and more monks came to his small country temple for instruction.*

Hakuin stressed that his monk pupils, after enlightenment, must continue with their post-enlightenment practice while returning to the world with great compassion. His Song of Meditation *is an example of how he continued to take his teachings directly to everyday people, and it has become one of the best-known and most succinct expressions of Zen.*

Song of Meditation

All living beings are originally Buddhas, just like water and ice:
Without water there is no ice, and outside living beings there is
    no Buddha.
Not knowing how near it is, people seek it outside themselves—
    what a pity!
Like someone in the middle of water crying out in thirst,
Or the child of a rich man, wandering around like a beggar,
We are bound to the six worlds because we are lost in the darkness
    of ignorance;
Following dark path after dark path, when shall we escape birth
    and death?

The Zen meditation of Mahayana Buddhism is beyond all words
    of praise;
The virtues of charity, morality, invoking the Buddha, repentance,
    training,
And all other worthy actions have their source in meditation.
Even those who sit in zazen only once will destroy evil karma;
How then can there be false paths? The Pure Land is now very close.
Listen with reverence to this teaching; praise, embrace it, and you
    will find merit;
Better yet, look within and find the self-nature beyond the self,
And you will transcend words and explanations.

When you open the gate of cause-and-effect,
You will discover a path beyond duality or multiplicity;
When you abide in the form that is no-form,
Whether going or returning, you will always be at home;

When you take thought as non-thought,
You will sing and dance to the music of Buddhist truth.
Boundless as the sky, radiant as the moon is the fourfold wisdom;
At this moment, what do you lack? Nirvana is right in front of you,
This very place is the Lotus Land, this body is the body of Buddha.

—Translation by Stephen Addiss

Figure 20. Hakuin Ekaku, *The Sound of One Hand* (detail)

25

Daigu Ryōkan (1758–1831)

Selected Poems in

Chinese and Japanese

One of the most beloved of all Japanese Zen monks is Ryōkan, who lived an extraordinarily simple and modest life in the mountains of western Japan. The son of a village headman in Niigata, at the age of eighteen he entered the local Sōtō sect Zen temple, leaving his younger brother to continue his father's duties. Four years later, Ryōkan moved to Entsū-ji in Okayama for further training under the monk Kokusen and trained there for twelve years. Ryōkan received Dharma transmission in 1790, and after his teacher's death he went on pilgrimage for several years. His father committed suicide in Kyoto in 1795, and Ryōkan traveled there for the memorial service. He then returned to live the rest of his life in his native province, far from the cultural centers of Japan.

Instead of serving and teaching in a temple, Ryōkan lived for many years in a simple mountainside hut. He begged for his food and preferred playing with village children to religious or social duties. He would enjoy games with them using a ball made up of wound-up cloth, or have them cover him with autumn leaves while he played dead. When he visited friends, he never lectured to them about Buddhism but rather helped in the kitchen or meditated quietly in the parlor. He was distrustful of verbal certainties, writing, "Forget about both knowledge and ignorance," "Buddha is merely a conception in your mind," and "When you attach yourself to anything at all, truth disappears."

Ryōkan was visited in 1809 by the Confucian scholar, painter, poet, and calligrapher Kameda Bōsai (1752–1826). According to one story, they were drinking saké at Ryōkan's hut when they ran out of it. Ryōkan volunteered to go down the mountain and get more, but after some time went by, Bōsai went out to look for him and found the monk sitting on a stone, totally absorbed in looking at the moon. At the time of the visit, Ryōkan was requested by a local Shinto shrine to write a large banner and surprised Bōsai by using the Japanese syllabary rather than more prestigious Chinese characters.

Like Ikkyū (see Chapter 21), over the years Ryōkan composed a number of poems in both Chinese style and the five-line Japanese waka *tradition, and he also composed a few haiku. He would write these out when people asked, always from memory, so sometimes there are different versions of the poems that were collected and published after his death. Ryōkan's calligraphy, although usually modest in size and format, is now highly prized by both collectors and museums; its simplicity does not entirely disguise his great mastery of standard, cursive, and Japanese scripts. Over the years, his poems in his own hand have also been carved into stone in various parts of Japan, particularly Niigata; for those who cannot afford an original work by Ryōkan, rubbings taken from these stele are available to everyone. As he wrote in one of his poems, "We meet and we part . . . all that remains are traces of brush and ink."*

I recall when I was young
I would read, alone in the empty hall,
Filling the lamp with oil again and again—
I never noticed the long winter night.

Since I first came to Entsū-ji,
How many winters and springs have passed?
In front of my gate, a village of a thousand homes,
But I don't know a single person.
When my robe is dirty, I wash it myself,
When I'm out of food, I go out begging.
I used to read the lives of great monks;
They spent their lives in the virtue of poverty.

On the Road in Shinshū

Since I set out from the capital
Twelve days have gone by,
And not one of these has been without rain—
How can I help but worry?
Wings of wild swans and geese grow heavy,
Peach blossoms droop lower and lower;
Boatmen can't ply their morning ferries,
Travelers at evening lose their way.
It's impossible to halt my journey;
I crane my neck and knit my brows.
Will it be like autumn last year,
When the wind blew three days on end,

Huge trees were uprooted by the roadside,
And thatch from rooftops flew into the clouds?
Because of that the price of rice soared—
Will it be the same this year?
If these rains don't let up,
What then?

Midwinter, the eleventh month,
Wet snow falls unceasingly,
All the mountains have become the same color;
On the myriad paths, human tracks are few.
My past journeys now all seem like dreams,
The door to my grass hut is deeply covered.
All night long I burn small chunks of wood
And silently read poems by masters from the past.

    In my grass hut
I stretch out my legs
    and listen happily
to the voices of frogs
in the mountainside paddies

The springtime breathes a quiet melody;
Swinging my staff, I enter the eastern town.
Newly green willows fill the gardens;
Buoyantly floating plants cover the ponds.
My begging bowl is fragrant with rice from a thousand hearths,
My heart renounces power and glory.
Following the path of past Buddhas,
I beg for food and travel on.

    It seems the autumn
that I waited for is here—
    tonight
from every clump of grass,
insect voices

    The dew clinging
to each clump of
    autumn grass—
could it be the tears of insects
who sang through the night?

Bleak and lonely, my little hut;
All day long, no friends to see—
I sit alone by the window
And hear only the sound of falling leaves.

From the mountain slope,
glistening maple leaves
come to rest here—
when the autumn passes,
will they be its memento?

Humans born into this floating world
Quickly become like roadside dust;
At dawn, small children,
By sunset, already white-haired.
Without inner understanding
They struggle without cease.
I ask the children of the universe:
For what reason do you pass this way?

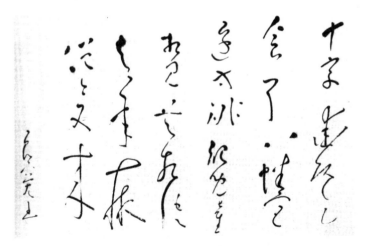

**Figure 21. Daigu Ryōkan, *Poetic Quatrain*
(Barnet and Burto Collection)**

I've finished begging at the village crossroads
And wander out west of the Hachiman Shrine;
A group of children see me and call to each other,
"That crazy monk from last year is coming here again!"

If my monk's robe
had wider sleeves
        I'd be glad
to shelter all the people
in this floating world

I see people endlessly striving,
Wrapped up in themselves like silkworms.
Totally motivated by the love for money,
They allow themselves no leisure;
As time passes, they lose their self-nature.
Year after year they become more foolish.
One day they will travel to the Yellow Springs
Where even their names are forgotten.
There are so many people like this—
Ah, I can't bear even to talk about it!

[At the early death of his only pupil.]

Here in this village,
there are so many people
        coming and going—
but when one of them isn't you
it can be very lonely.

Our human hearts are all different
Just as our faces are never exactly the same.
When we judge people by a fixed standard,
We create the alternations of right and wrong.
When someone is like us, wrong becomes right;
When different, right becomes wrong.
Good is seen from our own viewpoint,
Evil is judged by our personal standards.
Therefore right and wrong begin within themselves—
Deciding "the Way" does not come from nature.
Like trying to reach the bottom of the ocean with a pole,
We merely exhaust ourselves uselessly, losing our innate
        perception.

My begging bowl
totally forgotten—
        no one would steal it
no one would steal it
ah, this begging bowl!

We speak of falsehood as completely false
And of true as completely true;
But outside of truth there is no falsehood
And outside of falsehood, no special truth.
How can those who practice the Way
Diligently search for truth?
If we examine the depths of our own hearts,
There is delusion, and there is truth.

        In this world
it's not that I won't
        mix with people
but I much prefer
to enjoy my solitude

Illusion and enlightenment depend on each other,
Principle and actuality are ultimately the same—
All night long, sutras without words;
Through the night, Zen without sitting.
Warblers sing in the grove by the river,
A village dog barks at the moon.
I have no one to share my feelings,
So I just write what is in my heart.

        Mind itself
is the mind that leads
        mind into confusion
so never release the bridle
of the horse of your mind

A cold evening in my empty room,
Time flows by like incense smoke arising.
Outside my door, a thousand stalks of bamboo;
Above my bed, how many books—
The moon has come to whiten half my window,

Figure 22. Daigu Ryōkan, *Haiku*

Enough for a fire
the wind has brought me
maple leaves

The only sound in any direction is the singing of insects.
In this there is boundless feeling,
But as I encounter it, there are no words.

Sixty years have passed for this frail old monk
Living in a shrine hut, far from the world of men.
At the base of the mountain I'm nestled in during the evening rain;
The lamp flickers brightly in front of my old window.

—Translations by Stephen Addiss

26

Kyong Ho (1849–1912)

The Great Matter of

Life and Death (complete)

Kyong Ho is widely regarded as having given new life to Zen Buddhism in Korea after a three-hundred-year period of relative dormancy. After the early death of his father, he grew up in a temple with his mother, and by his late teens he had a strong foundation in Buddhist, Taoist, and Confucian studies. When he was twenty-three he began to lecture on sutras at Tonghak Temple and acquired a reputation as a brilliant and charismatic speaker. At the age of thirty he began a journey to visit one of his old teachers. On the way he passed through a village that had been ravaged by cholera. Shocked by this encounter with death, he realized that all of his learning amounted to nothing. He returned to his temple, dismissed his students, shut himself up in a room, and vowed not to leave it until he had solved the great question of life and death. After three months the attendant who brought him his daily meal was boasting of his Master's heroic meditation practice when a villager told him that if all his Master did was eat and sit he would be reborn as a cow with no nostrils. When the attendant reported this to Kyong Ho, he rose with a smile and strode out of the room. His enlightenment poem reads:

> I heard of the cow with no nostrils,
> And now the whole universe is my home.
> Yon-am Mountain is flat as a road.
> A farmer, done with his work, is singing.

Shortly after this he received transmission from Man Hwa and was given the name Kyong Ho ("Empty Mirror"). He spent about ten years as the resident Zen Master at Ch'ongjang Temple and then set out on a journey around Korea teaching at various mountain temples and encouraging his students to open new temples in cities and towns. He eventually settled at Haein-sa, where he oversaw a new printing of the Buddhist canon from the famous woodblock Tripitaka Koreana *stored at that temple. He was also renowned as a calligrapher and a poet. He gave Dharma transmission to five students, and then in 1903, at the height of his fame, Kyong Ho disappeared from public life and settled in a remote fishing village where he lived the rest of his life working as a laborer and teaching children their letters. When he was dying he summoned two of his students, Mang Gong and Su Wol, and wrote his death poem:*

> The moonlight of clear mind
> Swallows the whole world;
> When mind and light both go out
> What is this?

After his death his successors compiled his letters, poems, and speeches, including the selection here, an urgent injunction addressed to monastics to strengthen their practice.

It is no small thing for a person to become a Buddhist monk or nun. People do not become monks or nuns to eat and dress well. Rather, they want to be free from life and death by accomplishing Buddhahood.

To accomplish Buddhahood, one has to discover one's own Mind, which is already within one's own body.

To discover Mind, you should understand that your body is no more than a dead corpse and that this world is, for good or bad, nothing but a dream. Your death is like popping out in the evening of the same day that you have popped in during the morning. After death, sometimes one may be born in one of the hells, sometimes in the realm of animals and sometimes in the realm of ghosts. Then you must endure incalculable pains and sufferings.

Since this is true, do not concern yourself with the worldly life. Just examine and carefully observe your mind at all times. What does this which is now seeing, hearing and thinking look like? Does it have any form or not? Is it big or small? Is it yellow or green? Is it bright or dark?

Examine and observe this matter carefully. Let your examination and observation become like a mouse-catching cat; or like a hen sitting on her eggs; or like a desperately hungry, old, crafty mouse gnawing a hole in a rice bag.

The Great Matter of Life and Death, by Zen Master Kyong Ho. © The Kwan Um School of Zen. Reprinted by permission of The Kwan Um School of Zen.

Let your examination and observation be focused at one point and do not forget it. Keep it before you by raising doubt and by questioning yourself. Do not let this doubt go away while you are doing chores or the like. Do not let your question escape from you even while you are not doing anything special. By eagerly and sincerely practicing in this manner, finally there will be the moment of awakening to your own Mind.

Practice hard by raising your faith. Raising your faith is sincerely reexamining the matter just mentioned.

To be born a human being is most difficult. It is even more difficult to be born into favorable circumstances—harder still to become a monk or nun. It is the most difficult thing of all to find correct and righteous Dharma teaching. We should reflect on this matter deeply.

Shakyamuni Buddha once said, "One who is already a human being is as rare as a speck of dirt clinging to a fingernail, while one who has become an animal by losing his human form is as common as the dirt on the ground." If one loses the human form this time, then one will have to wait countless eons to recover it. When someone is in one of the many hells, he is unaware of it, as if playing games in a flower garden. Becoming a hungry ghost, *asura,* or animal, he acts like he is dwelling in his own home.

However, if one is awakened and has accomplished Buddhahood, he does not have to live or die. That is, he does not have to endure any kind of suffering again. These words should be carefully considered one by one.

Once, Zen Master Kwon began meditating from morning to night. As soon as the sun would set, he would beat his fists against the ground in frustration and cry out, "I have lost another day without realizing my Mind." He continued this way every day until he was fully awakened. Since there are many who have exhibited the determination of Master Kwon, it is impossible for me here to cite everyone who has had the determination to meditate until enlightened.

None of them were worried about living or dying, nor about eating, dressing well, nor sleeping. In our study, we should practice the same way. Consider this carefully!

Once Zen Master Dong Sal wrote: Do not seek noble titles nor wish to have possessions nor ask for prosperity. Wherever you happen to be, just live in accord with your karma here and now in this life. If your clothes wear out, patch them again and again. If there is no food, barely even search for it. When the warm energy under your chin grows cold, suddenly you become a corpse. What remains after death is only a hollow name. After all, how many days will this transient body live? Why work hard only to acquire useless things? That only makes your mind dark and causes you to forget your practice.

After awakening one's own Mind, one should always preserve its purity and tranquility. Cultivate this Mind without allowing it to be tainted by worldly things. Then plenty of good things (that is, pleasure which comes from awakening) will happen. Trust in this faithfully. When you have to die, there will be no more suffering or sickness. You can go freely to Nirvana or anywhere else you choose—you control your own life as a free person in the world.

Shakyamuni Buddha said, "If anyone—man or woman, old or young—has faith in these words and studies them, each will, as a result, become a Buddha." Why would Shakyamuni Buddha deceive us?

The Fifth Patriarch, Hung-jen Zen Master, said, "By examination and observation of mind, one will become enlightened naturally." Then he further promised us, "If you don't have faith in what I say, in future lives you will be eaten by tigers over and over again. On the other hand, if I have deceived you, I will fall into the dungeon of hell with no exit." Since the Patriarchs have said these words, should we not take them to heart?

If you take up this practice, do not agitate your mind; let it be like a mountain. Let your mind be like clear and empty space and continue to reflect on enlightening Dharma as the moon reflects the sun. Whether others think that you are right or wrong is not your concern. Do not judge or criticize others. Just be at ease and go on mindlessly like a simpleton or a fool; or, be like one who is struck deaf and dumb. Spend your life as if you cannot hear a thing, or like an infant. Then, sooner or later, all the delusion will disappear.

If one wishes to accomplish Buddhahood, it is useless to attempt to understand and master worldly life. It would be like one trying to fix food out of dung, or like trying to cut jade out of mud. It is totally useless for the accomplishing of Buddhahood. There is no reason for occupying oneself with worldly affairs.

See your own death in the death of others. Do not put your trust in this body. Rather, remind yourself again and again to not miss a moment to awaken your own mind.

Ask yourself repeatedly, "What does this mind look like?" In your daily rounds, continue to ask yourself, "What does this mind look like?" Reflect upon this question so intensely that you are like a starving man thinking of nothing but good food. Do not lose hold of your questioning at any time.

Buddha has said, "Whatever has a form, that is, everything, is all delusory." He also said, "Everything that the ordinary human being does is subject to life and death. There is only one way to be a true person and this is realization of your own mind."

It is said, "Do not drink liquor," since it will intoxicate and make your mind dull. Also, "Do not speak lies," since it will only accelerate delusive states of mind. Furthermore, "Do not steal," since it only helps to make your mind jealous and full of desires. You should observe these and all the precepts. Breaking the precepts can be very harmful for your cultivation and for your life itself. You should not cling to or incline yourself towards breaking any of them.

Master Ox-herder, Mokguja (Chinul), once mentioned that, "Indulging in craving and desire for property are as vicious as poisonous snakes. Watch your body and mind carefully when such desires arise and then understand them as they are. Detach yourself from them as much as possible."

These words are very important and they should be remembered. They will make your practice more effective. Buddha said, "Becoming angry even once raises ten million vicious sins. A student must simply endure and tolerate the angry mind." Many masters have also said that because of anger, one becomes a tiger, a bee, a snake, or some similar stinging or biting creature. From foolish-mindedness, one becomes either a bird or a butterfly. Depending upon his degree of low-mindedness, one becomes either an ant, a mosquito or the like. From craving things, one becomes a hungry ghost. The type of desire or anger molds the nature of hell into which one will accordingly fall. Each and every state of mind determines the kind of creature one is to become.

However, if one's mind is unattached, one becomes a Buddha. Even a "good" or positive state of mind is useless. Even though such a condition of mind can create a heavenly future life, it is still limited. As soon as one reaches heaven, he immediately begins descending to the hellish or animal realms in successive re-births. If no intention is held in the mind, then there is no place to be born again. One's mind is so pure and unconfused, it cannot go to the dark places. This pure and quiescent mind is the way of Buddha.

If one questions with one-pointed concentration, then this mind naturally settles down and becomes tranquil. By this one automatically realizes one's own mind as quiescent and tranquil. This is the same as becoming a Buddha.

This way is very direct and goes right to the point. It is the best way you can practice. Read and examine this talk from time to time and, on the right occasions, even tell other people. This is as good as reading eighty-four thousand volumes of scriptures. Practicing in this manner, you will accomplish Buddhahood in this lifetime. Do not think this talk to be some contrived encouragement or expedient deception. Follow these words with your whole-hearted mind.

In the deep canyon where the clear stream is flowing continuously, all kinds of birds are singing everywhere. No one ever comes to visit this place. It is called Sunim's dwelling place, and it is quiet and tranquil. Here is where

I sit and contemplate and examine what this mind is. Now, if this mind is not what Buddha is, then what else is it?

You have just heard a very rare talk. You should continue to study this great matter enthusiastically. Do not hurry, otherwise you might become sick or get a terrible headache. Calm yourself, then ceaselessly meditate. Most of all, be careful not to force yourself. Rather, relax and let your right questioning be within.

—Translation by the Kwan Um School of Zen

GLOSSARY AND CHINESE NAME CHART

Buddhist Terms

abhidharma (Sanskrit). The third part of the Buddhist canon (the sutras and the monastic rules are the other two parts), consisting of doctrinal commentary on the sutras; it became the mainstream of early Buddhist philosophy.

Amida (Japanese), **Amitabul** (Korean), **Amitabha** (Sanskrit). The Buddha who presides over the Western Pure Land.

Ananda (Sanskrit). Younger cousin and personal attendant of the historical Buddha Shakyamuni, credited with retaining in memory all of the Buddha's discourses; he succeeded Mahakasyapa as the Second Indian Patriarch.

asura (Sanskrit). A contentious demon, one of the six levels of existence (*devas, asuras,* humans, hell beings, hungry ghosts, animals).

Avalokitesvara (Sanskrit), **Kwan-yin, Guanyin** (Chinese), **Kannon, Kanzeon** (Japanese), **Kwan Se Um** (Korean). The Bodhisattva of Compassion.

Avatamsaka (Sanskrit). See *Hua-yen.*

bhikku (Sanskrit). A Buddhist monk.

bhikkuni (Sanskrit). A Buddhist nun.

bodhi (Sanskrit). Awakening, enlightenment.

Bodhidharma (Sanskrit), **Daruma** (Japanese). The monk considered the Twenty-Eighth Patriarch in India who became the First Patriarch of East Asian Zen.

Bodhisattva (Sanskrit). An enlightened being who foregoes nirvana in order to help others.

capping word. A phrase or verse, usually from Chinese classical poetry, that a student brings to confirm his or her understanding of a kōan; a short commentary to the main case or poem in a Zen text.

deva (Sanskrit). A heavenly being, a god; one of the six levels of existence (*devas, asuras,* humans, hell beings, hungry ghosts, animals).

dharani (Sanskrit). A comprehensive mnemonic summary of a teaching; also, a long mantra.

Dharma (Sanskrit). Cosmic law, reality, basic constituent of reality; the teachings of Buddha, Buddhist doctrine.

Esoteric Buddhism. Also known as Tantric Buddhism, esoteric schools of Buddhism developed in Tibet, China, and Japan under the influence of Hindu practices.

Teachings were often transmitted in secret and involved visualization of guardian deities, recitation of mantras, and other techniques used for both spiritual and material ends.

Four Noble Truths.   The first teaching of the Buddha: 1) existence is characterized by suffering, 2) the origin of our suffering is desire, anger, and ignorance, 3) this suffering can cease, 4) the Eightfold Path provides a way to the cessation of suffering (right view, right intention, right speech, right action, right livelihood, right effort, right mindfulness, right concentration).

gatha (Sanskrit).   A short poem, often providing a pithy summary of a teaching.

Hinayana (Sanskrit).   The "smaller vehicle," Mahayana term for the early form of Buddhism that has been dominant in Southeast Asia, stressing following the path of the historical Buddha.

host and guest.   Zen metaphor for the interactive relationship of the absolute and phenomenal.

Hua-yen (Chinese).   A philosophical school of Buddhism derived from a sutra of that name (also known as the *Avatamsaka, Kegon,* or *"Flower Garland" Sutra*), a very long, complex sutra that presents the interconnected nature of the universe as experienced by a Buddha, and the path of a Bodhisattva through the world.

hwa-du (Korean), *hua-t'ou* (Chinese).   Literally, "word-head," a phrase that embodies the essential point of a *kung-an* (kōan); a great question held as the object of meditation.

kalpa (Sanskrit).   An eon, the lifetime of a universe.

karma (Sanskrit).   The universal law of cause and effect, particularly the effect of an action done with moral intent.

kōan (Japanese), *kung-an* (Chinese), *kong-an* (Korean).   A "public case" of a Zen encounter; a meditation question given to Zen students in training.

Kwan-yin, Guanyin, Kannon, Kanzeon, Kwan Se Um.   See Avalokitesvara.

Lin-chi.   See Rinzai.

Lotus Sutra.   A major Buddhist sutra that includes the many paths, methods, and expedient means leading to enlightenment.

Mahakasyapa (Sanskrit).   A renowned disciple of Shakyamuni Buddha who smiled when the Buddha gave a wordless teaching, and who took over the *sangha* after the Buddha's death; regarded as the First Indian Patriarch of Zen.

Mahayana (Sanskrit).   The "greater vehicle," so called because it contains a great many Buddhist teachings and practices suited to a large variety of people; originating in the first century C.E., it became the dominant form of Buddhism in East Asia.

Maitreya (Sanskrit), **Miroku** (Japanese).   Literally, "Loving One," the Buddha of the future.

mani jewel (Sanskrit).   A jewel from the dragon king that responds to wishes and dispels evil.

Manjusri (Sanskrit).   The Bodhisattva of Wisdom.

mantra (Sanskrit).   A sequence of mystical syllables such as *Om Mani Padme Hum* or a devotional phrase such as *Namu Amitabul* (*Namu Amida Butsu,* Homage to Amida Buddha) recited continuously as a form of meditation practice.

net of Indra.   A conception of the universe, as in Hua-yen Buddhism, as a net with a jewel at each interstice, in which every element reflects every other element.

nirvana (Sanskrit).   The end of the cycle of rebirths and entry into state of being variously described as emptiness, stillness, bliss, and oneness with the universe.

Ōbaku (Japanese).   The third Zen sect in Japan, after Rinzai and Sōtō, begun when Chinese monks emigrated to Nagasaki in the mid-seventeenth century; the name comes from the Chinese Master Huang-po (died c. 850).

prajna (Sanskrit).   Wisdom, full consciousness, insight; with *samadhi* and *sila,* one of the three basic Buddhist practices.

Pure Land Buddhism.   A form of devotional Buddhism in which Amida Buddha will take the souls of dying believers to their Western Paradise.

Rinzai (Japanese), **Lin-chi** (Chinese).   One of the major Zen sects in Japan, tracing its history from the Chinese Master Lin-chi (died 866).

samadhi (Sanskrit).   State of concentration, mental absorption; with *sila* and *prajna,* one of the three basic Buddhist practices.

samsara (Sanskrit).   The cycle of existences until one reaches nirvana; the phenomenal world.

sangha (Sanskrit).   A Buddhist community, congregation.

Sariputra (Sanskrit).   One of the foremost disciples of the Buddha.

satori (Japanese).   Zen enlightenment.

sila (Sanskrit).   Buddhist precepts; ethics, morality; with *samadhi* and *prajna,* one of the three basic Buddhist practices.

skandhas (Sanskrit).   The five constituents of existence, which can be translated as form, sensation, perception, volition, and consciousness.

Sōtō (Japanese).   The numerically largest Zen sect in Japan, tracing its history from the Chinese Masters Ts'ao-shan and Tung-shan, and stressing gradual cultivation.

sunim (Korean).   Monk or nun.

sunyata (Sanskrit).   Emptiness, lack of an essential nature; one of the core ideas of Buddhism.

sutra (Sanskrit).   A scripture recording the discourses and teachings of the Buddha, originally composed in Pali or Sanskrit and preserved also in Chinese and Tibetan. The most important sutras for Zen are the *Heart Sutra,* the *Diamond Sutra,* the *Lotus Sutra,* the *Vimalakirti Sutra,* the *Avatamsaka Sutra,* and the *Surangama Sutra.*

Tathagata (Sanskrit).   "Thus come," the historical Buddha Shakyamuni.

Three Worlds.   The world of desire, the world of form, and the world of form-lessness; in some contexts: past, present, and future.

transmission.   Formal recognition by a Master that a follower is enlightened and ready to transmit Buddhist teachings.

Ts'ao-shan, Tung-shan.   See Sōtō.

Vairochana (Sanskrit).   The universal Buddha in Esoteric Buddhism, in Japan also considered the Sun Buddha.

Vimalakirti (Sanskrit).   A Buddhist layman who successfully debated with Man-jusri.

zazen.   Seated Zen meditation.

Chinese Names

In published translations of Zen texts, Chinese names and book titles are sometimes given in the traditional Wade-Giles Romanization, sometimes in the Chinese government-mandated Pinyin style, and sometimes in Japanese forms. This volume uses Wade-Giles, but the following list of names and book titles is given for further clarity.

Wade-Giles	Pinyin	Japanese
Ch'an	Chan	Zen
Kwan-yin	Guanyin	Kannon, Kanzeon
Hui-k'o	Huike	Eka
Seng-ts'an	Sengcan	Sōzan
Shih-t'ou	Shitou	Sekitō
Hui-neng	Huineng	Enō
Ma-tsu	Mazu	Basō
Ta-hui	Dahui	Daie
Pai-chang	Baizhang	Hyakujō
Chao-chou	Zhaozhou	Jōshū
Nan-ch'üan	Nanquan	Nansen
Huang-po	Huangbo	Ōbaku
Lin-chi	Linji	Rinzai
Hsueh-tou	Xuedou	Setchō
Te-shan	Deshan	Tokusan
Yün-men	Yunmen	Ummon
Yuan-wu	Yuanwu	Engo
Wu-men	Wumen	Mumon
Wu-men-kuan	*Wumenguan*	*Mumonkan*
Pi-yen-lu	*Biyan lu*	*Hekiganroku*
Hsin-hsin-ming	*Xinxinming*	*Shinshinmei*
Ts'an-t'ung-ch'i	Cantongqi	Sandōkai

SELECTED BIBLIOGRAPHY

Original Zen Texts

Bankei Yōtaku. *Bankei Zen.* Translated by Peter Haskell. New York: Grove Press, 1984.

———. *The Unborn: The Life and Teaching of Zen Master Bankei, 1622–1693.* Translated by Norman Waddell. San Francisco: North Point Press, 1984.

Bassui. *Mud and Water: A Collection of Talks by the Zen Master Bassui.* Translated by Arthur Braverman. San Francisco: North Point Press, 1989.

The Blue Cliff Record. Translated by Thomas Cleary and J. C. Cleary. Boston: Shambhala, 1977.

Blyth, R. H., trans. *Zen and Zen Classics.* Vols. 1–5. Tokyo: Hokuseidō Press, 1960–1962.

Bodhidharma. *The Bodhidharma Anthology: The Earliest Records of Zen.* Translated by Jeffrey L. Broughton. Berkeley: University of California Press, 1999.

———. *The Zen Teachings of Bodhidharma.* Translated by Red Pine. San Francisco: North Point Press, 1987.

Chao-chou. *The Recorded Sayings of Zen Master Joshu.* Translated by James Green. Boston: Shambhala, 1998.

Chinul. *The Korean Approach to Zen: The Collected Works of Chinul.* Translated by Robert Buswell. Honolulu: University of Hawaii Press, 1983.

Cleary, Thomas, trans. *Book of Serenity: One Hundred Zen Dialogues.* Hudson, NY: Lindisfarne Press, 1990.

———, trans. *Classics of Buddhism and Zen.* 8 vols. Boston and London: Shambhala, 2001.

———, trans. *The Five Houses of Zen.* Boston and London: Shambhala, 1997.

Dōgen. *Moon in a Dewdrop: Writings of Zen Master Dōgen.* Edited by Kazuaki Tanahashi. New York: North Point Press, 1985.

———. *A Primer of Sōtō Zen: Dōgen's Shōbōgenzō Zuimonki.* Translated by Reihō Masunaga. Honolulu: University of Hawaii Press, 1971.

———. *Zen Master Dōgen.* Translated by Yūhō Yokoi with Daizen Victoria. New York and Tokyo: Weatherhill, 1976.

———. *The Zen Poetry of Dōgen.* Translated by Steven Heine. Boston and Rutland, VT: Tuttle, 1997.

Ferguson, Andy. *Zen's Chinese Heritage: The Masters and Their Teachings.* Boston: Wisdom Publications, 2000.

Grant, Beata. *Daughters of Emptiness: Poems of Chinese Buddhist Nuns.* Boston: Wisdom Publications, 2003.

Hakuin Ekaku. *Embossed Tea Kettle.* Translated by R. D. M. Shaw. London: George Allen and Unwin, 1963.

Hakuin Ekaku. *The Essential Teachings of Zen Master Hakuin: A Translation of the* Sokkō-roku kaien-fusetsu. Translated by Norman Waddell. Boston: Shambhala, 1994.

———. *Wild Ivy: The Spiritual Autobiography of Hakuin Ekaku.* Translated by Norman Waddell. Boston and London: Shambhala, 1999.

———. *The Zen Master Hakuin: Selected Writings.* Translated by Philip B. Yampolsky. New York: Columbia University Press, 1971.

———. *Zen Words for the Heart: Hakuin's Commentary on the* Heart Sutra. Translated by Norman Waddell. Boston and London: Shambhala, 1996.

Heine, Steven, and Dale Wright, eds. *The Zen Canon: Understanding the Classic Texts.* New York: Oxford University Press, 2004.

———, eds. *Zen Classics: Formative Texts in the History of Zen Buddhism.* New York: Oxford University Press, 2006.

Huang-po. *The Zen Teaching of Huang Po.* Translated by John Blofeld. New York: Grove Press, 1958.

Hui-neng. *The* Diamond Sutra *and the Sutra of Hui Neng.* Translated by A. F. Price and Wong Mou-lam. Boulder, CO: Shambhala, 1969.

———. *The* Platform Sutra *of the Sixth Patriarch.* Translated by Philip B. Yampolsky. New York: Columbia University Press, 1967.

Ikkyū Sojun. *Ikkyū and the Crazy Cloud Anthology.* Translated by Sonja Artzen. Tokyo: University of Tokyo Press, 1986.

———. *Wild Ways: Zen Poems of Ikkyū.* Translated by John Stevens. Boston and New York: Shambhala, 1995.

———. *Zen-Man Ikkyū.* Translated by James Sanford. Chico, CA: Scholars Press, 1981.

Keizan. *The Record of Transmitting the Light: Zen Master Keizan's* Dentoroku. Translated by Francis H. Cook. Los Angeles: Center Publications, 1991.

———. *Transmission of Light* [The *Dentoroku*]. Translated by Thomas Cleary. Boston: Shambhala, 1990.

Lin-chi. *The Record of Lin-chi.* Translated by Ruth Fuller Sasaki. Kyoto: The Institute for Zen Studies, 1975.

———. *The Zen Teachings of Master Lin-chi (Lin-chi Lu).* Translated by Burton Watson. Boston: Shambhala, 1993.

———. *The Zen Teachings of Rinzai.* Translated by Irmgard Schloegl. Berkeley, CA: Shambhala, 1976.

Lu K'uan Yu [Charles Luk], ed. and trans. *Ch'an and Zen Teaching.* 3 vols. London: Rider and Company, 1960–1962.

Musō Soseki. *Dream Conversations on Buddhism and Zen.* Translated by Thomas Cleary. Boston and London: Shambhala, 1994.

———. *Sun at Midnight: Poems and Sermons.* Translated by W. S. Merwin and Soiku Shigematsu. San Francisco: North Point Press, 1989.

Nyogen Senzaki, ed. *The Iron Flute: One Hundred Zen Kōans.* Boston, Rutland, VT, and Tokyo: Tuttle, 2000.

The Original Face: An Anthology of Rinzai Zen. Translated and edited by Thomas Cleary. New York: Grove Press, 1978.

P'ang. *A Man of Zen: The Recorded Sayings of Layman P'ang.* Translated by Ruth Fuller Sasaki, Yoshitaka Iriya, and Dana Fraser. New York and Tokyo: Weatherhill, 1971.

Secrets of the Blue Cliff Record: Zen Comments by Hakuin and Tenkei. Translated by Thomas Cleary. Boston: Shambhala, 2000.

Sekida, Katsuki, trans. *Two Zen Classics:* Mumonkan *and* Hekiganroku. New York and Tokyo: Weatherhill, 1977.

Sharma, Arvind, ed. *Women Saints in World Religions.* Albany: State University of New York Press, 2000.

So Sahn. *The Mirror of Zen: The Classic Guide to Buddhist Practice by Zen Master So Sahn.* Translated by Boep Joeng and Hyon Gak. Boston and London: Shambhala, 2006.

Suzuki, Shunryu. *Branching Streams Flow in the Darkness: Zen Talks on the* Sandokai. Edited by Mel Weitsman and Michael Wenger. Berkeley: University of California Press, 1999.

T'aego. *A Buddha from Korea: The Zen Teachings of T'aego.* Translated by J. C. Cleary. Boston: Shambhala, 1988.

Ta-hui Tsung-kao. *Swampland Flowers: The Letters and Lectures of Zen Master Ta Hui.* Translated by J. C. Cleary. Boston and London: Shambhala, 2006.

Tōrei Enji. *The Discourse on the Inexhaustible Lamp of the Zen School.* Translated by Yoko Okuda. Tokyo: Tuttle, 1996.

Wu-men. *The Gateless Barrier.* Translation and commentary by Robert Aitken. San Francisco: North Point Press, 1991.

Yün-men. *Master Yunmen.* Translated by Urs App. New York and Tokyo: Kōdansha International, 1994.

Zen Dawn: Early Zen Texts from Tun Huang. Translated by J. C. Cleary. Boston and London: Shambhala, 1986.

Zenkei Shibayama. *A Flower Does Not Talk.* Translated by Sumiko Kudo. Rutland, VT: Tuttle, 1970.

———. *Zen Comments on the* Mumonkan. New York: Harper and Row, 1974.

Publications about Zen and Zen Arts

Addiss, Stephen. *The Art of Zen: Paintings and Calligraphy by Japanese Monks, 1600–1925.* New York: Harry N. Abrams, 1989.

———. *Ōbaku: Zen Painting and Calligraphy.* Lawrence, KS: Spencer Museum of Art, 1978.

Addiss, Stephen. *Zenga and Nanga: Paintings by Japanese Monks and Scholars.* New Orleans: New Orleans Museum of Art, 1976.

Awakawa, Yasuichi. *Zen Painting.* Tokyo: Kōdansha International, 1970.

Barnet, Sylvan, and William Burto. *Zen Ink Painting.* Tokyo and New York: Kōdansha International, 1982.

Brasch, Kurt. *Hakuin und die Zen Malerei.* Tokyo: Japanisch-Deutsche Gessellschaft, 1957.

Brinker, Helmut. *Zen in the Art of Painting.* London: Arkana, 1987.

———. *Zen: Masters of Meditation in Images and Writings.* Zurich: Artibus Asiae, 1996.

Covell, Jon Carter. *Unraveling Zen's Red Thread.* Elizabeth, NJ: Hollym International, 1980. [A discussion centering on Ikkyū.]

Dumoulin, Heinrich. *The Development of Chinese Zen after the Sixth Patriarch.* Translated by Ruth Fuller Sasaki. New York: The First Zen Institute of America, 1953.

———. *A History of Zen Buddhism.* Translated by Paul Peachey. New York: Pantheon Books, 1963.

Fontein, Jan, and Money Hickman. *Zen Painting and Calligraphy.* Boston: Museum of Fine Arts, 1970.

Hisamatsu, Shin'ichi. *Zen and the Fine Arts.* Tokyo: Kōdansha International, 1971.

Kapleau, Phillip. *The Three Pillars of Zen.* New York: Harper and Row, 1966.

Kashiwara, Yūsen, and Kōyū Sonoda, eds. *Shapers of Japanese Buddhism.* Tokyo: Kosei Publishing, 1994.

Kinsei Zenrin bokuseki. 3 vols. Kyoto: Shibunkaku, 1974. [Paintings and calligraphy by monks from 1600 to 1940, with large illustrations.]

Kraft, Kenneth, ed. *Zen: Tradition and Transition.* New York: Grove Press, 1988.

Kusan Sunim, *The Way of Korean Zen.* New York: Weatherhill, 1985.

Leggett, Trevor. *A First Zen Reader.* Rutland, VT and Tokyo: Tuttle, 1969.

McRae, John R. *Seeing through Zen: Encounter, Transformation, and Genealogy in Chinese Chan Buddhism.* Berkeley: University of California Press, 2003.

Miura, Isshū, and Ruth Fuller Sasaki. *Zen Dust.* New York: Harcourt, Brace and World, 1966.

Mu Soeng Sunim. *Thousand Peaks: Korean Zen-Tradition and Teachers.* Berkeley, CA: Parallax Press, 1987.

Munsterberg, Hugo. *Zen and Oriental Art.* Rutland, VT: Tuttle, 1965.

Nattier, Jan. "The *Heart Sutra:* A Chinese Apocryphal Text?" *The Journal of the International Association of Buddhist Studies* 15, no. 2 (1992): 153–219.

Omori, Sogen, and Katsujo Terayama. *Zen and the Art of Calligraphy.* London: Routledge and Kegan Paul, 1983.

Seo, Audrey Yoshiko. *The Art of Twentieth-Century Zen.* With Stephen Addiss. Boston: Shambhala, 1998.

Shambhala Dictionary of Buddhism and Zen. Boston and London: Shambhala, 1991.

Shigematsu, Soiku. *A Zen Forest: Sayings of the Masters.* New York: Weatherhill, 1981.

Shōkin Furuta. *Sengai: Master Zen Painter.* Tokyo: Kōdansha International, 2000.

Shrobe, Richard. *Don't Know Mind: The Spirit of Korean Zen.* Boston: Shambhala, 2004.

Stevens, John. *Sacred Calligraphy of the East.* Boulder, CO: Shambhala, 1981.

———. *Three Zen Masters: Ikkyū, Hakuin, Ryōkan.* Tokyo: Kōdansha International, 1993.

———. *Zenga: Brushstrokes of Enlightenment.* New Orleans: New Orleans Museum of Art, 1990.

Stryck, Lucien. *Zen Poems, Prayers, Sermons, Anecdotes, Interviews.* Garden City, NY: Anchor Books, 1965.

Stryck, Lucien, and Takashi Ikemoto, trans. *Zen Poems of China and Japan.* Garden City, NY: Anchor Books, 1973.

Suzuki, Daisetsu. *Essays in Zen Buddhism.* New York: Grove Press, 1961.

———. *Manual of Zen Buddhism.* New York: Grove Press, 1960.

———. *Sengai: The Zen Master.* Greenwich, CT: New York Graphic Society, 1971.

———. *Zen and Japanese Culture.* Princeton, NJ: Princeton University Press, 1959.

Takeuchi, Naōji. *Hakuin.* Tokyo: Chikuma Shoten, 1964. [More than 800 works of Hakuin's painting and calligraphy are illustrated and discussed.]

Tanahashi, Kazuaki. *Penetrating Laughter.* Woodstock, NY: The Overlook Press, 1984. [Paintings and calligraphy by Hakuin with translations and brief commentaries.]

Yamada, Kōun. *The Gateless Gate: The Classic Book of Zen Koans.* Boston: Wisdom Publications, 2004.